THE FOOD AND COOKING OF THE

MIDDLE EAST

THE FOOD AND COOKING OF THE MIDDLE EAST

A vibrant cuisine explored in 150 classic recipes: authentic dishes shown step by step in 600 vivid photographs

GHILLIE BAŞAN

HERMES HOUSE

This edition is published by Hermes House, an imprint of Anness Publishing Ltd, Blaby Road, Wigston, Leicestershire LE18 4SE; info@anness.com

www.hermeshouse.com; www.annesspublishing.com

Publisher: Joanna Lorenz
Editorial Director: Helen Sudell
Executive Editor: Joanne Rippin
Designer: Adelle Morris
Production Controller: Mai-Ling Collyer

A CIP catalogue record for this book is available from the British Library.

NOTES

Bracketed terms are intended for American readers.

For all recipes, quantities are given in both metric and imperial measures and, where appropriate, in standard cups and spoons. Follow one set of measures, but not a mixture, because they are not interchangeable.

Standard spoon and cup measures are level. 1 tsp = 5ml, 1 tbsp = 15ml, 1 cup = 250ml/8fl oz.

Australian standard tablespoons are 20ml. Australian readers should use 3 tsp in place of 1 tbsp for measuring small quantities.

American pints are 16fl oz/2 cups. American readers should use 20fl oz/2.5 cups in place of 1 pint when measuring liquids.

Electric oven temperatures in this book are for conventional ovens. When using a fan oven, the temperature will probably need to be reduced by about 10–20°C/20–40°F. Since ovens vary, you should check with your manufacturer's instruction book for guidance.

The nutritional analysis given for each recipe is calculated per portion (i.e. serving or item), unless otherwise stated. If the recipe gives a range, such as Serves 4–6, then the nutritional analysis will be for the smaller portion size, i.e. 6 servings. The analysis does not include optional ingredients, such as salt added to taste.

Medium (US large) eggs are used unless otherwise stated.

PICTURE ACKNOWLEDGEMENTS

The publishers would like to thank to the following picture agencies for the kind permission to use their images: Bridgeman Art Library; pp12t, 12b, 13bl, 13br. Corbis; p51. Getty p24. Alamy: 8b, 9b, 10b, 11t & b, 13t, 14b, 16t, bl & br, 17t, 18t, br & bl, 41tl, tr & tm, 42tc, bc & bl, 48t, 49tl, 49b, 50bc, 50tr.

PUBLISHER'S NOTE

CONTENTS

INTRODUCTION

The cuisines of Lebanon, Syria and Jordan are generally regarded as Arab food at its best. The Lebanese are proud of their appetizing mezze, a delicious range of little dishes to be shared by a group of diners, and kibbeh, torpedo-shaped mixtures of well-flavoured minced meat, herbs, spices and bulgur wheat. The Jordanians are renowned for their meat dishes, and for recipes that arrived with the many Palestinian refugees now living in their country. The Syrians lay claim to many of the more piquant specialities of the region, including muhammara, a hot pepper dip to be eaten with bread, and lahm bi ajeen, a spicy meat pie. Dairy produce, fruit, vegetables and pulses are of prime importance, resulting in hundreds of healthy, sustaining dishes. The food of the area shares not only a whole variety of fantastic colours, textures and flavours, but also the sense that preparing food is not just a duty but a joy.

THE FOOD OF THE FERTILE CRESCENT

The crescent-shaped area on the eastern fringes of the Middle East, comprising Lebanon, Jordan and Syria, has provided the world with one of the most distinguished culinary traditions. Although they have become separate entities, these three countries were once part of the Ottoman Empire, Greater Syria and the Fertile Crescent of Mesopotamia. They were bound by a common language and an ancient cultural heritage, which also encompassed Israel, Iraq and a portion of Turkey. Their shared culinary tradition is both fascinating and inspiring. Its roots in the peasant cooking of the fertile plains and mountains are combined with the more sophisticated Ottoman influences found in the bustling cities along the coast.

NATURAL ABUNDANCE

The name 'Fertile Crescent' is apt – the rich soil and climate allow for the large-scale production of grain and vegetables. Even in medieval times, the variety and abundance of the crops astounded visitors. Recording their impressions of the Bekaa and Jordan Valleys, these early travellers described olive trees bursting with fruit, figs, mulberries, sugar cane and aubergines in terraced fields, corn, beans, a variety of squashes, and plump purple grapes dangling from their vines. Specific regions were known for their vegetable specialities: Damascus produced the best asparagus; Ashqelon (a town on the coast of Palestine) was known for its onions; Tripoli was famous for its taro (a fleshy root vegetable); and the best cucumbers were cultivated in the Bekaa Valley.

Below: Vineyards in the spectacular Bekaa Valley, Lebanon's fertile area.

Right: An ancient olive tree still bears fruit in the North Lebanon.

TRADITIONAL FARMING

The grain-growing regions of the Fertile Crescent and Anatolia, the Asian part of Turkey, have changed little for hundreds of years. The land is still tilled by oxen, and groups of peasants, mainly women, work side by side in the fields, returning to their village as night falls. Orchards of peaches, apricots and pomegranates, and small vineyards often surround the villages, where carts laden with plump melons or tomatoes, or piled high with sunflower heads, sit outside the doorways of simple homes. Young boys often tend the goats or sheep while the women thresh the wheat or grind the corn. There is as much culinary activity on the rooftops as there is indoors: the flat roofs provide an ideal surface for apricots, figs, plums, raisins, wheat and corn to dry in the sun alongside trays of pulped tomatoes and peppers.

THE RISE OF CIVILIZATIONS

Greater Syria was located at the crossroads of major trade routes. This area witnessed many settlements and empires over the past centuries, from the early Egyptians, Canaanites, Hittites, Assyrians, Greeks, Romans, Arabs, Crusaders and Ottoman Turks right up to, more recently, the French and British occupation in the 20th century. These have all left an influential stamp on the geographical and culinary landscape. The first great civilizations of the world are known to have risen on this rich soil, where they were able to produce their own food with relative ease. The culinary culture of Lebanon, Jordan and Syria gives us a fascinating insight into the tremendous industry and creativity of early mankind. With a history of trading with far-flung countries and centuries of productive cultivation in the fertile fields, it is no wonder that the cuisine of the region grew and prospered with distinction.

FOOD CULTURE IN THE FERTILE CRESCENT

At times of political peace, travelling in Lebanon, Syria and Jordan is a joy. There is no better way to understand

Left: A shepherd on horseback leads his flock home in Syria.

the psyche of the local people than to observe and experience the role that food plays in their cultures every day, and it is an understatement to say that life here revolves around food. From the cradle to the grave, food is so subtly embedded in the mind and so neatly intertwined with life that there is a feast to mark every personal milestone and every act of faith. If ever there was a reflection of the human spirit, it is surely the culinary heritage of this region, as even among the rubble of a bombed neighbourhood, or in the dry heat of a simple Bedouin camp, there is always food being cooked, offered and shared in ancestral style.

HOW TO USE THE BOOK

This book is a celebration of the food of the Fertile Crescent, with recipes for all the most mouthwatering dishes of the region, and plenty of other fascinating information about the area. The first section gives an overview of the three countries that make up the Fertile Crescent – their climate, history and culinary heritage – to inspire the reader with a deeper knowledge of this beautiful part of the world. Daily life here is completely bound up with all aspects of food. It starts with the landscape, with its olive trees and grape vines, rows of succulent vegetables and herds of cows and sheep grazing on the lush grass of the valleys. Next come the lively markets with stalls crammed with all sorts of produce, from meat and fish to spices and herbs. At home, cooking pots bubble on the stove, containing delicious food for family and friends, who come together to eat, drink and talk. It is no surprise that when the important religious feast days come round each year the focus is on long celebratory meals as well as worship.

Many of the ingredients used every day in this region are less well known elsewhere in the world. The second section of the book is a detailed directory that is a comprehensive guide to these ingredients, with numerous hints and tips for using them in the typical ways found in any Arab kitchen. Most of the foods mentioned in the book can now be found in supermarkets or specialist food stores, and this section will help the keen cook to store and use the ingredients in the best way possible.

The third section of the book contains recipes of all kinds, from simple street snacks like falafel in pitta bread to elaborate dishes, such as spicy tartare balls, worthy of a banquet. These are fully explained, with complete lists of ingredients and step-by-step instructions. Colour photographs accompany each recipe to help you make an authentic dish that looks stunning and tastes delicious.

A love of food and a sense of satisfaction in sharing it with others is a big part of life in the Fertile Crescent. This book will provide all the information you need to recreate that experience in your own home.

Below: Family meals may have a more contemporary feel now, but the tradition of preparing and eating food together is still very important.

GEOGRAPHY AND LANDSCAPE

The three countries that make up the Fertile Crescent – Lebanon, Syria and Jordan – contain an amazingly diverse set of landscapes, from arid desert to green valleys, from flat flood plains to high mountain peaks. Although Lebanon is by far the smallest of these three countries, it is also one of the most productive, with a long sea coast and relatively few barren areas. Much of Syria and Jordan, on the other hand, is taken up with the vast and relatively unpopulated desert that borders Turkey, Iraq and Saudi Arabia.

Above: *The green curve of the fertile crescent is a stark contrast to the barren areas of desert in the region.*

LEBANON: A RICH AND VARIED LANDSCAPE

This small country divides quite naturally into three main regions, all running from north to south. First, in the coastal region, a mere 2 or 3 km of flat terrain gives just enough space for the major towns to gain a foothold before the mountains begin. These sea ports became important trading centres in the early medieval period, dealing in all kinds of foodstuffs. There is also room on the coastal strip for growing tender vegetables and fruit, particularly citrus fruits, with orchards and fields packed into this small fertile space.

The second region is the Lebanon Mountains, where the terraced lower slopes sprout almond and olive trees. These mountain peaks rise to over 3,300m (10,800ft) in the north of the range and most are topped with snow throughout the year. Crossing the mountains was a risky enterprise hundreds of years ago, but now routes through to Syria are well established.

The third main geographical area in Lebanon is the fantastically productive Bekaa Valley, nestled between the Lebanon Mountains to the west and the Anti-Lebanon Mountains to the east. This is a valley rich in agriculture of all kinds, from settled farming to nomadic herding. It has changed little over the centuries. The eastern Anti-Lebanon Mountains protect the Bekaa Valley from the heat of the desert in Syria, and the highest peaks of these mountains, like those of the Lebanon Mountains, are snow-covered for much of the year. This area is more thinly populated than the western side of the country, and the border with Syria snakes along the top of the range.

Left: A remote road in the beautiful Bekaa Valley, Lebanon.

SYRIA: A LAND OF CONTRASTS

Irrigation from two major rivers is a vital part of agriculture in this dry country. Flowing through the north-east of Syria is one of the great rivers of the Middle East, the Euphrates. This mighty waterway cuts through a dry, rocky, desert landscape, giving the river banks and flood plains sufficient moisture to grow wheat, cotton and sunflowers, as well as a variety of vegetables.

In the south, the mountains give way to a cultivated plain, the Al-Ghab, through which the Orontes River flows. Further south still, a high mountain range, the Jebel Libnan ash-Shariqiyya, separates the arid land of Syria from the fertile Bekaa Valley in Lebanon. The major Syrian cities of Damascus, Homs, Hama and Aleppo are surrounded by areas of intensive farming, including wheat and other cereal crops. Further inland to the east, away from the sea and the mountains, lies an enormous expanse of seemingly endless, stony desert, broken only by the oasis of Palmyra, which was, in ancient and medieval times, an important centre for camel caravans plying the trade routes.

Above: The lush date plantations of the Palmyra oasis, Syria.

JORDAN: RIVER PLAINS AND DESERTS

The River Jordan Valley, the east bank plateau and the desert are the three main geographical regions of Jordan. The most dominant feature being the fertile valley of the 251km (156 mile) Jordan River, which is fed by water from the Sea of Galilee, the Yarmouk River, and countless little streams from the high plateaux. The river valley forms part of the Great Rift Valley, and runs the entire length of the country, from the Syrian border in the north, past the Dead Sea, to the Gulf of Aqaba and the Red Sea in the south. The pine forests of the northern part of Jordan give way to cultivated slopes bearing eucalyptus, olive and banana trees. Most of the Jordan Valley is lush and fertile, providing a rich yield of citrus fruits and vegetables, and good grazing for livestock, although the Dead Sea area is too salty for cultivation.

Below: The stark beauty of Jordan's desert area, Wadi Rum.

The east bank plateau, which is divided by deep gorges, is home to the main cities of Jordan, including Amman and Karak. Crops such as cereals, pulses, olives, and fruit are grown in this region although the wadis (valleys) are often dry in the summer, and small plots and gardens require constant watering. The remaining 80 per cent of Jordan is purely arid desert, some of which is visually spectacular, such as Wadi Rum, but the only plants that grow there are cacti and the toughest of scrub grazing for the hardy sheep and goats that thrive in these regions.

THE CLIMATE OF THE FERTILE CRESCENT

Lebanon, Syria and Jordan are fortunate in having a perfect climate for many crops in the river valleys and flood plains, with long hours of sunshine for most of the year. In Lebanon, the winters are mild and rainy, allowing the ground to recover its fertility. In Syria and Jordan, on the other hand, the winters can be freezing cold, with snow on the plains as well as in the high mountains. It has always been more difficult to farm on a large scale in these two countries because of these extremes of climate. Most farmers and herders work in their own small area or travel around to find the best grazing for their animals season by season.

Throughout the Fertile Crescent, spring and autumn are the most pleasant times to visit. The sun warms the ground and the landscape suddenly bursts into life, with hundreds of wild flowers blooming everywhere except in the most extreme desert conditions.

The micro-climate of the Mediterranean coast

The coastal strip of Lebanon and Syria is hot and dry, but heavy dew often forms during the night to keep the fruit and vegetables well watered. When summer temperatures reach 45°C (113°F) or higher inland, it is time to escape to the coast, to resorts with their buzzing restaurants and cafés next to the sparkling sea, or to the cool green forests that spread up the mountain slopes.

A Culinary History

The research of archaeologists has confirmed that around 8,000BC agriculture was already being practised by the early settlements in the Fertile Crescent of Mesopotamia. This region is known as the 'cradle of civilization', and it could also be regarded as the cradle of Middle Eastern culinary culture. Wheat and barley were the principal grains, resulting in a variety of leavened and unleavened breads baked in clay ovens or on flat stones; meat was roasted whole over an open flame, or preserved in its own fat; milk was transformed into yogurt, cheese and butter; and olives were pressed for oil.

PHOENICIANS AND PERSIANS

As far back as the 12th century BC, the seafaring Phoenicians dominated the coastal colonies of the eastern Mediterranean, trading in shrubs and herbs, spices and perfumed oils, fruit, nuts and dried fish. The rise of the Persian Empire from 558 to 330BC, spanning a vast territory from Russia in the north to Egypt in the south, and from Greece in the west to India in the east, made an even bigger impact on the regional cuisine. Persia's merchants also spread the empire's culinary skills, using some wonderfully exotic ingredients such as pomegranates, saffron, aubergines and lemons, as well as the inherent belief in the art of pleasing the eye as well as the palate.

Khiyar-o anar (Pomegranate and cucumber salad)

This simple ancient Persian recipe is deliciously refreshing served as part of a mezze spread or as an accompaniment to grilled meats.

1 Cut 2 fresh pomegranates into quarters and take out the seeds, discarding any white pith.

2 Cut 1 peeled cucumber in half lengthways and slice it finely.

3 Cut 1 peeled golden or red onion in half lengthways, then in half crossways, and slice it with the grain.

4 Mix the pomegranates, cucumber and onion with a small bunch of shredded fresh mint leaves and stir to mix.

5 Just before serving, toss the ingredients in the juice of 1 lemon and season with sea salt and freshly ground black pepper.

THE ROMAN AND BYZANTINE EMPIRES

The Romans were the next great power to annexe the countries of the Fertile Crescent, and in doing so they linked India to Rome by sea, extending the trade routes even further. This was a period of industrious culinary productivity, with the discovery of many spices and scents and their uses in both food and medicine. When the Roman Empire split in two in AD 395, the eastern half became the Byzantine Empire, which governed Greater Syria until the early 7th century. The reign of Emperor Justinian I and Empress Theodora in the 6th century saw the spread of culinary traditions as their great feasts embraced Indian, Persian, Armenian, Greek and Syrian dishes.

Above: Pressing olives for oil probably dates back to 4,500 years ago in the regions of Jordan and Israel.

THE GOLDEN AGE OF ISLAM

The spread of Islam in the 7th century had a huge impact on the culture of the region and its cuisine. The vast Islamic empire gradually took hold of the region, spreading from Asia to North Africa and Spain. Along the way, the invading Arabs converted most of the diverse inhabitants to Islam and imposed religious restrictions on their

Below: Delegates from the subject lands of the Persian Empire, which included most of what is now Lebanon, Syria and Jordan, bear gifts for a ceremony, c.515BC.

Above: The city of Tyre was first settled 4,000 years ago and survived as a trading port through the rise and fall of the Persian, Roman and Ottoman empires.

culinary practices. Some Christian communities, however, hid in the mountains of Lebanon and in cave dwellings in Syria and Anatolia, holding on to their religious traditions.

The Golden Age of Islam flourished during the Abassid dynasty from the 8th to the 12th century. The culinary culture of this period included an emphasis on etiquette and tableware, as well as the visual creativity of the dishes. A number of culinary manuals were written during this period, with an emphasis on etiquette, diet and health, such as the 10th-century *Kitab al-Tabikh* by Ibn Sayyar al-Warraq.

Below: By the 1700s, drinking coffee had become an important part of the cultural life of the region.

THE OTTOMAN EMPIRE

In the year 1258, a son named Osman was born to the chief of a Turkish tribe in Anatolia. This boy later established the Ottoman Empire, which ruled a vast territory encompassing the Balkans, the eastern Mediterranean, Arabia and North Africa for the next 500 years.

The impact of the Ottoman Empire on the culinary culture of the region was particularly significant in the 16th century, when the Ottomans and the Spaniards came to an agreement that the goods brought back from the New World would be transported via the North African coast to Egypt and Constantinople. This convenient political arrangement meant that New World ingredients such as chilli peppers, tomatoes and corn were distributed throughout the Ottoman territories, finding their way into the cuisine with the greatest of ease. It was during this time, too, that coffee was discovered, probably in Ethopia, spreading by the middle of the 15th century, to Yemen, Arabia, and the rest of the Empire.

After ruling for half a century, the Ottoman Empire collapsed with the defeat of Turkey in the First World War, but its culinary legacy is evident in the cooking of the region today.

An Ottoman banquet

A list of the foods served at a feast held by Suleyman the Magnificent, Sultan of the Ottoman Empire from 1520 to 1566 is as follows: barberry and almond soups; noodles; pigeon, peacock, and mutton kebabs; savoury pastries; meatballs; savoury rice dishes; saffron rice pudding; carrot and quince jellies; sponge cakes soaked in syrup; sweet pastries; almond and pistachio sweetmeats; sweet preserves made from cherries, pumpkin, peaches, aubergines and melon; and many varieties of bread.

RECENT HISTORY

After the First World War, Lebanon and Syria became independent states, Jordan became a kingdom, and Palestine and Israel were partitioned. Since then the crescent-shaped region of Lebanon, Syria and Jordan has often been involved in political and boundary conflict, but culinary traditions have always been maintained through the worst of times, with a shared cultural history and an enthusiasm for food and cooking that has never wavered.

Below: Street vendors selling freshly baked bread have been a part of life in the region for centuries.

Feasts and Festivals

The Fertile Crescent is home to a colourful tapestry of ethnic and religious groups. Arabic is the principal language of the Levant, and the majority of the region's population is Muslim, with a minority that includes Christians, Jews, and breakaway Islamic groups. All of these add to the melting pot with their own traditional languages and dialects, as well as their particular cultural and culinary customs. In Lebanon, Syria and Jordan, the culinary calendar flows from one Islamic religious feast to another, interspersed with Christian celebrations.

A typical itfar meal for the month of Ramadan

- savoury pastries
- meatballs or kibbeh
- grilled lamb and chicken with rice
- stuffed vegetables
- sweet dishes such as baklava
- milk puddings
- fruit compotes
- ma'amoul, little walnut cakes
- drinks such as sherbets made from carob and tamarind
- dates

Above: Coffee and dates often begin the meal served at sunset during the festival of Ramadan.

CHRISTMAS

At this time of the year, the Christian communities of the region generally celebrate with an exchange of gifts and a roasted bird, or a leg of lamb, just like Christians in other parts of the world. One exception is the Armenian community, which celebrates Christmas on 6 January, the Epiphany, with mounds of sticky awamat, deep-fried fritters bathed in honey or syrup.

EASTER

This is the most important date of the Christian calendar. On Good Friday, when devout Christians abstain from meat, a variety of vegetable and pulse dishes are prepared, such as mujaddara, rice cooked with lentils, and a sour bulgur soup called shoraba zingool. The sourness of this soup is intended to remind Christians of the vinegar given to Christ on the cross. On Easter Sunday, platters of ma'amoul, semolina cakes stuffed with walnuts or dates, celebrate the end of Lent.

RAMADAN

As the vast majority of the population of the Levant is Muslim, the month of Ramadan plays a very important part in the year. During Ramadan, in the ninth month of the Muslim calendar, all adult Muslims fast between sunrise and sunset to mark the revelation of the Koran to the Prophet Mohammad. A simple meal, suhur, is prepared before dawn and is designed to fill the stomach for the daylight hours ahead. It normally comprises a hearty soup and bread. Itfar, the meal that is consumed once the sun has gone down, is much more extensive. Dates are always placed on the table as a reminder that they were the only food for the Prophet when he was fasting in the desert. The purpose of Ramadan is to teach self-discipline, and to instil understanding and compassion for the poor who experience hunger all year round.

EID AL-FITR

Once the month of Ramadan comes to an end, it is time to celebrate with a great deal of merriment and feasting over a three-day period. Friends and neighbours exchange gifts, buy new clothes, and visit their relatives to share good food of all kinds.

ST HELENA'S DAY

One of the most celebrated feast days among the Christian communities is Eid al-Salib, or St Helena's Day, on

Left: The festival of St Helena's Day, Eid al-Salib, is marked with huge firework displays over Lebanese towns and cities.

Islamic food rules
In the holy book of Islam, the Qur'an, there are four categories of food that are strictly forbidden:

- any animal that did not have its throat cut
- products made from the blood from an animal's body
- pork
- the meat of an animal sacrificed in the name of any other God

The consumption of other creatures, such as reptiles and beasts of prey, is not officially banned, but Islamic scholars consider them harmful so they are not usually on the Muslim menu. Also, although it is considered lawful 'to fish in the sea and consume the catch', not all Arabs happily tuck into shellfish. The Koran also forbids any form of alcoholic drink, although the text refers to 'wine', leaving room for argument amongst those who wish to consume arak or other spirits.

8 September. Legend says that Queen Helena, the mother of the Roman Emperor Constantine, found the True Cross of the crucifixion on a hillside above Jerusalem and demanded that fires be lit in watchtowers all the way to

Below: Baklava is made in huge quantities for many Islamic feast days.

Above: Pomegranates are referred to in the Qur'an as the fruit of paradise.

Constantinople. To commemorate this legend, bonfires and fireworks light up the sky as Christians, and Muslims too, gather together to dance and feast in the streets, and vendors sell kibbeh and other delights late into the night.

EID AL-BARABARA

Another Christian celebration that Muslims also enjoy is Eid el-Barabara, which marks the end of the harvest. The children dress up in masks and devour bowls of kamhiyeh, wheat or barley sweetened with sugar and decorated with pomegranate seeds.

EID EL-KURBAN

This is another feast day that is respected throughout the Muslim world, and marks the near-sacrifice of Isma'il. To celebrate, each family that can afford to buy a ram will take it home and share it among the family members and sometimes with the poor in their area. The meat is cooked in soups, stews and kibbeh, the intestines are stuffed and grilled, and the tail is boiled and served as a delicacy with pitta bread and yogurt. Nothing is wasted.

FAMILY FEASTS AND TRADITIONS

Food is also associated with different events in life, such as birth, marriage and death. When a baby is born, a traditional cinnamon-flavoured rice pudding, meghlie, is served to family members and visitors. When the baby's first tooth comes through, the family prepares sachets of sugar-coated almonds and chickpeas to give to friends and family.

Wedding feasts are lavish affairs, often involving an entire village. Stuffed vine leaves, pastries, pilaffs, kibbeh and puddings are all prepared for the event, and some dishes symbolize fertility or prosperity for the new couple.

Funerals, on the other hand, vary from region to region, as some families mark the occasion with a feast, while others simply prepare a traditional halva to offer to those who have come to pay their respects.

Sugar-coated chickpeas

1 Toss a batch of dried chickpeas into a pan and fill with cold water.

2 Bring the water to the boil, then simmer for about 20 minutes, until the chickpeas are tender.

3 Drain the chickpeas and spread them out in a flat pan lined with kitchen paper – leave them to dry.

4 Heat 30–45ml/2–3 tbsp olive or sunflower oil in a heavy pan and stir-fry the chickpeas for about 5 minutes until toasted and crisp.

5 Drain the chickpeas again on kitchen paper, tip them into a bowl and sprinkle with 30–45ml/2–3 tbsp sugar. Toss and serve.

CULINARY CUSTOMS

The Arab traditions of hospitality and kindness are deeply ingrained in the psyches of most of the region's population, especially the nomadic Bedouin, the people who perhaps have the least to share. Over the last few centuries, writers and travellers have commented on the dignity and courtesy of the Bedouin, often describing their gracious hospitality when they have stopped at a tent in the middle of the desert. Nowadays there is increasing polarization within the Levantine society as a whole as many families gravitate toward a Western outlook, and some of the young people question the traditional values and concepts of honour that can impinge upon their freedom. The Bedouin, however, still have their nomadic roots in the desert, and their way of life and hospitable habits have barely changed with the passing of time.

MY HOUSE IS YOUR HOUSE

When it comes to culinary culture, most of the traditional customs are still observed. Even the youngest members of the family are deeply courteous and hospitable. Hospices, guest-houses and private homes have provided free food and shelter for travellers throughout the

Below: A Bedouin woman makes bread in her tent, Syria.

Above: A mezze table.

region's history and they still do so to this day. When a host welcomes a guest it is normal to hear the words 'bayti, baytak' (my house is your house), and usually it is sincerely meant.

It is polite to offer food and drink to strangers. It is also usual to offer them the best cuts of meat, which may include the coveted eyeballs, brains or testicles, and it is impolite to refuse! Sometimes great mounds of food are consumed, which can be difficult for the guest, but it is acceptable to leave food on your plate, proving to the hostess that she has provided you with more than enough to eat.

TABLE ETIQUETTE

In most households, meals are eaten sitting on floor cushions, often with everyone gathered around trays of food raised off the ground. In some traditional families the grandparents may be served in one room with the male head of the house, while the women eat with the children; in other households, the women and men may eat separately. This is not necessarily for religious reasons. In some areas, eating separately is simply a time-honoured tradition for the family.
In more modern families, however, mealtime is a sociable, family event and all the members and their guests eat together, including the very young and the elderly.

SHOPPING FOR FOOD

The food markets of Lebanon, Syria and Jordan played a major role in the culinary life of the Islamic and Ottoman empires and still do so today. These markets are the heart and lungs of every community, and typify all that is best about the food culture of the Fertile Crescent. They range from the sprawling clusters of historic bazaars in Damascus and Amman to the rural, makeshift stalls of the mountain villages of Lebanon. In the larger indoor suqs, the shops are grouped together according to their trade in the manner of the medieval guild system, and as you walk through them you can observe artisans making kibbeh and other delicacies. If you're feeling hungry, you can buy some kebabs or falafel tucked into pitta bread, or roasted, salted pumpkin seeds in a cone of newspaper.

THE MEZZE TRADITION

This is one of the most enjoyable and relaxing features of the culinary culture of the Levant. Nothing quite beats eating mezze under the shade of an old

Below: Kibbeh is cooked by a street vendor in the city of Amman, Jordan.

fig tree, or on a balcony overlooking the cobbled streets of an old town, or at a table by the sea, watching the sun sink below the horizon, or indoors seated comfortably on cushions around a low table set with a tantalizing array of little dishes. The city of Zahleh, in the heart

Above: An outdoor market in Sidon, in one of the ancient little streets of the city, typical of those found all over Lebanon, Syria and Jordan.

of the Bekaa Valley, is particularly renowned for its superb mezze served in the open-air restaurants on the banks of the river.

The concept of mezze is an old one. The word is thought to be derived from either the Persian word 'maza', meaning 'taste' or 'relish', or from the Arabic verb, 'mazmiz', 'to nibble at food'. The ancient Greeks and Romans enjoyed a tradition of nibbling nuts, herbs, seeds and raw vegetables, accompanied by wine. The medieval Arabs and Ottoman Turks added to the quality and variety of appetizing dishes but, under the rules of Islam, they were usually offered with non-alcoholic drinks. However, in Lebanon the drinking of wine and arak, the aniseed-flavoured spirit, was not banned, and the Christian monasteries produced their own wine. In Lebanon and Syria, snacks and appetizers that are served with a non-alcoholic drink, such as a glass of tea or a sherbet, are generally referred to as muqabbalat.

A Social experience

One thing that all mezze have in common is that the dishes are served in small quantities on individual plates, and everyone helps themselves. The joy of mezze lies in admiring different colours and textures, dipping bread into creamy dips, and popping succulent nibbles into your mouth. It is a wonderful way to eat and can form an entire meal, but it is also easy to forget that this spread of dishes is very often only a prelude to the ensuing meat, rice and vegetable dishes, so a degree of restraint has to be mastered.

Bizr laktin muhammas (roasted pumpkin seeds)

1 Heat 15ml/1 tbsp sunflower or olive oil in a heavy pan.

2 Add a knob of butter and throw in 250g/9oz pumpkin seeds.

3 Stir-fry until they are crisp and lightly browned.

4 Drain on kitchen paper and sprinkle with sea salt. Serve warm.

Typical mezze dishes

- a simple bowl of plump marinated olives or nuts
- hot savoury pastries
- miniature versions of main-course dishes, such as meatballs, kibbeh, stuffed vegetables, grilled shellfish and Arab pizzas
- salads of root and leafy vegetables
- cold dishes prepared with eggs, beans, truffles, fish and lamb's brains
- succulent spinach-filled pastries (see below)
- garlicky chickpea and smoked aubergine dips
- salads of herbs and bulgur
- melting morsels of fried halloumi cheese sprinkled with zahtar spice mix

Cooking Methods and Tools

For millennia, waves of seafaring traders passed by these countries, bearing goods and spices from India, the South Seas and China, and bringing with them all their own culinary traditions. This abundance also fostered long periods of peace and all the benefits of a stable society. It would be easy to assume that the illustrious and inventive culinary history of the Fertile Crescent has led to the development of fairly sophisticated kitchens, with all the latest tools, rows of pots and pans, drawers full of gadgets and gleaming worktops. Yet the kitchens of the poor and rural communities have barely changed since the birth of civilization. They often consist of a simple hearth made by piling up a few stones to contain a fire, situated in a dark room at the back of the house or outdoors. The wealthier, more modern households may possess a fixed brick range, or an electric cooker with an oven, but even in the most up-to-date buildings, the kitchen remains fairly basic and the cooking utensils completely traditional.

In the medieval period, it used to be the custom for a father to give his daughter a gift of useful household items on the eve of her marriage. This mainly consisted of basic copper pans, a baking tray, ladles and dishes. Neither the custom nor the utensils themselves have changed much, and each newly married couple is still grateful to receive a selection of traditional utensils to furnish their own kitchen.

Above: The traditonal way of making coffee and tea, in a Bedouin tent beside Qusair Amra castle in Jordan.

COOKING TECHNIQUES

Regardless of how intricate and time-consuming some of the dishes can be, they do not require sophisticated utensils. Of course, wealthier and more cosmopolitan members of society may have sophisticated aids such as electric

Food preparation

The cooking process is kept fairly simple, with a few solid pots and good quality smaller utensils.

Knives: a selection of sharp knives of different sizes is needed for preparing and carving whole joints of meat, filleting fish and chopping vegetables and herbs.

Wooden spoons: these are often carved with beautiful patterns.

Ladles: a large curved spoon is absolutely vital for ladling soup or rice from the dist, the large cooking pot found on every stove.

Skewers: metal grilling skewers are needed for kebabs cooked on the manqal, or barbecue.

Draining dish: a dish or tin with a perforated base, like a colander, used for draining vegetables or rice or bulgur.

Rolling pin: bread-making requires a long, thin rolling pin for the wide flat breads so typical of the region.

Mortar and pestle: used for many kitchen tasks, such as grinding spices and coffee beans, crushing garlic, and pounding pulses.

Coffee and tea pots: many people still use traditional elegant metal pots with decorated lids.

Below: A small traditional bakery making flat bread in Safi Jordan.

Below: A huge copper pot, called a dist, is used here for making carob.

Above: A Lebanese migla.

Above: The manqal, used for grilling.

Above: A typical copper pan.

mixers, but to achieve the genuine taste of good Arab food, simple tools are all that is required. The techniques of simmering, frying and baking remain the same whether the cook is using a built-in cooker in a city apartment or a tiny fire in an open hearth next to a Bedouin tent.

Pilaffs, stews and preserves

Many households reserve pride of place in the kitchen for a large copper pot, known as a dist. This substantial utensil is used for simmering mixtures gently on the stove top. It is ideal for making all sorts of recipes, from preparing savoury rice or a bulgur pilaff, to producing a large quantity of tomato paste from the summer crop, traditional kawurma, meat preserved in its own fat, or a seasonal batch of fruit jam and molasses. These pots are lined with tin and supported by two handles to make them easier to carry to the table when full. The copper base means that the heat of the stove is quickly transferred to the food simmering inside. The hefty size of a dist means that is an extremely useful piece of equipment, as it can contain a large amount of soup or even a whole sheep cut into joints for a feast. The dist typifies the hospitable nature of cooks from Lebanon, Syria and Jordan, who are always ready to cook for a crowd. A smaller version of this pot, used for everyday dishes in smaller households, is the traditional tanjara, which is also fashioned from copper and tin-lined, with one or two handles and a lid.

Roasted spices and kibbeh

A basic roomy frying pan, called a miqla, made from heavy tin-lined copper or cast iron, is another important utensil for cooking eggs and omelettes, for dry-roasting spices, and for frying meatballs and kibbeh. It is also ideal for cooking pieces of meat or fish quickly on the stove top.

Below: Most houses have a permanent grill or barbecue for roasting kebabs.

Baked savoury and sweet treats

For oven-baked savoury dishes such as spicy meat pies and kibbeh, most households use a circular metal tray with raised sides, known as a siniyya. This is also ideal for baking sweet pastries, such as baklava. It is made of strong, solid metal that will not buckle in the oven at high temperatures.

Many households still do not have their own built-in oven for baking. Villages and towns are generally provided with communal ovens, known as the furn, where people can purchase bread or take their home-prepared dough and other dishes to be baked. Large cuts of meat or whole beasts are also roasted in the local furn for special occasions such as religious feasts or weddings. A furn is often made from clay and is fired by wood. Flat breads can also be prepared outdoors on hot stones in the desert areas, or in the kitchen on a heavy iron griddle, known as a saaj.

Succulent barbecues

A charcoal grill, the manqal, made out of copper, clay or metal, is frequently used for grilling meat and fish. This is often a permanent fixture in the kitchen or in the enclosed yard of a rural house. When it is made freestanding and fashioned out of metal, it becomes portable so that it can be used on balconies, in gardens or even taken to the countryside for picnics.

SPICES, HERBS AND FLAVOURINGS

With the Phoenician and Persian legacy of trading and the art of hospitality inherited from the Arabs and the Ottoman Empire, it is not surprising that the stylish and vibrant cuisine of the Levant is rich in flavour and colour. Spices and herbs, nuts and seeds, scented flavourings and syrups play an important role in every dish.

The herbs, spices and flavourings mentioned below are the standard ingredients kept in a munay, the food cellar or larder of a traditional kitchen in a typical Lebanese, Syrian or Jordanian house. These ingredients can all be found in well-stocked supermarkets or Middle Eastern stores.

Medicinal spices

The ancient Chinese theories of yin and yang filtered through to the Fertile Crescent in the medieval period. This involved balancing the warming and cooling properties of foods in every meal, as well as utilizing their particular medicinal properties.

Warming spices such as cumin, cinnamon, allspice, cloves (above), and chilli peppers are believed to improve the appetite and aid digestion.

Generous quantities of fresh herbs, particularly mint, dill and parsley, are often mixed together as a warming trio to balance the cooling properties of some vegetable dishes and salads.

Garlic is believed to be beneficial to the circulation of the blood.

AROMATIC SPICES AND SYRUPS

Well-flavoured spices and syrups are an integral part of the Middle Eastern kitchen. Individual spices are usually bought whole and ground at home with a mortar and pestle. Spice mixes are made in batches from subtle combinations of spices and kept for short periods, ready to be added to many delicious traditional dishes.

Carob molasses

This is a thick, dark syrup obtained from the carob trees that grow in the dry soil of the desert areas in Syria, Jordan and Lebanon. Traditionally, the syrup was used instead of sugar to sweeten drinks, puddings and stews. A sweet paste made with carob molasses and tahini is often served with bread for breakfast, or for a snack, but it can also be transformed into a savoury dish to be served as part of a mezze spread by spiking it with crushed garlic, lemon juice and dried mint.

Pomegranate molasses

Unlike sweet carob molasses, this syrup is very sharp. It is prepared from sour pomegranate juice, which is boiled until it thickens and darkens. The syrup is used in salad dressings and marinades, and is often drizzled over dishes to add its exquisite fruity, sour note.

Mastic

This is the aromatic gum from a small evergreen tree (Pistacia lentiscus) that grows wild all over the Mediterranean region. The droplets of resin form little crystals, which are pulverized with sugar in a mortar and pestle. Traditionally, the distinctive flavour of mastic is added to milk puddings, jams, ice cream, marinades and the local aniseed-flavoured spirit, arak.

Below: Mastic crystals.

Above: Rose water and diluted pomegranate syrup.

Sumac

This deep red-coloured condiment is prepared by crushing and grinding the dried berries of a bush (Rhus coriaria) that grows wild in the mountains of Lebanon and the arid regions of Syria and Jordan. The ground spice has a sharp taste and is often used as a

Below: Pomegranate molasses.

Above: Sumac.

substitute for lemons in salads and savoury dishes. It is also a component of zahtar, the popular spice mix.

Cinnamon

This spice was first brought to the region by Arab traders from Ceylon and the Spice Islands, and quickly became absorbed by the culinary culture of the region. The Ottomans added cinnamon to savoury rice dishes, stuffed vegetables, milk puddings and sweet pastries. In Lebanon and Syria it is used in a variety of sweet biscuits, cakes, and sweetmeats, as well as savoury stews and soups.

Coriander seeds

These have a slightly peppery taste and emit a delicious nutty fragrance when roasted. They are used in seed form or ground to a powder to be added to stews and marinades.

Lebanese pomegranate and sumac salad dressing

1 Whisk together 30ml/2 tbsp olive oil with 30ml/2 tbsp pomegranate syrup and 5–10ml/1–2 tsp ground sumac.

2 Pour the dressing over a salad made up of leafy greens, or shredded vegetables, and toss just before serving.

Grinding spices Dried spices are at their most pungent when stored in seed, bark or pod form and ground as required. The best way to grind spices is by hand, using a mortar and pestle, as this enables the natural oils to be released, but you can also use a food processor.
Roasting spices Place the seeds, bark or pods in a heavy pan and stir-fry them over medium heat until they brown a little and emit a nutty aroma.

Cumin

These seeds have a distinctive taste and emit a delightful nutty aroma when roasted. They are best stored in seed form and ground when needed as the ground spice loses its pungency fairly quickly. Cumin is believed to aid digestion, and is therefore used in a number of dishes that might cause a degree of indigestion or flatulence, such as ful medames, the Egyptian-inspired dish of brown beans. Along with cinnamon and coriander, cumin is one of the principal flavourings in the Arab spice mixture, baharat.

Saffron

The only spice in the world to be measured by the carat, being worth its weight in gold, genuine saffron is very special indeed. It is formed from the dried orangey-red stigmas of the purple crocus (*Crocus sativus*), which only

Below: Baharat and zahtar spice mixes.

Above: Cinnamon.

flowers for two weeks every October. Although only mildly perfumed when first picked, the stigmas come to life when soaked in water and impart a magnificent yellow dye with a hint of floral notes. In Lebanon, the cheaper alternative of turmeric is employed for colour in some rustic soups and stews and in the sweet cakes, sfouf, while best-quality saffron is added to the more sophisticated dishes in French-style restaurants and at weddings or religious feasts.

SPICE MIXES: BAHARAT AND ZAHTAR

The ground spice mix known as baharat is used to flavour meat stews throughout the Middle East. It includes eight spices: black pepper, coriander seeds, cumin, cinnamon, cloves, nutmeg, paprika and cardamom (the cardamom is often omitted in Lebanon). Another much-loved spice mixture is known as zahtar, the Arabic word for thyme, which grows wild in the hills of Lebanon. It is sprinkled over bread, cheese, yogurt and salads and is a favourite seasoning used by street vendors throughout Egypt and the Fertile Crescent. It is added liberally to beans, cooked meats, kibbeh and other hot savoury snacks. Simply mix 75–90ml/5–6 tbsp dried organic or wild thyme, 45ml/3 tbsp ground sumac and 15ml/1 tbsp sea salt, and rub with your fingers to release the aroma before sealing in a sterilized jar.

Above: Fresh and dried red chillies.

FRESH HERBS AND AROMATIC VEGETABLES

Middle Eastern cooking is full of green leafy herbs for freshness, and pungent garlic or chillies for a zingy flavour. Many of these plants have been cultivated in the region for hundreds of years, and newer additions such as fiery chilli peppers have been adopted with enthusiasm.

Parsley

Flat leaf parsley forms an integral part of many dishes, including:

- fattoush, a toasted bread salad with sumac
- ful medames, a peasant dish with brown beans
- baba ghanoush, a delectable dip of smoked aubergine (eggplant)
- tabbouleh (below), the famous Lebanese dish – a parsley salad with bulgur tossed through it, rather than the other way round.

Above: Coriander (cilantro).

Chillies

These fiery little peppers reached the eastern Mediterranean in the 16th century, when the Ottomans and Spaniards brought them into the region, along with tomatoes and corn. Since then, chillies have developed a leading role for themselves, particularly in Jordan and Syria, where some dishes are very fiery compared to the subtler notes of Lebanese cooking. Unripe green chillies are used mainly in salads, kebabs and grilled dishes. Some of these are tiny and extremely hot, while others are long, twisted and fairly mild. The ripe red ones are often left to dry in the sun and then chopped finely or ground to a powder. Long red chillies are the most common as they are extremely fruity, with just a hint of fire, and can be finely chopped and sprinkled over blocks of cheese, creamy dips, salads or grilled foods.

Below: Ramiri chilli peppers.

Garlic and cumin marinade

This is a traditional marinade that can be rubbed over a whole fish or pieces of lamb before grilling.

1 Grate a whole onion and sprinkle it with salt. Leave it to weep and then squeeze all the juice out of it into a bowl.

2 Discard the onion flesh, and combine the juice with 2–3 crushed cloves of garlic and 5–10ml/1–2 tsp cumin seeds.

3 You can add sumac to the marinade if you wish for an extra sharp flavour.

Coriander (cilantro)

The coriander plant has been used in the eastern Mediterranean for medicinal and culinary purposes since ancient times. Coriander leaves have a fresh

Below: Garlic.

Above: Mint.

smell, with a citrus taste which works particularly well in marinades, meat and poultry dishes, and as a garnish.

Flat leaf parsley

This is probably the most popular fresh herb in the eastern Mediterranean. Large bunches of flat leaf parsley are stacked so high in the market stalls that they hide the stall-holder. Although it is used liberally in numerous dishes, parsley is also served on its own to sharpen the appetite, to cleanse the palate, or to freshen the breath. The flat leaf variety has a very distinctive strong aroma and taste.

Garlic

Indigenous to the Fertile Crescent, garlic is used for both medicinal and culinary purposes. It appears in mezze dips, nut sauces, pickles, marinades for fish and meat kebabs, and most stews and soups. In the villages of Lebanon, Syria and Jordan, whole heads of plump, healthy, strong garlic are threaded on to kebab skewers with strips of fat from the sheep's tail and grilled over an open fire. Because of its pungency, garlic is believed to hold magical powers, and strings of garlic bulbs are often hung in people's doorways to ward off evil spirits.

Mint

This well-known herb grows prolifically in the eastern Mediterranean, finding its way into numerous salads, dips, soups (such as chilled cucumber and yogurt soup, shorbet khyar bi laban) and sweet dishes. With its refreshing and digestive qualities, fresh mint is one of the most useful herbs for cold dishes. The dried herb is found more often in soups and stews. Infusions are believed to relieve nausea, stomach pain and sore throats.

Above: Rose petal sherbet.

Rose

The origins and culinary uses of rose petals can be traced back to the ancient Egyptians, who bathed in an infusion of roses, and the Romans, who made wine from the flowers, but the invention of distilled rose water for culinary purposes is attributed to the Persians. This spread throughout the region, from the sumptuous medieval dishes prepared for the banquets of Baghdad to the sophisticated dishes of Istanbul. In Lebanon, rose petals are mainly used as a garnish for puddings, and rose-flavoured syrups are used in a variety of sweet dishes and drinks.

Right: Mint infusion.

Medicinal infusion of mint: Believed to aid digestion, this makes a refreshing drink.

1 Place several sprigs of fresh mint in a glass or a teapot, and pour on hot water.

2 Add sugar to taste. Leave the mixture to infuse (steep) for at least 5 minutes before drinking.

Rose petal sherbet (Sharab al ward)

This refreshing rose-flavoured drink is offered to guests in Lebanon as they arrive at the house.

1 Put 300ml/10fl oz cold water and 350g/12oz granulated sugar in a heavy pan and bring the liquid to the boil, stirring all the time until the sugar has dissolved.

2 Reduce the heat and simmer for 5–10 minutes until the syrup coats the back of the spoon.

3 Add 90ml/6 tbsp rose water and simmer for 2–3 minutes more.

4 Leave the syrup to cool, then pour it into a sterilized jar and store in a cool place.

5 To serve, chill the glasses and measure roughly 15ml/1 tbsp rose syrup into each one. Dilute with cold water and serve with ice, if you like.

OLIVES, TRUFFLES AND PRESERVES

A handful of olives, a chunk of cheese and some bread makes a meal that has sustained the peasants and nomads of the Fertile Crescent since ancient times, and the custom has not changed. These are the simplest of foods, made by methods handed down from one generation to the next. In the mountain pastures of Lebanon and the fertile plains of Syria, local herders and travellers still feed themselves on local wild produce and whatever they have preserved from the autumn harvest.

OLIVES

A Lebanese dinner table would be incomplete without a bowl of locally harvested olives, which are often marinated in olive oil, thyme and lemon juice, and are invariably served as part of a mezze spread. They are eaten for breakfast, lunch, supper or just as a snack. Evergreen olive trees thrive in the dry soil and stony hillsides of Lebanon, Jordan and Syria, where they bear fruit for a long time, sometimes hundreds of years. There is an old Arab saying that the olive tree is a bedawiyya, implying that, in spite of hardship and neglect, it is like a loyal, hard-working wife. A huge variety of olives are available in the markets of the eastern Mediterranean, and certain villages are renowned for particular kinds of olives and their superb olive oil pressed from the harvest.

Below: A selection of olives.

Above: A simple meal of bread, cheese and pickled vegetables.

OLIVE OIL

Collectively, Lebanon, Syria, Jordan and Turkey are the main producers of olive oil in the eastern Mediterranean and the Middle East. Olive oil is the principal cooking oil of these countries, where it has been produced for thousands of years. The Romans used it as fuel for lamps and cooking, while the ancient Hebrews used it for religious ceremonies. The cooks of the Ottoman kitchens devised recipes where olive oil was not only the cooking fuel but also the principal flavouring ingredient, requiring the dish to be served at room temperature to appreciate its characteristic aroma. In the Middle Ages the olive oil of Syria was much sought after, but nowadays Turkey has superseded Syria as the main producer of quality oils in the region. Generally, olive oil is used in salads and in dishes where the flavour is intended to predominate, whereas sunflower or nut oil is used for frying.

Lebanese barbecued truffles

1 Cut the truffles into cubes and marinate them in olive oil, lemon juice, dried thyme and sea salt.

2 Thread them on to skewers and grill (broil) over a fire or barbecue.

TRUFFLES

Although truffles are more commonly associated with the cuisines of France and Italy, they have been enjoyed in Lebanon and Syria for centuries. Some varieties of Lebanese truffle, kama, are found at the roots of particular trees on the hillsides, but the Syrian variety is found in the desert. The best truffles, which are gathered and distributed throughout the eastern Mediterranean, grow in profusion around the oasis of Palmyra, situated on the ancient caravan route from Damascus to the Euphrates River. The Bedouins collect them and eat them boiled with buttermilk, or roasted in the ashes of the fire. Medieval recipes call for truffles to be boiled and dressed with oil and crushed thyme, or to be cooked with eggs or lamb. The black and white

Below: Truffles.

Above: Red cabbage and chilli pickle.

Above: The classic green pepper pickle.

Above: Pickled cauliflower with peppers.

truffles of the driest regions are mild in aroma and taste and they are sold in the markets still covered in desert sand.

PRESERVES AND PICKLES

Preserving food is a vital process in the Fertile Crescent, and there are many different techniques for making sure there is plenty of food for the lean months. This seasonal activity used to be part of daily life in the region and still is in many rural homes, but most of these products are now also commercially produced in the cities. In Lebanon, Syria and Jordan, the knowledge of preservation techniques was inherited from the medieval Arabs, who were, in turn, influenced by the civilizations of Greece and Rome.

PICKLED VEGETABLES

When pickled fruit and vegetables were a necessary part of the region's diet, a wide variety of ingredients were preserved in this way, often in colourful combinations. Nowadays, fresh produce is distributed all year round in the region, but pickling remains a popular tradition, partly because the results are so delicious and attractive. Individual pickles include jars of green beans, white cabbage, green chilli peppers, okra, green tomatoes, green walnuts, green almonds and beetroot (beets).

Combined pickles can range from cabbage with apricots and green almonds to slices of aubergine (eggplant) wrapped around garlic or apricots, and tied in a bundle with a thin ribbon of leek or celery. Other popular combinations include pickled turnip with a few slices of beetroot to turn them a pretty a shade of pink. Similarly, the addition of red cabbage to cauliflower produces a purple hue.

Pickling liquids

Vine leaves, cloves of garlic, coriander seeds, cinnamon sticks, parsley stalks, allspice berries and small, thin, hot chillies are often added to pickling jars with the vegetables. These are then filled to the brim with apple vinegar or white wine vinegar, sometimes diluted with water and often seasoned with salt. The pickling juice is drunk to quench the thirst on a hot day.

Below: Pickling spices.

Preservation methods

An amazing variety of preservation methods are included in the culinary techniques of the Fertile Crescent.

Type of food	Method of preservation
meat	preserved in its own fat
fleshy fruits such as apricots, peaches, pears and figs	dried in the sun
sour pomegranates and grapes	boiled down to a syrupy molasses
vine leaves	preserved in brine
tomatoes and bell peppers	reduced to a paste
red chilli peppers	dried in the sun and ground to a powder
yogurt	drained, rolled into balls and bottled in oil
butter	clarified so that it keeps for months
olives	crushed to make oil, or preserved in salt
fish	dried and salted, or pickled while still raw
wild herbs	tied in loose bunches and hung up to dry
fruit and nuts	conserved in jams and pickles
vegetables and pulses	pickled or dried in the sun
rose petals and orange blossom	distilled to make flavoured water

Dairy Products

Milk and its by-products have a central part in the culinary world of Lebanon, Jordan and Syria. In accordance with Islamic customs, milk is rarely consumed fresh, and more commonly appears in the form of by-products, such as butter, clarified butter, yogurt, cheese and cream. Some of the Bedouin use camel's milk; however, in general, the milk supply comes from sheep, goats and cows.

Cooking with yogurt

A number of regional dishes call for yogurt to be used as a cooking liquid. It needs to be stabilized first, otherwise it curdles. While heating the yogurt, it is traditional to stir it in one direction only. It is also important to keep the pot uncovered to prevent steam from disturbing the balance.

1 Tip 600ml/1 pint thick yogurt into a pan and beat until smooth.

2 Gently whisk an egg white and stir it into the yogurt, using a wooden spoon.

3 Add 15ml/1 tbsp cornflour (cornstarch) to 30ml/2 tbsp water and blend to a smooth paste, then add this to the pan. Add 5ml/1 tsp salt and stir well.

4 Heat gently until simmering but not boiling; stir in one direction.

5 Reduce the heat to as low as possible and simmer, uncovered, for 10 minutes. The yogurt is now ready to be cooked with.

Above clockwise from top right: two types of halloumi, feta, labna, and ewe's milk cheeses.

Each country in the Fertile Crescent has a particular region where the milk, cheese and yogurt are regarded as superior to everywhere else, such as the Bekaa Valley in Lebanon or the Euphrates Valley in Syria. In Lebanon, the women from the villages used to travel to the nearest town and go from door to door, selling their own milk, cheese and yogurt from large trays balanced on their heads, but nowadays there are well-established dairy farms, and most products are distributed to towns and cities by truck.

Yogurt

Yogurt has been enjoyed in this region since ancient times and has formed an important part of the basic diet, being easily digestible and nutritious. A bowl of yogurt is often served with a meal, particularly with rice and pulse dishes, or it can be combined with other ingredients, such as herbs, garlic and

Yogurt cheese

Generally, yogurt cheese (labna) is enjoyed with fresh herbs and salad. It is also drizzled in olive oil and sprinkled with the spice mix zahtar or paprika, and served with bread. It is very simple to make.

1 Combine 600ml/1 pint natural (plain) yogurt with 5ml/1 tsp salt.

2 Set the mixture to drain for about 48 hours through muslin. This should produce a firm cheese which can be stored in the refrigerator for 4–5 days.

Yogurt drink

In Lebanon this nutritious yogurt drink is known as laban. It is very popular in Lebanon, Jordan and Syria. It can be served plain, or with a light sprinkling of dried mint, a pinch of the spice mix zahtar, or a dusting of cinnamon.

1 Whisk 600ml/1 pint chilled thick, creamy yogurt with 600ml/ 1 pint cold water until foamy. Season with about 5ml/1 tsp salt.

2 Drop several ice cubes into each glass and pour the yogurt mixture over the top.

3 Scatter the surface with mint, zahtar or cinnamon as required and serve immediately.

vegetables, to form a dip or salad. It is also served mixed with water and a little salt to produce a refreshing drink.

The yogurt of this region is generally thick and creamy, but for certain dishes, it is strained through muslin to produce an even thicker cream-cheese consistency which is ideal for dips and mezze dishes.

CHEESE

Records of cheese-making can be traced back to the ancient Egyptians, Greeks and Romans as well as to the early pastoral societies of the Fertile Crescent. Cheese appears in various guises, from soft white goat's cheese to hard yellowish blocks prepared from ewe's milk. The set white kind is the most versatile as it can be used in mezze dishes, in sweet and savoury pastries, in fillings for flat breads, or simply drizzled with olive oil for a quick snack or for breakfast. For most dishes in this book, the firm white cheese of the eastern Mediterranean can be substituted with the readily available feta, or the salty, springy cheese, halloumi (hallum), which is popular in Lebanon and Jordan.

BUTTER

Traditionally, butter was made in a churn fashioned from the tanned skin of a whole goat. The skin was partially filled with milk, and then suspended by four ropes which were secured to the legs of the skin. The woman of the household would then sit beside the skin and jerk it to and fro until the milk was churned – an age-old tradition that is still used in the remote rural villages and by the Bedouin in their temporary camps. Depending on where you are in the eastern Mediterranean, butter can be made from the milk of sheep, goats or buffalo. It can have quite a strong, almost rancid smell and taste, which some people prefer.

Butter was used lavishly in the medieval kitchens and still is by some cooks, but olive oil and a variety of vegetable oils have superseded butter in most areas. Aleppo in Syria is well known for its delicious creamy butter, and Hama, also in Syria, has gained a reputation for its clarified butter, samna.

Left: Cheese and yoghurt dip.

Clarified butter

Butter is clarified by melting it until it froths and then straining it through muslin to remove the impurities, before pouring it into a container to cool and solidify. Clarified butter is much enjoyed for its nutty taste and aroma, is easy to make at home, and can be stored in a cool place for months. Because the milk solids have been removed, it can reach higher temperatures before burning, so is perfect for frying.

Below: Fried halloumi cheese.

Nuts and Seeds

Since ancient times, nuts and seeds of all kinds have played a huge role in the culinary cultures of the eastern Mediterranean. The plants and their fruits are even a favourite subject for decorating ceramic tiles and crockery. The cuisine of the Fertile Crescent boasts numerous sweet treats and snacks prepared with these delicious, nutritious ingredients, and they are added liberally to pilaffs, puddings, pastries and mezze dishes.

Almond milk sherbet

A traditional drink in the Levant is a refreshing sherbet prepared from almond milk.

1 Tip 250g/9oz ground almonds on to a piece of muslin or cheesecloth. Gather up the corners and tie them together to form a loose sack.

2 Pour 850ml/18 pints water into a bowl and place the sack in it for at least 1 hour, shaking and squeezing it from time to time so that the flavour from the soaked almonds penetrates the water.

3 Give the sack a final squeeze and lift it out of the water. This will leave a fragrant milk that can be used in sweet and savoury dishes.

ALMONDS

The ancient Greeks are the first people known to have cultivated almonds, and the Romans, who consumed them in vast quantities, referred to them as a Greek nut. In the early Arab cooking manuals, there are records of almonds being poached and pressed for their delicate milk, which was then used in puddings and drinks.

Immature green almonds are picked while their husks are velvety soft and the whole fruit, including the husk, is eaten as a snack with a sprinkling of salt, or preserved in vinegar. Mature almonds, on the other hand, are prised from their hardened shells and then blanched, roasted, flaked or ground and employed in numerous sweet and savoury dishes, such as the dried fruit and nut compote, khoshaf, a dish of medieval origins that is popular throughout the eastern Mediterranean.

CHESTNUTS

Sweet, soft chestnuts in their prickly husks grow prolifically in the eastern Mediterranean and the large, hardy trees live for a long time. When they are finally felled, the strong, flexible wood is used to make orchard ladders and garden tools. They bear ripe fruit in the months of October and November, and so chestnuts are always associated with the colder months. Street-vendors roast chestnuts on open braziers, and the shops sell boxes of delectably moist chestnuts preserved in syrup, the Middle Eastern marrons glacés. The Palestinian tradition is to add chestnuts to their famous makloub, 'upside-down' dishes, in which the rice is first cooked on top of layers of meat and chestnuts. The whole dish is served turned over so that the delicious meat and nut juices permeate the rice.

PINE NUTS

In ancient times in the Fertile Crescent, pine nuts were included in ceremonial cornucopias of fruit placed on statues to symbolize the wealth and status of individual towns and cities. The medieval Arabs added them liberally to both savoury and sweet dishes; the Ottomans added them to fillings for stuffed vegetables and vine leaves, and roasted them to scatter over puddings and dips. With such a pine-nut heritage on their doorstep, the cooks of the eastern Mediterranean could hardly

Below: Almonds.

Below: Chestnuts.

Roasting pine nuts

A number of savoury and sweet dishes call for pine nuts to be roasted. Place them in a heavy pan over medium heat, shaking until they turn golden brown and a little oily. Watch them carefully, as they burn easily. Tip them on to a plate to cool.

ignore this ancient pine cone seed. Pine nuts are scattered over a variety of dishes and are pounded to make a creamy tartare sauce for fish. The nuts have a mild resinous taste and are deliciously crunchy when roasted.

PISTACHIOS

The pistachio tree is native to the Levant, parts of Anatolia, Iran and Afghanistan. With the influence of Persia on medieval Arab cuisine and the later Ottoman Empire, the popularity of pistachios spread to Lebanon, Jordan and Syria. The name comes from the Persian word pesteh, and the genus also includes the trees from which the edible resin, mastic, is harvested. The nut can be used in all sorts of creative ways, both sweet and savoury, such as in Turkish delight and baklava, salads, rice dishes and stuffed meatballs.

SESAME SEEDS

These tiny, teardrop-shaped seeds seem almost indispensable in the Arab culinary world. They are sprinkled over a variety of savoury pastries and breads, such as the bread rings, semit, which are sold on every busy street, on the quayside, in bus stations and markets. Sesame seeds are added to salads, marinades and spice mixes such as zahtar, and they are crushed for their oil and ground to a versatile creamy paste called tahini. The seeds are harvested while still immature as they tend to burst out of their pods and scatter everywhere when they are ripe – hence the famous command 'Open sesame!' in 'Ali Baba and the Forty Thieves'.

Above: Pistachio nuts.

Sesame paste

Tahini (or tahina) can be found in light or dark varieties. The darker, coarser one is prepared from roasted sesame seeds and their husks, and has a nuttier flavour than the lighter, creamier version. It is used in chickpea puree, hummus, and the smoked aubergine (eggplant) mezze dish, baba ghanoush. It is also combined with lemon and crushed garlic to make a sauce or as a delicious sweet dip for bread.

Above: Sesame seeds.

WALNUTS

These larged, wrinkled nuts have long been regarded as the 'king of nuts', in accordance with the Latin and Greek myths that the gods ate walnuts, while mere mortals lived on acorns. The immature green nuts are often pickled or preserved in syrup, while the ripened ones are pressed for their rich, pungent oil, or used in a variety of puddings, sweet pastries and salads. Perhaps their most famous role in the eastern Mediterranean is in the popular mezze dish muhammara, in which the walnuts are pounded with garlic, red peppers, olive oil and breadcrumbs to make a delicious dip.

Below: Walnuts.

VEGETABLES

Since ancient times, vegetables have featured prominently in the cooking of the eastern Mediterranean. They appear in many guises, as mezze dishes, pickles, salads, stews, pilaffs, jams and puddings. Numerous dishes are dedicated to vegetables alone, or they might be combined with fruit in stews, or stuffed with meat and rice. They are held in such high esteem that they have become the focus of Arab sayings, such as 'A table without vegetables is like an old man devoid of wisdom'.

Below: Carrots are often eaten raw.

Above: Peppers, aubergines and courgettes are the staple ingredients of many recipes in the region.

AUBERGINES (EGGPLANT)

The most useful vegetable of all is the aubergine, which is known throughout the region as 'poor man's meat'. Aubergines first appeared in Persia, where the conquering Arabs fell under their spell in the 7th and 8th centuries. During the Ottoman period, palace chefs were known to have prepared aubergines for feasts in at least 40 different ways.

Generally, the aubergines of the region are purple, or almost black in colour, and range from large, bulbous ones to small, teardrop-shaped ones that are lovely when smoked.

Aubergines find their way into numerous stews and grain dishes, as well as Arab fatta dishes with pitta bread and yogurt, which could be regarded as soul food for the Lebanese, Jordanians and Syrians. Dried aubergines are reconstituted in water, stuffed with an aromatic pilaff, or spicy bulgur, and then poached in a little olive oil and lemon juice – a speciality of Syria. Pickled aubergines, often stuffed with walnuts or hot peppers, are another speciality of the eastern Mediterranean.

CARROTS

Wild red and purple carrots are believed to have originated in Afghanistan. Somewhere along the carrot's journey into Europe, 17th century Dutch horticulturalists cultivated orange carrots as they were regarded as more

Smoking aubergines

To smoke aubergines effectively, you need a gas flame or a griddle.

1 First, place the whole aubergine directly over the gas flame or on a heated griddle. Leave to soften, turning over from time to time.

2 When the aubergine is soft, place it in a plastic bag to sweat for a few minutes.

3 To extract the flesh, either slit the aubergine open lengthways and scoop it out, or hold the aubergine by its stalk under a running cold tap and peel off the skin. If you do the latter, make sure you squeeze out the excess water at the end.

4 The distinctive-tasting flesh of smoked aubergines is mixed with olive oil and lemon juice, or yogurt and garlic, and served with bread.

appealing in colour and superior in taste. Nowadays, we are completely familiar with the orange carrot, but the red, purple and yellow varieties are still grown in Syria and southern Turkey. Carrots contain a fair amount of natural sugar, making them both pretty to look at and sweet to taste. They are used in many ways: grated or chopped and combined with yogurt; tossed in salads and pilaffs; cooked with lentils, beans or other vegetables in stews; sliced and pickled; steamed and puréed.

COURGETTES (ZUCCHINI)

Both courgettes and marrows are believed to be cooling to the blood, and therefore require balancing with warming herbs such as dill and mint. The smallest, freshest courgettes are crisp and slightly perfumed, and taste best tossed raw in salads or cooked very lightly. Young courgettes are often sold with their papery yellow-orange flowers, which are then stuffed with aromatic rice or bulgur.

Larger courgettes are cooked with tomatoes in stews or egg dishes, such as the Arab bread and courgette omelette eggah bi eish wa kousa. They can also be stuffed with savoury mixtures of aromatic rice or minced lamb, or with a sweeter herb mixture and cooked with fruit, for instance in kablama, a dish of stuffed courgettes cooked with apricots. Large marrows are served stuffed with minced meat, or cooked in stews, and marrow seeds are roasted and eaten as a snack like pumpkin seeds.

CUCUMBER

These are perhaps one of the oldest cultivated vegetables in the region, and have been utilized throughout the centuries for their refreshing qualities. Generally, the cucumbers of the region are much the same size as courgettes – short and stubby, and almost seedless. The skin is quite bitter, so they are usually peeled or partially peeled before eating. Strips of peeled cucumber sprinkled with salt make a popular mezze dish in Lebanon and Syria, and finely chopped cucumber is often mixed with yogurt and garlic to make a dip. In Lebanon cucumber and yogurt are also combined in a soup, shorbet khyar bi laban, which is served cold.

Above: Melokhia.

GLOBE ARTICHOKES

These regal-looking vegetables were once regarded as luxury foods for the wealthy and noble, in fact, globe artichokes are simply glorious thistles, a cultivated version of the ancient cardoon, which has grown wild in the eastern Mediterranean for centuries. Fresh artichokes are sold on their long stems in the markets so that they can be kept in a bucket of water at home, like a bunch of flowers.

In Lebanon, where they are particularly popular, ready-prepared artichokes can be bought at the markets. They are poached in olive oil or stuffed with broad (fava) beans or a minced lamb filling.

Preparing artichokes

To prepare artichokes for cooking, remove the stalk and scales first, then the hairy choke. Rub lemon juice over the heart and the fleshy bottoms before plunging them in cold water to prevent them from discolouring.

Above: Okra.

MELOKHIA

The leaves of the melokhia plant are particularly popular in Egypt, Jordan and Lebanon. It is a member of the mallow family, and is sometimes referred to as 'Jew's mallow'. The leaves are sold in the markets fresh or dried and taste a little bit like sorrel. The texture is similar to okra, with a sticky quality which is much sought after by locals but is not always to the taste of foreigners. Generally, the leaves are prepared and cooked like spinach but tend to be restricted to soups or stews.

OKRA

This is another member of the mallow family. Each pod contains compartments filled with seeds, and a gummy substance that gives okra its glutinous character when cooked. Immature okra is picked while still small and hung on strings to dry. The dried pods are first rubbed in a cloth to remove the hairs before being added to soups and stews for their tart flavour.

Onion garnish

This garnish is used for serving with kibbeh and roast meat.

1 Roast 30ml/2 tbsp pine nuts in a heavy-based pan until golden brown. Transfer to a plate and stir 30ml/2 tbsp olive oil and a knob of butter into the hot pan.

2 Add 2 onions, chopped, and sauté until golden brown. Return the pine nuts to the pan and season with salt and pepper. Spoon the mixture over kibbeh or a cut of roasted lamb.

Mature pods should be bought when they are fresh, firm and bright green in colour. When tossed in lemon juice and left whole they remain crunchy, but once the pods have been sliced they should be cooked quickly. The Arab dish of sautéed, lightly caramelized whole okra in sugar and lemon juice is a popular mezze dish.

ONION

All types of onion are available in the markets, from round and bulbous varieties in their varying shades of red, purple, and gold to pearly white small onions, pink shallots and long green spring onions (scallions). Large onions are often hollowed out and stuffed with an aromatic rice and minced lamb filling, while smaller purple and red onions are particularly favoured for salads and mezze dishes as they are slightly sweet. Shallots are used in stews or threaded on to kebab skewers.

Above: Onions.

Long onion tops are chopped and sautéed in butter with a squeeze of lemon, as a topping for an omelette.

PEPPERS

The bell-shaped capsicum pepper arrived in the eastern Mediterranean from the New World in the 16th century. The most common (bell) peppers are small and green, the immature fruit of capsicum pepper plants. These firm, slightly tart peppers are favoured for stuffing with rice or meat in dishes such as mahshi filfil hilu, or slicing raw in salads. More mature, long, sweet red peppers are used in stews or grilled, skinned and marinated in olive oil. They are also dried in the sun and then ground into fruity paprika powder,

Below: Red peppers.

Above: Pumpkin.

made into paste, or re-softened in warm water to be stuffed with rice or bulgur wheat in the winter.

PUMPKIN

This is another vegetable that came to the eastern Mediterranean from the New World. The pumpkin is particularly linked to the cuisines of the Armenians

Red pepper paste

Dried sweet red peppers are pounded with chillies, olive oil and salt to form a thick paste used in dishes or simply spread on bread.

1 Soak 8–10 dried red peppers and 2–3 dried red chilli peppers in warm water for about 2 hours.

2 Peel, remove any seeds and, using a mortar and pestle, pound the flesh to a paste. Add 30ml/2 tbsp olive oil and salt and mix. Chill and store for up to 2 weeks.

Baked pumpkin with spices
The beautiful orange flesh of pumpkin comes into its own when roasted, as it develops a rich sweetness and flavour. This is a favourite side dish in Lebanon.

1 Cut a seeded pumpkin into slices and place in a baking tin.

2 Drizzle with olive oil and sprinkle with crushed coriander, cumin and sesame seeds, ground cinnamon and allspice.

3 Dab a little butter on each segment and sprinkle with sugar and salt. Bake in a medium oven for about 40 minutes. Serve with grilled or roasted meats.

Below: Spinach, yogurt and pine nuts.

Above: Spinach.

and the Kurds, who prepare a variety of sweet dishes with them, such as baked pumpkin with honey and spices, or a sweet rice dish with cinnamon. Other pumpkin dishes include soups, stews, pilaffs, savoury pastries, jam and baklava, and the seeds are roasted and eaten as a snack. The most impressive dish of all is baked pumpkin stuffed with jewelled pilaff, containing pine nuts, pistachios, currants, orange zest and apricots. In some villages of the Levant, a hollowed-out pumpkin is often used as a cooking or serving vessel for soups or stews.

SPINACH

Originally from Persia, where it was considered more as a herb than a vegetable, spinach is regarded by Arabs as the 'prince of vegetables'. There are even medieval Arab recipes for spinach to be used in sweet dishes, combined with honey, spices and nuts. Spinach is rich in vitamins and minerals and grows all year round in the temperate climate of the Fertile Crescent. One of its principal savoury roles is in the filling for Arab fatayer pastries, often combined with cheese and dill or walnuts and raisins. It is also a popular choice for fatta dishes, topped with yogurt and nuts.

TOMATOES

These are another 16th-century import, yet tomatoes are so entwined in the cuisine that it is difficult to imagine how the people of the eastern Mediterranean

Above: Tomatoes.

ever managed without them. Tomato harvests are abundant, and the bright red, flavoursome fruits come in a variety of shapes and sizes.

Generally, tomatoes are skinned and seeded before being served in mezze dishes and salads, such as Lebanese fattoush, made with left-over bread. Whole tomatoes are stuffed with rice, bulgur or minced meat, in the same manner as peppers. Ripe tomatoes are crushed to a pulp, which is poured into trays and thickened in the sun to form a paste that is used in soups and stews and in the meat filling for Arab pizzas, lahma bi ajeen. The unripe green fruit at the end of the season is often pickled with whole garlic cloves, green almonds and chillies.

Below: Tomato and bread salad.

FRUIT

The variety of fresh fruit in the markets of the Fertile Crescent is quite stunning. Piled high on the stalls are juicy peaches, grapes, pomegranates, mulberries, apples, oranges, melons, green plums, apricots, dates, figs, quinces and lemons. Although ripe seasonal fruits are mainly enjoyed fresh and uncooked, this is by no means the only way fruit is eaten. Several favourite puddings feature poached and dried fruits. Cherries, grapes, plums, figs and apricots are also added to savoury stews and roasted meats in their fresh or dried forms. Sherbet, which today and historically, is perhaps the most widespread drink in the Arab world, is prepared in many households as a way of using up a fruit glut. Unripe fruits are preserved as pickles and jam.

Above: Apricots.

Poached apricots in syrup

These are ideal for stuffing with almond paste or cream.

1 Soak dried apricots in water overnight. The soaking water is then used for the syrup, so strain it into a heavy pan and add roughly 350g/12oz sugar to each 600ml/1 pint water.

2 Bring to the boil, stirring all the time, until the sugar is dissolved. Reduce the heat and simmer for 5–10 minutes, until the syrup coats the back of the spoon.

3 Add several tbsp lemon juice or scented water such as rose or orange flower water to the syrup.

4 Add the soaked apricots and simmer for 15 minutes. Leave the apricots to cool in the syrup.

APRICOTS

These little fruits come in varying colours and sizes, although the most common is orange-yellow with a velvety skin. When harvested, soft, sun-ripened fresh apricots are eaten fresh as a snack, but many are set aside to be dried on the flat roofs in rural areas so that they can be consumed throughout the year. Naturally sun-dried apricots are dark orange in colour, with a slightly caramelized flavour. Reconstituted dried apricots are often stuffed with savoury rice and minced lamb, added to meat stews, or combined with other dried fruits and nuts in pilaffs and compotes. Unripe apricots are added to mixed pickles along with green almonds.

Below: Cherries.

CHERRIES

Both sweet and sour cherries are native to the eastern Mediterranean. Ladders made from chestnut wood are used to harvest the fruit which, in the case of sweet cherries, matures only in June and the first half of July. Most of the cherries in the region are deep red in colour, although there are also black ones in Syria. Sweet, juicy cherries are devoured in quantities for breakfast, for dessert or for a little refreshment at any time of day. Sour cherries, on the other hand, have a number of culinary uses. Poached with sugar, they are made into jam or a syrup used as the basis of a refreshing sherbet drink. They are also puréed and dried for adding to pilaffs and to stews such as lahma bil karaz.

DATES

These have long been a staple food in desert regions of the Middle East and, at times, the only source of food for nomadic herdsmen and the Bedouin, who can thrive on a diet of dates and fermented milk for long periods. In the eastern Mediterranean, dates fall into three main categories: the soft, juicy ones which are eaten fresh, dried, ground to a powder or compressed into

Below: Fresh dates.

Stuffing dates

To make a delicious sweet snack, moist dried dates can be stuffed with blanched almonds, or with a paste prepared with ground almonds or pistachios. Buy plump, succulent dates, such as medjool, for stuffing.

1 Using a sharp knife make a slit along the top of the date to prise it open and remove the stone, keeping the end intact.

2 Fill the cavity with a blanched almond, half a walnut, a mixture of chopped nuts, or marzipan made from pistachios or almonds.

blocks or date paste – this is the main type for export; the dry, fibrous fruit known as 'camel' dates, which are one of the staple foods of the nomads; and semi-dry dates, which are slightly tart.

Most of the dates in the regional markets come from Syria, Jordan, Iraq, Saudi Arabia and Egypt. They are often sold stuffed, or pounded with rose water and cinnamon to form a paste for filling cakes, biscuits and pastries. Dried dates are also added to savoury dishes, such as fruity pilaff prepared with nuts and apricots or vegetables and meat.

FIGS

Mohammad is reputed to have adored figs and commented that they must be heaven-sent. Fresh figs really need to

Above: Lemons.

mature on the tree under a hot sun to be at their moist, ultra-sweet best. They are generally eaten as a snack and sometimes cooked in desserts, whereas the dried fruits find their way into compotes, jams, savoury stews and roasts. Unripe green figs are picked for a delectable honey-flavoured jam.

GRAPES

There are paintings of vines on the walls of early Egyptian tombs, and Noah was reputed to have planted vines in the foothills of Mount Ararat when the Great Flood subsided. The Phoenicians spread the vine wherever they settled and the Romans cultivated it for wine, as well as for its fresh, sweet fruit. Today in the eastern Mediterranean

Below: Figs.

Above: Dried limes.

there are many varieties of grape grown for the table and for wine, with some specially grown to make dried fruit. Fresh grapes are also puréed, dried flat, or pressed for their juice, which is boiled to form a useful fruit molasses. Tart green grapes are sometimes added to savoury stews, and the dried fruits are used in sweet and savoury dishes.

LEMONS AND LIMES

Before the cultivation of lemons and limes in the eastern Mediterranean began in Roman times, pomegranate juice or fermented grape juice was used as a souring agent. Today, however, lemons are grown in abundance and harvested all year round. They appear in some form at almost every meal – in dressings, marinades, sherbet drinks, or syrup for sweet pastries; as an accompaniment to melon, olives, grilled lamb or sautéed liver; or squeezed into mezze dishes. Limes are often used as a substitute for lemons, but are also used in cooking savoury soups and stews when dried.

MELON

Although not of the same family, fresh melon and watermelon are sold beside one another in the markets. Watermelons thrived in the region long before the modern melon, which was not cultivated there until after the fall of the Roman Empire. Both kinds of melon grow at speed, like weeds, and sprawl over the soil, providing plenty of fruit to harvest in both summer and winter.

Choosing melons
When choosing mature sun-ripened melons at the market, the simplest test of ripeness is to press the end opposite the stem to see if it yields, and sniff it for its perfume. The flesh should be golden-yellow or orange, depending on the type. Watermelons should have a rich, hollow sound when tapped and the flesh should be a vibrant reddish-pink when cut open, with a sweet, fresh taste, and a texture that is not too watery.

Above: Melon.

Perfectly ripe melon is often served cut into cubes and served as a mezze dish. The seeds can be soaked, dried and then roasted and salted, and eaten like pumpkin seeds. Golden melons, such as the Galia and Casaba varieties, are often served with cubes of feta cheese; watermelon cubes can be lightly tossed in rose water to give them a perfumed aroma. Unripe melons and watermelons are pickled in vinegar or poached with sugar to make a conserve.

ORANGES

Seafaring Arabs brought sour oranges to the eastern Mediterranean from China and India, but the sweet orange did not arrive there until the 15th century. Oranges of both kinds are used in sweet and savoury dishes, such as the Turkish and Arab salad salata naranj, and whole oranges, or just the peel, are preserved in syrup. The blossoms of the bitter orange are distilled to make a fragrant essence, which in its diluted form is sold as orange blossom water.

Below: Oranges.

POMEGRANATES

This fruit has a rich and ancient history. The goddess Aphrodite is said to have planted a pomegranate tree in her birthplace in Cyprus, and the Romans, who referred to the fruit as the 'apple of Carthage', consumed it in vast quantities and made wine from the fermented juice. In medieval times,

Below: Pomegranates.

Bitter orange-peel preserve
This preserve will keep in a cool place for several months. Serve spooned over milk puddings.

1 Take 8 oranges, and, using a sharp knife, peel off a wide strip of skin all the way around each orange, so that you have a long ribbon of orange peel.

2 Remove any pith from the peel strips and divide each one into 3 or 4 pieces. Roll each piece into a tight bud and pack tightly, so they do not unravel, into a sterilized jar.

3 Cover them with cold water and leave to soak for about 12 hours. Meanwhile, squeeze the peeled oranges and save all the juice.

4 Drain all the orange-peel buds and place them in a pan. Cover with about 600ml/1 pint water and bring it to the boil. Reduce the heat and simmer for an hour.

5 Add 350g/12oz sugar to the water with the reserved orange juice and the seeds of 3–4 cardamom pods.

6 Bring to the boil, stirring all the time until the sugar has dissolved, then reduce the heat and simmer until the buds turn almost transparent. Leave to cool, then pack the buds into a sterilized jar and cover with the syrup.

Above: Stuffed vine leaves.

Islamic mystics believed pomegranates could elevate the soul and purge it of hate, anger and envy.

Both sweet and sour pomegranates were cultivated during the Ottoman period. The sour variety was valued for its juice, which was used to make a refreshing drink and as a souring agent before the arrival of lemons in the region. Today the juice of sour pomegranates is still used to make a sherbet drink, but it is also used to prepare a special molasses known as dibs, which is used in Syria for dressing salads or as a marinade for poultry. Pomegranate juice is also boiled, then dried in flat strips, an excellent way of preserving the tart and fruity flavour for adding to dishes throughout the year. The seeds of the sweet pomegranate are sometimes sprinkled with a little rose water and served as a dessert, and they are also added to both savoury and sweet dishes as a vivid garnish.

Below: Pomegranate salad.

QUINCES

Related to the apple and the pear, the quince is similar in appearance, although larger and pale yellow in colour. Quince fruit and seeds are both extremely high in pectin, and transform their poaching juices to a jelly. The flesh of the fresh fruit is firm, mildly perfumed, and slightly tart. However, the fruit really comes to life when cooked, as it emits a delightful floral fragrance and lends a honeyed taste to any dish. Quinces are generally cooked with lamb or poultry, stuffed with rice and minced lamb, or poached with sugar to make jam or a fruit pudding.

Below: Quinces.

VINE LEAVES

Leaves from vines are sold fresh in piles in the markets, or preserved in brine. The leaves have a slightly malted taste and are used for wrapping around poached or grilled fish, cheese and stuffed artichokes. Their most famous role is in the mezze dish of wrapped vine leaves, stuffed with a mixture of aromatic rice or minced meat.

Preparing vine leaves

Fresh vine leaves should be plunged into boiling water for a minute to soften, then drained and refreshed in cold water. Preserved leaves have already been softened but must be soaked several times in boiling water to rid them of salt. Place the leaves in a bowl and pour boiling water over them, making sure it gets between the layers. Leave them to soak for about 15 minutes, drain and repeat. Make sure they are thoroughly drained before use.

FISH AND SHELLFISH

Lebanon, Jordan and Syria are in the enviable position of having a regular supply of fish on their doorstep, principally from the Mediterranean and the Red Sea.

In the early cooking manuals of the eastern Mediterranean, recipes rarely specified the type of fish to be used. This was probably because people tended to use whatever fish was available and, in the case of Jordan and Iraq, that was more likely to be of the inland freshwater variety. The most popular fish caught off the coast of Lebanon and Syria, as well as in the Gulf of Aqaba off the Jordanian coast, include sea bass, red snapper, garfish, grouper, sardines, swordfish, tuna, grey mullet, red mullet and sole.

Right, from top: sea bass, red snapper, sardines and prawns.

Tahini sauce

This simple tahini sauce makes a delicious accompaniment to any type of fried fish.

1 Pound the 1–2 cloves of garlic in a mortar and pestle with a little salt, until you have a paste.

2 Beat 150ml/¼ pint/⅔ cup tahini paste in a bowl together with the juice of 1 lemon and the juice of 1 orange, until thick and smooth with the consistency of pouring cream.

3 Beat the garlic paste into the tahini, and season to taste. Serve spooned over fried fish, with lemon wedges.

SEA FISH

Most firm-fleshed fish are interchangeable in soups, kibbeh and stews, and are equally ideal for barbecuing and baking. A popular Arab speciality found throughout Lebanon and Syria is sayadieh samak, a dish of any sea fish combined with walnuts and pomegranate seeds.The most common way of cooking fish in the Fertile Crescent is to grill (broil) it whole over charcoal. Alternatively it can be baked in the oven and served with a tahini sauce, lemon wedges or herbs. However, it is rarely cooked with milk or served with yogurt or any kind of cheese, as there is a widespread belief that such a combination could render the dish harmful to those who eat it.

Sole

Favoured by the Romans, sole is named after Moses (samak Moussa), as it is believed that when he divided the Red Sea, this particular fish was cut in half and remained thin and flat ever after. In Lebanon, sole is cooked French-style, fried quickly with almonds, and is at its best when lightly cooked. It can also be rubbed with garlic and ground sumac, salt and pepper, briefly grilled (broiled) and served with a wedge of lemon.

Below: Red mullet.

Below: Fried sole.

Preserving fish

Drying and salting fish is an ancient tradition in the Levant and a very practical one, enabling it to be transported inland and cooked out of season. Whole fish or boned fillets are hung up on makeshift lines to dry, like socks hanging on a washing line, and then rubbed in salt to preserve them. The Orontes River in Lebanon made a name for itself during the Ottoman Empire as the place to buy salt-cured fish, which was in demand throughout the eastern Mediterranean. Nowadays, salted fish is a delicacy rather than a necessity and is consumed with bread for a simple snack.

Red mullet

This is the most prized fish in Lebanon and Turkey, where it is generally grilled or fried whole so that its pink, dappled skin and juicy flesh can be enjoyed in its full glory. In Lebanon it is often served with strips of fried pitta bread and a bowl of tahini sauce.

Grey mullet

This is an expensive fish, which is highly prized in the eastern Mediterranean for its roe. This is almost as valuable as caviar from the Caspian Sea. Arab cooks make a traditional delicacy called batarekh, which involves salting, pressing and drying the roe, and encasing it in beeswax to preserve it. The Lebanese, in particular, enjoy the roe preserved in this manner, and serve it cut into very thin slices, drizzled with a little olive oil and lemon juice.

Above: Sea bass.

Sea bass

With its firm flesh and subtle flavour, sea bass is an incredibly versatile fish employed in all sorts of dishes that call for firm chunks and fillets. It is particularly popular in the chilli-flavoured dish samak harra. Sea bass is also a practical fish for stuffing and, as it is such a fleshy fish, it is ideal for flaking to make the tasty fish kibbeh which are so popular in Syria and Lebanon.

Mackerel

The oily, richly flavoured flesh of mackerel is also ideally suited to the kibbeh of Syria, Jordan and Lebanon. Another Ottoman speciality is uskumru dolmas, a whole mackerel stuffed with a filling of nuts and spices combined with its own cooked flesh.

FRESHWATER FISH

The fish from the rivers and inland waters, such as trout, eel, carp and barbell, end up in the rural markets, or are sold by lone fishermen standing by the roadside. In Lebanon there is a leaping carp with a pale pink flesh, just like the leaping salmon of other countries, which is highly prized when available. Frogs and snails are also eaten to some extent in parts of the Levant, particularly in Lebanon and Syria, where the French have left their mark on the cuisine. Most Muslims will not touch these creatures for religious reasons, but a number of Christians do eat them. It is not uncommon to come across recipes in the Christian communities for fried frogs' legs cooked with rice, or simmered in a tomato-based ragout. Snails were often regarded as the food of the poor and were sold in the markets at a low price. Nowadays, though, they are back on restaurant menus, often served with a garlicky nut sauce, a tahini sauce or, as in France, with garlic butter.

SHELLFISH

These are mainly enjoyed by people in the coastal regions, although many Muslims will not eat anything with a shell. Squid, mussels and lobster are consumed in some parts of Lebanon and the Gulf of Aqaba in Jordan. In the same category is a species of crab which has a penchant for white mulberries and can be caught while climbing the mulberry trees to devour the fruit. These were considered a great delicacy by the French and other Europeans during their occupation of Lebanon. The crabs are often steamed and served as a delicacy during Lent in the Christian communities. Prawns (shrimp) are perhaps the most common of all shellfish and are generally baked, sautéed, or threaded onto kebab skewers with pieces of bell pepper and cherry tomatoes. They also blend very well with rice dishes and salads.

Below: Prawns.

MEAT AND POULTRY

Throughout the history of the eastern Mediterranean, the preferred meat for everyday meals has traditionally been mutton or lamb. Pork is never eaten by Muslims and is practically unknown in this region, and beef is more expensive than lamb. Ever since the early nomads herded their sheep for sale into the villages and towns, lamb and mutton have been included in the daily diet, although still somewhat sparingly by the majority of the population – vegetables and pulses were cheaper. The wealthy have always indulged in huge portions of meat, often roasting a whole sheep for banquets, but the poorer communities have had to rely on devising recipes that enable small quantities of meat to go far, hence the abundance of stews, kebabs and kibbeh in traditional Arab cuisine.

Above: Skewered lamb cooked on hot coals is universally popular.

WILD GAME

In medieval times, hunting played a big role in the lives of the poor and the rich alike. The areas known as Anatolia and Greater Syria were blessed with many edible wild animals, such as rabbit, hare, gazelle, wild boar, porcupine, and a whole range of game birds. The Shuf, a scenic part of the Lebanon Mountains inhabited mainly by the Druze people, has provided ample hunting grounds for small game birds, such as pigeon and quail. The sight and aroma of these small birds being marinated in a pomegranate sauce and then grilled over charcoal is just as common now as it was in medieval times. These tasty morsels are available to buy in the rural markets and are favourite treats for picnics in the hills.

Below: Pigeon is a favourite game bird in Lebanon and Syria.

LAMB AND MUTTON

Throughout Lebanon, Syria and Jordan, a whole lamb roasted on a spit is the festive dish most commonly made for special occasions, such as weddings, family gatherings, the visit of an important guest, and religious feasts.

Below: Mutton needs marinating and long slow cooking.

Medieval pomegranate sauce

This sauce works well as a marinade or a dressing for grilled poultry and game birds.

1 Using a mortar and pestle, crush and grind 2 cloves of garlic with 1 tsp salt to a smooth paste.

2 In a bowl, combine the creamed garlic with 2 tbsp olive oil and 4 tbsp pomegranate molasses.

3 Add a small bunch of fresh mint leaves, finely chopped, and/or 1–2 tsp ground sumac. Use as a marinade, or serve with grilled or roast chicken or game.

Daily fare includes a variety of stews, which have been the mainstay of the region's cooking since medieval times. The dish often takes its name from the principal ingredient, such as mishmishiya, lamb stew with apricots, and safarjaliya, a stew containing quince. Needless to say, mouth-watering lamb kibbeh are prepared daily, and street vendors and kebab shops serve lamb shawarma, the Arab equivalent of Turkish döner kebabs.

The most highly prized lamb and mutton comes from the hardy and resilient Awassi breed of sheep, as it produces an excellent, strong-tasting meat. Not just the flesh, but every part of the sheep is used in the kitchens of the region – the head, eyes, brain, tongue, lungs, heart, stomach, intestines, testicles and feet – and all have their favourite recipes.

Above: Goats at a watering hole in Wadi Rum, Jordan.

Above: Awassi sheep, highly prized for their fatty tails.

Above: Chickens on a farm in Beirut, ready to be transported to market.

Sheep's tail fat is perhaps the earliest and most primitive cooking oil, and is still in use today. It is rendered from the sheep's podgy bulbous tail. Capable of surviving in hot, dry climates, these Awassi sheep rely on the fat stored in their tails to provide them with the sustenance they need in a similar way to the hump of a camel. In the rural and mountainous regions of Lebanon, Jordan and Syria, sheep's tail fat is still the preferred cooking fuel for its taste, and chunks of it are often threaded on to kebab sticks to flavour the meat.

OTHER MEAT

The addition of beef and veal to the diet in this region is relatively recent, as traditionally cows and oxen were valued solely for their milk and their labour in the fields. Nowadays, beef may be used in stews and meatballs, but lamb still remains the preferred choice for rituals and celebrations. In some rural regions, a whole goat or camel may be roasted for special occasions.

POULTRY

The delicate meat of chickens and other poultry was so highly regarded in the medieval Arab kitchen that numerous chicken recipes, flavoured with rhubarb, mulberries, almonds, walnuts and pomegranates, were recorded. During the Ottoman period, more exotic and interesting poultry recipes were created, resulting in a vast choice of chicken dishes in the eastern Mediterranean. Chicken, turkey duck, pigeon, pheasant, partridge and quail were all used, and once the Ottomans introduced turkey from the New World, it too gained a place in the repertoire.

Today, chicken features in the daily diet of the region almost as frequently as lamb. It is popular in kebabs, stews, grilled and roasted, as a main course for dinner and as a street snack.

Below: Roast stuffed turkey.

For the most part, chickens are free range and fed on corn, so the meat is lean and tasty. Turkeys remain a popular choice for Christian religious feasts, whereas Muslim feasts invariably involve a whole ram or goat. Quail is spit-roasted at street stalls and at picnics in the countryside, and pigeon stew is popular in parts of Jordan and Lebanon close to the Egyptian border, where pigeon dishes are common.

Diet and religion

For the Muslims of the eastern Mediterranean there are certain dietary restrictions that must be adhered to regarding meat. The Qur'an forbids an animal to be slaughtered in any other manner than by cutting its throat; it forbids the consumption of an animal's blood; it forbids the consumption of an animal slaughtered for any other god; and it forbids any form of pork. The Muslims also engage in the ritual sacrifice of a ram during the Islamic festival called Eid-el Kurban in Arabic, which marks the near-sacrifice of Isma'il (Isaac in the Bible).

Above: Basterma.

Above: Sucuk.

Above: Spiced chicken with sumac.

CURED MEAT

There are two main types of cured meat in the eastern Mediterranean. One is a cured fillet of beef, basterma in Arabic, which is encased in a wonderfully pungent paste prepared with ground fenugreek, garlic and red pepper. The Armenians of the region are said to make the best basterma of the region as they have been involved in the curing process since the days of the Ottoman Empire. Sliced finely, this cured meat lends a strong aroma of fenugreek to many bean and pulse dishes, and it is popular cooked with eggs, or served as a mezze dish with cheese and melon.

The other cured meat that is found in the markets of the region is a spicy sausage prepared with beef or lamb. Each region has its own version, such as the cumin-flavoured sucuk of Turkey or the spicy maqaniq of Lebanon. These well-flavoured sausages are usually simply grilled, then sliced and enjoyed as mezze, or added to bean and pulse dishes for the subtle spicy flavour they impart to the dish.

Preserved meat in fat

This is a traditional delicacy in Arab and Anatolian cooking, and consists of any meat, most often lamb, preserved in its own fat. Following an ancient method of preserving, the meat is cut into small cubes and fried, then stored in more rendered fat in earthenware jars. These tasty morsels are reserved for flavouring eggs, soups and grain dishes in the winter months, or at any time when meat is scarce.

TRADITIONAL MEAT DISHES

Classic meat dishes from the region are universally enjoyed, and have been cooked in homes and villages for centuries. Three of the most popular are kibbeh, shawarma and mansaf.

Below: Kibbeh.

Kibbeh

This is often regarded as the national dish of Lebanon, although it is, in fact, just as popular in Syria. The Jordanians, who call it kubba, enjoy it too. Whenever you meet someone from Lebanon living abroad, one of the first things they will tell you is how much they miss home-made kibbeh. Just the very thought of this dish will bring on a bout of nostalgia as their minds spiral back to a memorable childhood, much of which must have been spent consuming stuffed kibbeh, grilled kibbeh on skewers, baked kibbeh, raw kibbeh and a host of other dishes. When a guest is invited into a Lebanese or Syrian home, kibbeh is the traditional offering of hospitality, and it is always cooked for special occasions.

This versatile dish with its endless variations is most commonly a combination of minced lamb and bulgur with grated onion and a variety of herbs and spices; however, minced beef can also be used and some Armenians make it with minced pork. There are also meatless versions based around lentils, vegetables or fish. The kibbeh mixture can be eaten raw, moulded into balls and grilled (broiled) or fried, or baked in the oven like a meat loaf.

Some kibbeh are filled with a mixture of minced lamb, spices and nuts, to which pomegranate seeds, fruit molasses and yogurt cheese can also be added. There are recipes that call for the kibbeh balls to be cooked in a yogurt sauce, kishk, or pomegranate juice, bitter oranges, or tahini, and they are also simmered in stews, in recipes that date from medieval times, with sour cherries, plums, quinces or apricots.

The origins of kibbeh are ancient, possibly dating back to Mesopotamia. The word itself is derived from the Arabic verb meaning 'to form a lump or ball'. In Lebanon, Syria and Jordan, women are judged by the quality of their kibbeh. The pounding and shaping of this traditional dish requires practice and patience, as well as a degree of strength if using the stone mortar and heavy wooden pestle, and the procedure can be lengthy and arduous. In Turkey, similar meatballs are called kofte and generally do not contain bulgur, although there is one variant intriguingly known as mother-in-law's kofte which is prepared with bulgur.

Shawarma

Delicious at any time of day, as a snack or a meal, shawarma is prepared on a long vertical spit which is threaded with marinated pieces of lamb or chicken, interspersed with pieces of fat to keep the meat moist. The spit is then rotated in front of a charcoal fire, as the cook deftly slices off the meat with a very sharp knife so that the fine slices are deliciously moist and tender. The pieces of meat are packed into a pitta bread pocket, or laid on top of flat bread, and smothered in tahini or yogurt. The whole mixture is topped with onions, tomatoes, pickles and leafy herbs, such as coriander, parsley and mint.

Onion marinade

The juice of pulped onions can be used as a simple but very delicious marinade for all types of roast and grilled meats.

1 Peel 2 onions, then grate the flesh into a bowl. Use the end of a rolling pin to mash to a pulp.

2 Sprinkle the pulp with 5ml/1 tsp salt and leave to stand, then press through a sieve (strainer). Retain the liquid, discard the pulp.

3 Mix the juice with crushed cumin seeds and use to marinate or coat meat before cooking.

Mansaf

The Bedouin of the region prepare their own festive dish, mansaf, meaning 'big dish'. This consists of a large tray, sometimes as large as 1.8m (6ft) in diameter, lined with sheets of flat bread, followed by a layer of rice, on top of which sit chunks of boiled or roasted lamb. The whole dish is flavoured with a traditional sauce, jameed, which is prepared from the juices of the boiled or roasted lamb thickened with the dried curds of sheep or goat's milk yogurt. The dish, which is prepared for wedding feasts, state banquets and presented to distinguished guests, can reach mammoth proportions. Other roasted meats can be used too. It is not unusual for a young camel to be stuffed with a whole sheep, which in turn is stuffed with a turkey, which is stuffed with a chicken – a bit like a Russian doll. This dish, also enjoyed in Syria, is regarded as the national dish of Jordan.

Below: Lamb shawarma.

Below: Dala'mashi is a domestic variation of the Bedouin mansaf.

RICE, WHEAT, LENTILS AND BEANS

No household in the Fertile Crescent is complete without a little grain in the kitchen. There will always be enough wheat to grind for bread, enough bulgur to prepare some delicious kibbeh, or enough pulses to prepare a stew. With these ingredients alone the stoical people of the eastern Mediterranean know they can survive all sorts of shortages and inclement weather.

Wheat has been a principal crop of the region since ancient times and is at the root of many classic dishes, such as flat bread, pastry-based snacks, bulgur salads and pilaffs, and, of course, kibbeh, the national dish of Lebanon. The Bekaa Valley, which acted as an important granary for ancient Rome, still provides Lebanon with most of its grain, and the plains of Syria and Anatolia are also major producers of wheat for the whole region. Lentils, beans and chickpeas have long been associated with the diet of the less well-off rural population in this region, as they are filling and nutritious but also cheap. However, they are enjoyed by everyone, from the wealthiest to the poorest, in many mouthwatering dishes.

Above, clockwise from top left: dried broad beans, bulgur, rice, Egyptian brown beans, brown lentils, red lentils, freek and chickpeas.

RICE

The ancient Greeks and Romans first brought rice to the eastern Mediterranean region from China, but as it was such an expensive commodity, it was enjoyed exclusively by the wealthy and the nobility, and was often cooked for medicinal rather than culinary purposes. During the Ottoman period there was a growing demand for rice, and it had to be imported from India and Egypt, resulting in such high prices that it was still considered a luxury, cooked sparingly for festive feasts and wedding ceremonies. Now that rice is cultivated in the region, it is part of everyday fare. However, in the rural areas, wheat is still the cheaper and more accessible grain. Cooks in the Fertile Crescent consider it essential to produce rice or some other grain at every meal, and if there is no grain, there must be plenty of bread.

There are several types of rice available, some requiring longer cooking times than others. Generally, the rule is that the long and medium grains are used in pilaffs, while the short grains are used for stuffing vegetables and for milk puddings. The Arabic name for plain rice is roz mufalfal, meaning 'peppered rice', because the cooked grains should be plump and separate, resembling white peppercorns.

Below: Rice.

Below: Rice flour.

Rice flour

White rice can also be ground to a fine powder which is employed in numerous milk puddings, such as the traditional muhallabia, to thicken them and give them body. Another popular pudding prepared with rice flour is meghlie, which is flavoured with spices and served to celebrate the birth of a baby.

Rice flour needs to be kept in an airtight container to retain its colour and elasticity. Before adding rice flour to a hot liquid, it is important to slake it with a little warm water first, forming a smooth paste, which is then beaten into the hot liquid. This should avoid any lumps forming.

Cooking rice

The preparation of rice is simple once you have grasped the best method. This is termed the 'absorption method' in cooking circles, as it allows the grains to absorb all the liquid they are cooked in, thus retaining all their nutritional goodness and keeping the desired texture. Rice cooked in this manner is termed a pilaff. In the Levant it can be simply flavoured with clarified butter or aromatic spices, or it can be a more elaborate mixture containing vegetables, pulses, nuts, strips of liver, lamb or chicken.

1 Before cooking plain rice, the grains should first be rinsed thoroughly and drained before tipping them into a heavy-based pan and covering them with double the quantity of water (ie 1 cup of rice to 2 cups water).

2 Once the water has been brought to the boil, stir in a little salt, put on the lid, reduce the heat and simmer for 10–15 minutes, until all the water has been absorbed.

3 Turn off the heat, cover the pan with a clean dish towel, add the lid on top, and leave the rice to steam for a further 10 minutes.

4 Fluff up the grains with a fork and serve.

Above: Bulgur.

Above: Kishk.

BULGUR

This is a staple food of many peasant communities and a great favourite among the Druze and Maronite communities of Mount Lebanon and the peasant communities of Syria and Anatolia. When wheat is harvested in the Levant, some of it is par-boiled, drained, and then dried and rubbed to remove the bran before crushing it into the grains known as bulgur. Traditionally, this was achieved by laboriously boiling the whole-wheat grains first, then spreading them on trays which were placed on the flat roofs of houses to dry in the sun, and finally crushing them. Nowadays, though, bulgur is prepared commercially for sale in rural and city markets and has become popular all over the world.

The bulgur grains can be coarse, medium or fine, and vary in colour from light to dark brown. They require soaking or boiling in water before eating, and the resulting taste is nutty, with a springy texture. Bulgur is highly nutritious and performs much the same role in a dish as rice, making a solid base on which to build a meal of meat or fish, or an accompanying salad or pilaff. Its primary role in Lebanon, Jordan and Syria is as the foundation for all kibbeh.

Below: Bulgur salad.

KISHK

In the wheat-growing areas of Lebanon and Syria, bulgur is mixed with yogurt and spread out on clean cloths on trays to dry in the sun. As the bulgur grains soak up the moisture, they are rubbed between the palms to break them up until they resemble fine breadcrumbs. Known as kishk in Arabic, these dried, fermented grains are used to flavour and thicken soups and stews, or to make a kind of porridge which is often enjoyed for breakfast.

FREEK

This is another type of wheat that is popular in the diet of the eastern Mediterranean. Freek is the immature wheat grain and is still green in colour. There are a variety of elaborate recipes employing freek in medieval manuals, but modern recipes cook it simply to retain the nutty flavour, and serve it with roasted meats and poultry.

SEMOLINA

The harvested wheat grain can also be coarsely milled to produce the brittle grains of semolina which, when cooked, have a light, slightly gritty texture. These grains are popular in some puddings, such as the Syrian ma'mounia, a sweet porridge-like dish. They are also used in breads and cakes. They can be ground to an even finer texture to produce a superfine flour which is used to make best-quality couscous and noodles. Couscous, more associated with North African cuisine, is found in some parts of the eastern Mediterranean but it is not such a traditional dish here. In Lebanon the principal couscous dish consists of chicken or meat cooked with chickpeas on a couscous base. The dish is known as mughrabiyya, meaning 'from the Maghreb', the coastal area of North Africa.

Above: Freek.

LENTILS

These are the best-known legumes of antiquity. Lentils have been endowed with various characteristics throughout history. The Egyptians, who were the first to cultivate them, believed they could cheer up children; the Persians thought they had a calming effect on the mind and metabolism; and the Romans maintained that they reduced rage and encouraged mildness. In fact, one Roman general blamed a defeat by the Persians on these pulses as his troops, who had run out of wheat, had survived on a diet of lentils, and he was sure that this had resulted in slow reactions and sluggishness.

Crossing all classes of society, lentils form part of the daily diet of the poor because they are cheap, but are also enjoyed in a variety of popular family and festive dishes. The most common lentils of the area are the tiny reddish-orange ones, sometimes referred to as Egyptian lentils, but the pale yellow, brown and larger green varieties are popular too. Two of the best-known lentil dishes of the region are moujadara (or mdardara), a rice pilaff with brown lentils and crispy onions, which the Christian communities serve during Lent, and imjadra, a spicy bulgur pilaff combined with red or green lentils.

Below: Semolina.

Below: Red lentils.

Below: Brown lentils.

BEANS

Probably because there are so many different kinds of beans, most of which can be either fresh or dried, they are perhaps even more popular than lentils. Although they have been considered a staple food from ancient times, they are still appreciated for their nutritional value, a fact that is summed up in the Arab saying: 'Beans have even satisfied the Pharoahs'.

There are so many types of bean to enjoy in the eastern Mediterranean, such as black-eyed beans, haricot beans, soya beans, speckled borlotti beans, broad beans, long green beans and Egyptian brown beans. In spite of the fact that they have long been regarded as a staple food of the poor, they have proved irresistible to the wealthy too. Another well-known proverb runs: 'The man of good breeding eats beans and returns to his breeding'.

Many types of fresh and dried beans feature, like lentils and chickpeas, in salads, soups, and stews. Of particular note are fresh broad (fava) beans, which are often served as a salad tossed in olive oil, or mashed to a puree and served as a seasonal dip. These are known as besara in Arabic and fava in Turkish. The more unusual Egyptian brown beans, ful medames, are generally tossed with cumin and parsley and served as a snack or as a breakfast dish in Lebanon and Jordan.

CHICKPEAS

Another staple food of the rural population of this region, chickpeas were first grown in ancient Egypt and the Fertile Crescent. The small bushy plants bear pods that are dried and threshed to release the two or three seeds – the chickpeas – that are contained inside each one. These freshly harvested chickpeas are then dried in the sun to rid them of moisture. Before being cooked, chickpeas need to be soaked in plenty of water for at least six hours to absorb liquid and increase in size.

The Arabic word for chickpea, hummus, is also the name of one of the most famous mezze dishes of the entire region, now an internationally known dish. Hummus is primarily prepared with crushed or puréed chickpeas, olive oil, tahini, lemon juice and a little garlic. Crushed chickpeas are also often used to make falafel, the spicy balls that are a great favourite in Lebanon and Jordan. They are also popular simply boiled in water and served in salads, stews, and Arab fatta dishes.

COOKING PULSES

Chickpeas: For most dishes, dried chickpeas need to be soaked for at least 6 hours prior to cooking. They are then boiled for 40 minutes for tender chickpeas, or up to an hour for really soft ones.

Lentils: Unlike chickpeas, these do not require pre-soaking, nor do they require long cooking. In general, if they are to be used in a salad or pilaff, they only need to be cooked for 20–25 minutes, until they are tender, or for about 30 minutes for a purée.

Dried beans: These, on the other hand, have rules of their own. Haricot and borlotti beans need to be soaked for at least 6 hours before cooking, followed by an hour's cooking. Black-eyed beans do not require any soaking and need only 30 minutes' cooking. Dried broad (fava) beans and Egyptian brown beans need an even longer soaking and cooking.

Salt: This should never be added to beans while cooking, as it makes them tough. Instead, season them once they have been added to the dish.

Below: Chickpeas.

Below: Haricot beans.

Below: Black-eyed beans.

BREAD

A meal without bread in Lebanon, Jordan and Syria would be comparable to a Chinese meal without noodles or rice – in other words, it is almost unthinkable. An essential component of every meal, leavened or unleavened bread is employed as a scoop to raise and transport tasty morsels to the mouth, as a mop for soaking up the divine oily cooking juices on the plate, as a dipper to sink into a puréed, garlicky mezze dish, or as an all-round table companion to munch on throughout the meal.

A RUSTIC TRADITION

Since medieval times, bread has been prepared with barley, millet and wheat, but corn was introduced from the New World during the Ottoman era and became a common ingredient in loaves made in the rural areas. The industrious bread-making and amazingly diverse recipes of the Ottoman Empire were remarked upon in the diaries and letters of a number of travellers who passed through the Fertile Crescent. From the middle of the 17th century until the occupation of the French after World War I Armenians monopolized the bread-making industry in Lebanon and Syria, baking bread and other goods and selling them in their shops and on street stalls. Under the influence of the French, soft white baguettes and some of the delicious specialities of French patisserie made an appearance in the cafés and cosmopolitan homes of the city of Beirut.

A MEDLEY OF SHAPES

Bread does not come in one simple form in the Levant. The dough is used to make tasty snacks such as the famous Arab pizza, lahm bi ajeen, which is so popular in Lebanon and Syria that both claim it as their own, and manakakeish bil zahtar, little flat breads smeared with a herby paste made from thyme and sumac.
A favourite street snack in Lebanon is kahk, sesame-covered miniature bread rolls, which are shaped either like thick bracelets or like handbags with a little handle. These shapes are particularly loved by children; they are the equivalent of the ubiquitous Turkish simit and just as popular. Trays piled high with kahk are carried proudly on the heads of the vendors as they walk through the streets.

The most common bread in the eastern Mediterranean is called khubz arabi, or simply khubz. This is a round, flat, slightly leavened loaf that comes in different sizes, sometimes with a hollow pouch. It is the ubiquitous everyday loaf. On the other hand, the bread of

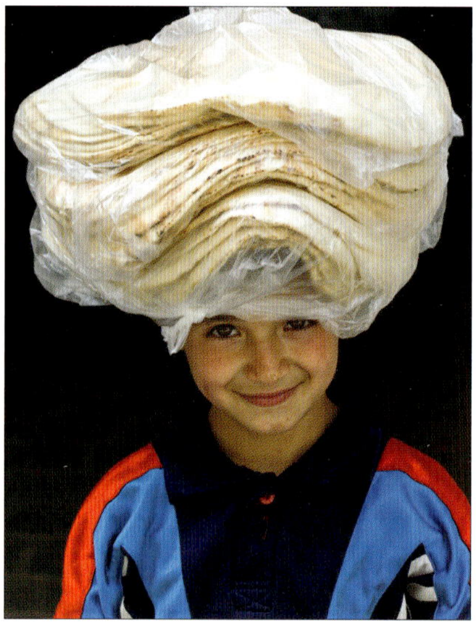

Above: A boy carries flat breads home in Aleppo, Syria.

Below, clockwise from top left: markouk khubz, pitta, shrak and kahk.

Sacred gift

In the Arab world, bread is seen as sacred. It is even regarded as a gift from God, and because of this there are various rules to follow; bread should be broken by hand, as to cut it with a knife would be like raising a sword against God. If a piece of bread should accidentally fall to the ground, it is picked up and symbolically pressed to the lips and forehead as a mark of respect.

Above: A bakery in Hama, Syria.

Above: Flat bread, cheese and sumac.

the mountain regions, markouk, is much thinner and is generally prepared in a saaj, a slightly curved griddle pan. This is the loaf that the Lebanese and the Syrians are most proud of and see as part of their food heritage. The Jordanians and Palestinians produce a similar thin loaf called shrak.

A TREASURED FOODSTUFF

Leftover bread is never thrown away; that would be a waste of this precious food. Instead it is used up in a number of sweet and savoury dishes. In Lebanon, Syria and Jordan, the famous bread salad fattoush and tasty fatta dishes are delicious ways of using up stale bread. The word fatta describes bread broken into pieces, which is the basic element of the dish. The broken pieces are toasted and soaked in broth to form the basis of this tasty all-in-one recipe. The next step is to add some meat, vegetables or pulses to the bread base, and then yogurt and nuts are spooned over the top.

BREAD-MAKING TECHNIQUES

Traditionally bread was baked at the communal oven, the furn, or on a domed oven made out of clay, called a tanur. In some rural areas, a small pit dug in the ground was used as the oven and flat breads were cooked over the fire on a saaj, a type of griddle. The communal baking at the village furn was often a social outing for the women of the village, who gathered around the oven preparing bread loaves of different proportions and shapes, while they chatted and sang.

All of these methods of baking bread are still in use today, particularly in the rural areas, but in the towns and cities most neighbourhoods are blessed with a local bakery that produces batches of freshly baked bread several times a day. Even in the busiest and most modern parts of the main cities, most people buy their bread every day, freshly made and still warm from their neighbourhood baker. Furthermore, they often buy fresh bread two or three times a day, so that each meal is graced with a fresh loaf.

Left: Baking bread on the traditional dome-shaped hot plate.

Snacks with khubz markouk

In the rural areas of the Levant the wide, flat, thin sheets of bread known as khubz markouk are used to make quick, impromptu snacks. Farmers and shepherds often carry leather bags over their shoulders containing several sheets of this flat bread, some crumbled cheese and a few olives, which they put together to make a good meal whenever they get peckish. Raw or cooked vegetables are sometimes included, or jam and honey. Another popular snack prepared with this flat bread is arus, 'the bride', which consists of a sheet of bread spread with traditional yogurt cheese, drizzled with olive oil, sprinkled with zahtar and rolled up to eat.

TRADITIONAL DRINKS

Lebanon, Syria and Jordan all share similar traditions of hospitality when it comes to offering drinks. For example, it is usual to give a cup of coffee or tea to a guest to welcome them into a home. On a hot day, the drink might be a cold sherbet instead. Similarly, it is polite to accept the drink, otherwise it looks as if the guest is rejecting the host's kind offer of refreshment.

Above: Roasted coffee for sale in Syria.

COFFEE

The introduction of coffee from Yemen to the eastern Mediterranean in the 15th and 16th centuries made a significant impact on the social life of the region. Coffee-drinking became primarily a male pastime in the men-only coffee houses, although women who could afford it enjoyed coffee in their own homes. Some of these coffee houses were set up as extremely luxurious establishments, private meeting places for the noble and rich; others were less sophisticated but no less pleasing, as the locations were selected for their small scented gardens, or for the shade of several large trees. In the evenings some coffee houses provided entertainment with professional dancers, singers, musicians and story-tellers. In Lebanon, particularly in Beirut, there are now a number of modern French-style cafés, which welcome women as well as men.

Below: A traditional coffee seller on the streets of Damascus, Syria.

There are two styles of coffee served in the region: Turkish and Arabic. Turkish coffee is very finely ground and brewed in a long-handled pot, a rakwi. The thick, grainy coffee can be prepared sweet (hilweh), medium-sweet (wassat), and without sugar (murra). Arabic coffee, on the other hand, is generally prepared in two pots, known as dallahs. The first pot is used for making the brew of ground coffee beans and boiling water, which is then poured into the second pot, leaving the grains behind. Cloves, cardamom pods, cinnamon sticks and orange flower water or rose water are often added to enhance the flavour of Arabic coffee.

Whether it is Turkish or Arabic, coffee is always served in tiny ornate cups. The most decorative are inlaid with real strands of gold or silver, and they may have both handles and/or saucers.

It is the custom to serve a glass of water with the thick, strong brew. Among the Bedouin, coffee flows like the wine of ancient Rome, and if your cup is empty, it will always be filled up. The Bedouin of Syria and Jordan thrive on their strong coffee, which they grind by hand, prepare in a pan over the open fire, and drink black and bitter.

TEA

Although it is surrounded by fewer customs and rituals, tea holds its own significance in the culinary and social culture of the region. Generally, tea is

Fortune-telling

Reading fortunes from the sediment left at the bottom of the coffee cup is a popular pastime throughout the region. First the cups are inverted onto the saucers to allow the grains to drip downward and form rivulets and patterns on the inside of the cup. Readings are then made first from the lines and patterns on the cup, and then from the patterns on the saucer.

made strong and is sweetened with sugar, either by stirring it into the hot liquid, or by holding a sugar lump between the teeth and sipping the tea through it. In Jordan and Lebanon, herbs and spices are added to the tea, and there are numerous herb and floral teas, such as thyme, lemon verbena, hibiscus, jasmine and camomile. Some teas are medicinal, thought to be good for colds or to aid digestion; others are said to increase fertility.

SHERBET DRINKS

Some sherbets are served on specific occasions, but all are popular as welcoming drinks for guests, or simply as a refreshing interlude in the day. One of the most unusual sherbet drinks in the region, a recipe known to be hundreds of years old, is prepared from a syrup of mint and vinegar, but the more common sherbets are made from the infinite variety of seasonal fruits, nuts, pods and blossoms. These include lemons, sour cherries, pomegranates, mulberries, rose and orange blossom waters, almond milk and tamarind pods.

ALCOHOLIC DRINKS

Although wine was enjoyed by the ancient Egyptians, Phoenicians and Romans, its consumption was curtailed

Below: Lebanese wine.

Above: Glasses of tea served with the almost inevitable lumps of sugar.

by the introduction of Islam and its religious prohibitions. Arabs had enjoyed wine before the Islamic revolution and Lebanon was regarded as one of the prime producers of arak, the local spirit, but excessive drunkenness and gambling led to prohibition in the early 20th century. The production of wine continued in the region, however, through the Christian and Jewish communities. Not all Muslims were strict converts to the new restrictions on alcohol, and the most frequent offenders were often the noblemen, caliphs and judges.

Below: Arak.

Aniseed tea (Shay bi yansun)

1 Put 600ml/1 pint water into a pan with 30–45ml/1–2 tbsp aniseed and 2 cinnamon sticks.

2 Bring to the boil, then reduce the heat and simmer for 10–15 minutes. Sweeten to taste with sugar or honey. Strain into glasses and drink as a digestive.

Naturally, when the French occupied Lebanon after World War I, they took advantage of the fertile soil and wonderful climate, and set about producing wines there. Lebanon is still admired to this day for its quality wines and flourishing grape vines, some of which are reputed to date back to the Crusaders. The fertile soil of the Bekaa Valley produces excellent grapes, and wines are still made in private homes and Christian monasteries in Lebanon.

Other alcoholic beverages of Lebanon, Jordan and Syria include beer and arak, a clear spirit distilled from grapes and flavoured with aniseed, which turns cloudy when water is added, just like the raki of Turkey and the ouzo of Greece. Although beer is mentioned in some early records, it was really only during the post-Ottoman period that it began to be mass-produced, with each region boasting its own light, refreshing beer. The enjoyment of arak, on the other hand, has been well documented for centuries, and it remains hugely popular as the drink to accompany mezze – or maybe the mezze is a necessary accompaniment to the arak.

Mezze and Salads

The tradition of mezze is one of the most enjoyable features of the culinary culture of the eastern Mediterranean. The pursuit of leisure is ingrained in the region's social life, whether it is playing backgammon in a teahouse or smoking a hubble-bubble in a coffee-house, often served with a little light refreshment. Nothing beats a delicious array of mezze spread on a table in the shade of an old fig tree, at a sea-front café, or sitting on cushions at home.

YOGURT CHEESE BALLS IN OLIVE OIL

AN AGE-OLD TRADITION THROUGHOUT THE EASTERN MEDITERRANEAN IS TO DRAIN YOGURT OF ITS LIQUID CONTENT UNTIL IT RESEMBLES CREAM CHEESE. IF DRAINED FOR ABOUT 3 DAYS, IT BECOMES FIRM AND A LITTLE DRY, WHICH IS THE PERFECT CONSISTENCY FOR THESE DELICATE YOGURT CHEESE BALLS, CALLED LABNA BI ZEIT, A GREAT FAVOURITE ON THE MEZZE TABLE.

SERVES SIX

INGREDIENTS

- 1kg/2¼ lb Greek (US strained plain) yogurt
- 5ml/1 tsp salt
- olive oil
- paprika, to serve

1 In a bowl, stir the yogurt with the salt, then pour the yogurt into a piece of muslin suspended above a bowl, or lining a colander set over a bowl.

2 Fold the cloth over the yogurt and leave it to drain in the refrigerator for 3 days, pouring off the whey as needed.

3 After 3 days, when the straining is complete, remove the drained yogurt from the cloth, stand it on a plate and leave to dry out for about 6 hours. Then lightly oil your fingers and palms and divide the cheese into small pieces.

4 Roll the pieces into 2cm/¾ inch balls. Place on a tray, cover, and refrigerate for 6–12 hours. Pack the balls into a sterilized jar and pour in enough olive oil to cover. Store in a cool place for 2–3 weeks. Serve sprinkled with paprika.

Energy 177kcal/740kJ; Protein 10g; Carbohydrate 13g, of which sugars 13g; Fat 10g, of which saturates 4g; Cholesterol 18mg; Calcium 333mg; Fibre 0.0 g; Sodium 461mg.

OLIVES SPICED WITH CHILLIES AND THYME

Whether you are in Jordan, Syria, Lebanon or Turkey no mezze table is complete without a bowl of olives. Fleshy and juicy, this recipe bathes them in olive oil, flavoured with herbs and chilli. They are delicious, whether eaten on their own with an apperitif, or served with fried halloumi, little cubes of feta cheese, or labna.

SERVES FOUR

INGREDIENTS

- 250g/9oz fleshy green olives, soaked in water for 24 hours
- 1 fresh hot red chilli, seeded and finely chopped
- 15ml/1 tbsp fresh thyme leaves
- 100ml/3½ fl oz olive oil
- juice of half a lemon
- sea salt

1 Drain the olives and, using a sharp knife, cut 3 slits in each one, placing them in a large bowl as you work.

2 Add the chopped chilli and thyme leaves to the bowl, and toss in the olive oil and lemon juice. Season with salt and stir well so that all the olives are coated in the oil and flavourings.

3 Cover the bowl and leave the olives to marinate for 1–2 hours before serving as needed. These olives will keep in a jar, refrigerated, for 3–4 weeks.

Energy 291kcal/1196kJ; Protein 1g; Carbohydrate 0g; Fat 32g, of which saturates 5g; Cholesterol 0mg; Calcium 44mg; Fibre 1.8g; Sodium 1407mg.

AUBERGINES WITH HONEY AND POMEGRANATE MOLASSES

There are many different ways of presenting aubergines – smoked, grilled, fried, and baked. Versions of this medieval Arab salad, batinjan bil rumman, appear in Syria and Jordan, and the common denominator is the combination of pomegranate molasses and honey.

SERVES FOUR

INGREDIENTS

- 1 large aubergine (eggplant), peeled, cut in half lengthways and sliced into half-moons
- sea salt
- 45–60ml/3–4 tbsp olive oil
- 1 red onion, cut in half lengthways and finely sliced with the grain
- 15–30ml/1–2 tbsp sultanas
- 15–30ml/1–2 tbsp pomegranate molasses
- juice of half a lemon
- 10ml/2 tsp fragrant, runny honey
- 150ml/5fl oz boiling water
- sea salt
- 1 bunch flat leaf parsley, and a few mint leaves, chopped, to garnish

1 Sprinkle the aubergine slices with salt and leave them to weep for about 15 minutes. Drain, then rinse off the salt and pat the slices dry.

2 Heat the oil in a heavy pan and sauté the aubergine slices until they are golden brown and cooked through.

3 Add the sliced onions and sultanas to the pan and cook for a further 1–2 minutes to soften.

4 In a small bowl, mix together the pomegranate molasses, lemon juice, honey and a little salt.

5 Add the boiling water to the bowl and mix.

6 Pour the mixture into the pan and cook gently for 10–15 minutes until the aubergine is tender. Garnish with the parsley and mint and serve warm, or at room temperature.

Energy 228kcal/948kJ; Protein 2g; Carbohydrate 21g, of which sugars 19g; Fat 16g, of which saturates 2g; Cholesterol 0mg; Calcium 56mg; Fibre 3.0 g; Sodium 10mg.

Spicy Bean Balls

Ideal street food, falafel are one of the most popular snacks in Lebanon and Egypt, eaten plain with pickles, or tucked into pitta bread with onions and yogurt. They can be served as a mezze dish with a tahini sauce, with garlic-flavoured yogurt and lots of parsley, or with a salad.

SERVES FOUR TO SIX

INGREDIENTS

- 250g/9oz/1 cup dried broad (fava) beans, soaked overnight
- 115g/4oz/½ cup chickpeas, soaked overnight
- 10–15ml/2–3 tsp ground cumin
- 10ml/2 tsp ground coriander
- 1 red chilli, seeded and chopped
- ½ onion, chopped
- 1 red or green (bell) pepper, chopped
- 4 cloves garlic, crushed
- 1 small bunch fresh coriander (cilantro), chopped
- 1 bunch flat leaf parsley, chopped
- 5ml/1 tsp bicarbonate of soda (baking soda)
- sunflower oil for deep-frying
- sea salt and ground black pepper
- lemon and yogurt, to serve

1 Drain the beans and chickpeas and place in a blender with the dried spices. Blend to a paste, then add the chilli, onion, pepper, garlic and herbs. Season well, then whizz until smooth. Transfer to a bowl, beat in the bicarbonate of soda, cover, and leave for 15 minutes.

2 With wet hands, mould the mixture into small, tight balls.

3 Heat enough oil for deep-frying in a pan and when it is hot enough, fry the balls in batches until golden brown.

4 Drain the falafel on kitchen paper and serve them warm or at room temperature, with lemon wedges to squeeze over them, and a dollop of yogurt flavoured with chopped fresh mint if you like.

Energy 303kcal/1282kJ; Protein 18.5g; Carbohydrate 44.7g, of which sugars 5.2g; Fat 6.9g, of which saturates 1.2g; Cholesterol 0mg; Calcium 88mg; Fibre 7.2g; Sodium 16mg.

FRIED HALLOUMI WITH ZAHTAR

AVAILABLE IN ARAB MARKETS AND MOST SUPERMARKETS, HALLOUMI IS A SALTY, FIRM WHITE CHEESE. IN LEBANON, IT IS MADE FROM COW'S MILK AND MATURED IN WHEY, SOMETIMES COMBINED WITH NIGELLA SEEDS, MINT OR THYME. GENERALLY, IT IS USED IN PASTRIES, OR SLICES ARE GRILLED OR FRIED AND SERVED AS A MEZZE. SERVE STRAIGHT AWAY, AS IT BECOMES RUBBERY WHEN COOL.

SERVES TWO TO FOUR

INGREDIENTS

- 45–60ml/3–4 tbsp olive oil
- 250g/9oz plain halloumi cheese
- 15ml/1 tbsp zahtar
- lemon wedges and Lebanese flat bread, to accompany

1 Rinse the block of halloumi under cold running water and pat dry with kitchen paper.

2 Using a sharp knife, cut the halloumi into thin slices.

3 Heat the oil in a heavy pan. Fry the halloumi slices for 2 minutes until golden, then flip over and fry the other side. Drain on kitchen paper.

4 Transfer the hot halloumi on to a serving dish and sprinkle with zahtar. Eat immediately, with some Lebanese flat bread and a squeeze of lemon.

Energy 328kcal/1356kJ; Protein 16.2g; Carbohydrate 1.7g, of which sugars 0g; Fat 28.6g, of which saturates 13.1g; Cholesterol 48mg; Calcium 311mg; Fibre 0g; Sodium 331mg.

Spicy Tartare Balls

Prepared with lean, fresh raw lamb, these tartare balls, or 'kibbeh naye', are enduringly popular in the Eastern Mediterranean. Flavoured with a multitude of spices, perhaps to render the meat more digestible, the raw lamb and bulgur balls are invariably served with sprigs of parsley to chew on to cut the spice, and wedges of lemon to refresh them. They are also served with small lettuce leaves in which they are often wrapped and popped into the mouth. In Syria and the southern region of Turkey, where they are called çi köfte, these tartare balls are said to contain 30 different spices.

SERVES FOUR TO SIX

INGREDIENTS

- 225g/8oz best-quality, preferably organic, lean minced (ground) lamb
- 125g/4½oz fine bulgur, soaked in boiling water for 20 minutes
- 2 small onions, finely chopped
- 4 cloves garlic, finely chopped
- 1 red chilli, seeded and finely chopped
- 10ml/2 tsp tomato purée (paste)
- 5ml/1 tsp paprika
- 5ml/1 tsp ground coriander
- 2.5ml/½ tsp ground cumin
- 2.5ml/½ tsp ground cinnamon
- 2.5ml/½ tsp ground allspice
- 2.5ml/½ tsp ground fenugreek
- sea salt
- freshly ground black pepper
- 1 bunch flat leaf parsley, chopped
- 1 bunch flat leaf parsley sprigs
- roughly 12 lettuce leaves
- 1–2 lemons, cut into wedges, to serve

1 Put the minced lamb into a bowl. Knead it and slap it down into the base of the bowl to knock out the air.

2 Squeeze out the bulgur and add it to the lamb with the onions, garlic and chilli. Knead well.

3 Add the tomato purée and spices to the lamb mixture, and knead well again. Season with salt and pepper and add the chopped parsley, and knead once more until everything is mixed together.

4 Moisten your fingers and the palms of your hands with water, and roll small portions of the mixture into balls.

5 Make a small indentation with your finger in each ball and place them on a serving plate with the parsley sprigs and lettuce leaves. Serve with the wedges of lemon that are squeezed into the dip.

Energy 148kcal/618kJ; Protein 11g; Carbohydrate 19g, of which sugars 2g; Fat 4g, of which saturates 1g; Cholesterol 28mg; Calcium 40mg; Fibre 0.7 g; Sodium 112mg.

CHEESE AND YOGURT DIP WITH ZAHTAR

Cheese and yogurt are made in the villages of Lebanon from the milk of goats, ewes, or cows. Labneh is thick, creamy yogurt obtained by draining the everyday set yogurt through muslin. This combination of village cheese and labneh is creamy and slightly sour. Sprinkled with thyme or zahtar, it is popular as a dip or with toasted flat bread.

SERVES SIX

INGREDIENTS

- 250g/9oz feta cheese
- 250g/9oz/generous 2½ cups Greek (US strained plain) yogurt
- 30ml/2 tbsp olive oil
- 15ml/1 tbsp zahtar

COOK'S TIP

You can buy strained yogurt or strain it yourself by draining it through muslin (cheesecloth), as on page 54. The longer it is left, the thicker it gets. Labneh is delicious drizzled with olive oil and sprinkled with herbs or spices.

1 Drain and rinse the feta cheese and pat dry with kitchen paper.

2 Place the feta in a bowl and mash it well with a fork.

3 Using a wooden spoon, beat the strained yogurt into the mashed feta to form a thick paste.

4 Spread the mixture in a shallow dish and drizzle the olive oil over the top.

5 Sprinkle the zahtar over the top before serving with toasted bread.

Energy 192kcal/797kJ; Protein 9.5g; Carbohydrate 2.3g, of which sugars 1.5g; Fat 16.7g, of which saturates 8.4g; Cholesterol 29mg; Calcium 217mg; Fibre 0g; Sodium 631mg.

SMOKED AUBERGINE DIP

THERE ARE VARIATIONS OF THIS CLASSIC AUBERGINE DISH, 'BABA GHANOUSH', ALSO KNOWN AS 'MOUTABAL'. SOME COOKS ADD CHOPPED FLAT LEAF PARSLEY OR CORIANDER (CILANTRO), WHILE OTHERS LIGHTEN IT WITH A LITTLE YOGURT OR LEMON JUICE. THE DISH HAS A STRONG SMOKY FLAVOUR, WHICH IS BEST ENJOYED WITH CRUSTY BREAD, OR PITTA, TO DIP INTO IT.

SERVES FOUR TO SIX

INGREDIENTS

- 2 large aubergines (eggplants)
- 30–45ml/2–3 tbsp tahini
- juice of 1–2 lemons
- 30–45ml/2–3 tbsp Greek (US strained plain) yogurt
- 2 cloves garlic, crushed
- 1 bunch flat leaf parsley, chopped
- sea salt and ground black pepper
- olive oil, for drizzling

COOK'S TIP

If grilled over charcoal the aubergine (eggplant) skin toughens, and it is easier to slit it open and scoop out the softened flesh.

1 Place the aubergines on a hot griddle, or directly over a gas flame or charcoal grill, turning them from time to time, until they are soft to touch and the skin is charred and flaky.

2 Place the aubergines in a plastic bag for a few minutes to sweat. When cool enough to handle, hold them by the stems under cold running water and peel off and discard the skin. Squeeze out the excess water and then chop the flesh to a pulp.

3 In a bowl, beat the tahini with the lemon juice – the mixture stiffens at first, then loosens to a creamy paste.

4 Beat in the yogurt and then, using a fork, beat in the aubergine pulp.

5 Add the garlic and parsley (reserving a little to garnish), season well with salt and pepper and beat the mixture thoroughly. Transfer the mixture to a serving dish, drizzle a little olive oil over the top to keep it moist and sprinkle with the reserved parsley.

Energy 91kcal/375kJ; Protein 1g; Carbohydrate 2.2g, of which sugars 1.5g; Fat 8.8g, of which saturates 1.4g; Cholesterol 8mg; Calcium 8mg; Fibre 1.4g; Sodium 52mg.

Spicy Walnut and Yogurt Dip

The wonderful spicy walnut dip, 'muhammara', has been an Arab favourite since medieval times. Prepared with pomegranate syrup, chillies and garlic, it is delicious served as a mezze dish with strips of toasted Arab flatbread and it can be served as sauce for steamed and roasted vegetables and meat. An extended version of this dish is the Syrian muhammara labneh, a combination of the classic muhammara ingredients and strained yogurt, which is served as a thick, creamy dip for toasted flat bread and crudités. The labneh needs to be prepared well in advance – at least 48 hours – or you can buy ready prepared labneh in Middle Eastern stores.

SERVES SIX

INGREDIENTS

For the labneh

- 450g/1lb Greek (US strained plain) yogurt
- 2.5ml/½ tsp sea salt

For the muhammara

- 2 red (bell) peppers
- 1 red chilli, seeded and finely chopped
- 2 cloves garlic, crushed with sea salt
- 125g/4½oz walnuts, roughly chopped
- 30–45ml/2–3 tbsp toasted breadcrumbs
- 15ml/1 tbsp pomegranate molasses
- juice of ½ a lemon
- 5ml/1 tsp sugar
- 45ml/3 tbsp olive oil
- sea salt

1 To prepare the labneh, beat the yogurt with the salt and tip it into a piece of muslin lining a colander.

2 Pull up the four corners of the muslin, tie them together and suspend the bundle from the handle of a wooden spoon placed over a deep bowl, a bucket, or the sink.

COOK'S TIP
Roast the peppers in a high oven if you don't have a gas flame.

3 Leave the yogurt to drain in a cool place for at least 48 hours. Pour off the whey that collects in the bowl as necessary.

4 When the yogurt has reduced to half the original amount (roughly 225g/8oz) and is the consistency of cream cheese, transfer to a clean bowl.

5 To prepare the muhammara, place the peppers directly over a gas flame, or over a charcoal grill, and roast them until the skin is charred and buckled.

6 Place the peppers in a plastic bag to sweat for 5 minutes and loosen the skins. Remove from the bag, peel off the skins and remove the stalks and seeds. Chop the pepper flesh into very small pieces.

7 Using a mortar and pestle, pound the chopped peppers with chopped chilli, garlic, and walnuts to a fairly smooth paste. You could use a food processor for this, but pulse rather than blend for a rough, chopped consistency.

8 Beat the breadcrumbs, the pomegranate molasses, lemon juice and the sugar into the pepper and walnut paste.

9 Drizzle the oil into the mixture, beating all the time, until the consistency is thick and creamy.

10 Add the muhammara to the bowl of labneh and combine. Check the seasoning, drizzle a little olive oil over the top and serve with sticks of carrot, celery, bell pepper and spring onions.

Energy 319kcal/1327kJ; Protein 9g; Carbohydrate 17g, of which sugars 13g; Fat 24g, of which saturates 4g; Cholesterol 8mg; Calcium 188mg; Fibre 1.8 g; Sodium 332mg.

TAHINI DIP WITH PARSLEY

QUICK AND SIMPLE, THIS POPULAR DIP IS OFTEN SERVED WITH WARM PITTA BREAD AS AN APPETIZER. IT IS ALSO SERVED AS A DIPPING SAUCE FOR FALAFEL, STEAMED VEGETABLES AND GRILLED FISH. IN JORDAN, SYRIA, AND SOUTHERN TURKEY, A VARIATION OF THE DISH IS PREPARED WITH A FRUIT MOLASSES, SUCH AS GRAPE, DATE OR CAROB, COMBINED WITH DRIED MINT.

SERVES THREE TO FOUR

INGREDIENTS

- 150ml/5fl oz tahini
- 2 cloves garlic
- juice of 2 lemons
- cold water
- sea salt and ground black pepper
- 1 small bunch flat leaf parsley, finely chopped

1 Beat the tahini in a bowl until smooth. Using the flat edge of a knife, crush the garlic to a creamy paste with the salt.

2 Add the garlic paste to the tahini. Gradually beat in the lemon juice – the mixture will thicken at first, then loosen. Add several teaspoonfuls of cold water to lighten, until thick and creamy.

3 Adjust the taste by adding a little more salt or lemon to suit your palate.

4 Stir in most of the parsley, and a little pepper, then spoon the mixture into a serving bowl and garnish with the rest of the parsley.

Energy 231kcal/956kJ; Protein 7g; Carbohydrate 1g, of which sugars 1g; Fat 22g, of which saturates 3g; Cholesterol 0mg; Calcium 258mg; Fibre 3.1 g; Sodium 106mg.

CHEESE AND CUCUMBER DIP

THIS DISH, CALLED MICHOTET, IS SAID TO BE OF EGYPTIAN ORIGIN. PREPARED WITH A CRUMBLY WHITE CHEESE, SUCH AS FETA, THIS DISH IS OFTEN SERVED ON ITS OWN WITH WARM PITTA BREAD OR AS PART OF A MEZZE SPREAD. IT IS ALSO EATEN WITH THE BEAN DISH FUL MEDAMES, ALSO THOUGHT TO HAVE ORIGINATED IN EGYPT, AND MUCH ENJOYED IN LEBANON AND JORDAN.

SERVES THREE TO FOUR

INGREDIENTS

- 1 small cucumber, or half a large one, partially peeled
- sea salt
- 225g/8oz feta, rinsed and drained
- 30ml/2 tbsp olive oil
- juice of 1 lemon
- 2 spring onions (scallions), white and green parts finely chopped
- sea salt and ground black pepper
- 1 small bunch fresh dill, finely chopped
- 1 small bunch fresh mint, finely chopped

1 Finely dice the partially peeled cucumber, and place on a plate. Sprinkle with a little salt. Leave to weep for about 15 minutes, then squeeze out the excess water with your hands and place on kitchen paper.

2 In a bowl, mash the cheese well with a fork and then, with a wooden spoon, beat in the olive oil and lemon juice.

3 Add the spring onion and cucumber to the beaten cheese, and season to taste with salt and black pepper. Fold in the herbs and serve with warm pitta bread or a selection of crudités.

Energy 219kcal/907kJ; Protein 10g; Carbohydrate 2g, of which sugars 2g; Fat 19g, of which saturates 9g; Cholesterol 39mg; Calcium 252mg; Fibre 0.5g; Sodium 913mg.

Lebanese Chickpea Dip

Hummus is a classic dip that can, of course, be bought ready-made, but made at home it can be varied widely to taste – some enjoy it spiked with cumin, garlic or chilli; others prefer it light and lemony. There are dense versions thickened with tahini and refreshing versions flavoured with orange juice or fresh herbs.

Serves four to six

INGREDIENTS

- 225g/8oz dried chickpeas, soaked in water for at least 6 hours, or overnight
- 45–60ml/3–4 tbsp olive oil
- 1–2 cloves garlic, crushed
- juice of 1 lemon
- juice of 1 Seville orange, or half a large orange
- 45–60ml/3–4 tbsp tahini
- sea salt and ground black pepper
- pitta bread or crudités, to serve

To garnish

- 15ml/1 tbsp olive oil
- 1 small bunch fresh coriander (cilantro), finely chopped

1 Drain the chickpeas and place them in a pan with plenty of water. Bring to the boil, reduce the heat and simmer, covered, for about 1½ hours, until soft.

2 Drain the chickpeas, reserving a few spoonfuls of liquid, and discard any loose skins.

3 Put the chickpeas and liquid into a blender or food processor, and whizz to a thick paste. Add the olive oil, garlic, lemon and orange juices and tahini, and blend thoroughly. Season to taste.

4 Transfer the hummus to a serving bowl and drizzle a little oil over the top. Sprinkle with a little coriander and serve with warm pitta bread or crudités.

Energy 265kcal/1101kJ; Protein 10g; Carbohydrate 12.6g, of which sugars 0.8g; Fat 19.7g, of which saturates 2.8g; Cholesterol 0mg; Calcium 210mg; Fibre 4.7g; Sodium 15mg.

Toasted Bread Salad with Sumac

This salad, fattoush, is one of the classic Lebanese dishes that were devised to make use of leftover bread, and actually works better with day-old flat bread than with fresh. Sumac, the deep red, fruity spice ground from the berries of a bush native to the eastern Mediterranean, is an essential component.

SERVES FOUR TO SIX

INGREDIENTS

- 1–2 flat breads, such as pitta breads
- ½ cos or romaine lettuce
- 2–3 tomatoes, skinned
- 1 carrot, peeled
- 5–6 small radishes, trimmed
- 1 red or green (bell) pepper
- 4–5 spring onions (scallions)
- 60–75ml/4–5 tbsp olive oil
- juice of 1 lemon
- 1–2 cloves garlic, crushed
- 1 small bunch flat leaf parsley
- 10–15ml/2–3 tsp ground sumac
- sea salt and ground black pepper

1 Toast the bread briefly on both sides, then break it into bitesize pieces. Set aside. Trim and chop the lettuce leaves.

2 Seed and chop the skinned tomatoes, thinly slice the carrot and radishes, seed and chop the pepper, and trim and slice the spring onions. Place all the vegetables in a large bowl.

3 In a jar or a small bowl, whisk the olive oil with the lemon juice and garlic to make the dressing.

4 Add the parsley to the bowl, together with the pieces of bread, then pour the dressing over. Sprinkle the sumac over the top and season.

5 Toss the salad well, making sure the bread is well coated. Serve immediately as part of a mezze spread, or on its own as a snack or light lunch.

Energy 120kcal/499kJ; Protein 2.4g; Carbohydrate 7.7g, of which sugars 7.5g; Fat 9.1g, of which saturates 1.4g; Cholesterol 0mg; Calcium 54mg; Fibre 3g; Sodium 18mg.

BEAN SALAD WITH GARLIC AND CORIANDER

THIS TRADITIONAL SALAD, KNOWN AS 'FOUL MOUKALA', IS POPULAR AS A MEZZE DISH, BUT IT IS ALSO SERVED AS AN ACCOMPANIMENT TO GRILLED MEATS. IT IS USUALLY MADE WHEN FRESH BROAD BEANS ARE IN SEASON, BUT IT IS ALSO VERY GOOD WHEN PREPARED WITH FROZEN BEANS.

SERVES FOUR TO SIX

INGREDIENTS
- 500g/1¼lb/3½ cups shelled broad (fava) beans
- 5ml/1 tsp sugar
- 30–45ml/2–3 tbsp olive oil
- juice of ½ lemon
- 1–2 cloves garlic, crushed
- sea salt and ground black pepper
- 1 small bunch fresh coriander (cilantro), finely chopped

COOK'S TIP

This salad is also good eaten while the beans are still warm. In this case, simply drain them without refreshing under cold water, toss the beans in the oil, then add the other ingredients and serve immediately.

1 Put the shelled beans in a pan with just enough water to cover. Stir in the sugar to preserve the colour of the beans, and bring the water to the boil.

2 Reduce the heat and simmer, uncovered, for about 15 minutes, until the beans are cooked but remain al dente.

3 Drain the beans and refresh them under running cold water, then drain again and put them in a bowl.

4 Toss the beans in the oil, lemon juice and garlic. Season well with salt and pepper to taste, and stir in the chopped coriander, reserving a little to sprinkle over before serving.

Energy 111kcal/464kJ; Protein 6.8g; Carbohydrate 10.7g, of which sugars 2g; Fat 4.8g, of which saturates 0.7g; Cholesterol 0mg; Calcium 64mg; Fibre 5.8g; Sodium 10mg.

Lebanese Country Salad

Each region has its own version of this classic salad, which is often described as originating with shepherds, gypsies or, in some cases, monks. This one, salatah Lebanieh, is a typical country salad that can be served as an accompaniment or as part of a mezze.

SERVES FOUR TO SIX

INGREDIENTS

- 1 cos or romaine lettuce
- 1 cucumber
- 2 tomatoes
- 2–3 spring onions (scallions)
- 1 bunch fresh mint leaves
- 1 bunch flat leaf parsley
- 30ml/2 tbsp olive oil
- juice of ½ lemon
- sea salt

1 Cut the lettuce leaves into bitesize chunks and place in a bowl.

2 Partially peel the cucumber and cut into small chunks. Place in a bowl.

3 Skin the tomatoes and dice the flesh, and add to the cucumber. Trim and slice the spring onions and add them to the bowl too.

4 Wash and finely chop the mint and parsley, discarding the stalks, and add to the vegetables.

5 Toss in the olive oil and lemon juice. Season with salt, and serve straight away before the lettuce and herbs wilt.

Energy 51kcal/210kJ; Protein 1.1g; Carbohydrate 2.5g, of which sugars 2.4g; Fat 4.1g, of which saturates 0.6g; Cholesterol 0mg; Calcium 36mg; Fibre 1.3g; Sodium 8mg.

Aubergine with Pomegranate Seeds

Variations of this dish, batinjan rahib, can be found throughout the eastern Mediterranean. Serve it either warm or at room temperature to make the most of the subtle, smoky flavour of the aubergine and the sharp crunch of the pomegranate seeds.

SERVES FOUR TO SIX

INGREDIENTS

- 2 aubergines (eggplants)
- 2 tomatoes, skinned, seeded and chopped
- 1 green (bell) pepper, chopped
- 1 red onion, finely chopped
- 1 bunch flat leaf parsley, finely chopped
- 2 cloves garlic, crushed
- 30–45ml/2–3 tbsp olive oil
- juice of 1 lemon
- 15–30ml/1–2 tbsp walnuts, finely chopped
- 15–30ml/1–2 tbsp pomegranate seeds
- sea salt and ground black pepper
- wedges of pomegranate, to garnish

1 Place the aubergines on a hot griddle, or directly over a gas flame, and leave to char until soft, turning occasionally.

2 Hold the aubergines by their stems under running cold water and peel off the charred skins, or slit open the skins and scoop out the flesh.

3 Squeeze out the excess water from the aubergine flesh then chop it to a pulp and place it in a bowl with the tomatoes, pepper, onion, parsley and garlic. Add the olive oil and lemon juice and toss thoroughly. Season to taste with salt and pepper, then stir in half the walnuts and pomegranate seeds.

4 Turn the salad into a serving dish and garnish with the remaining walnuts and pomegranate seeds.

Energy 90kcal/374kJ; Protein 2.2g; Carbohydrate 7.3g, of which sugars 6.3g; Fat 6g, of which saturates 0.8g; Cholesterol 0mg; Calcium 39mg; Fibre 3.1g; Sodium 10mg.

PARSLEY AND BULGUR SALAD

THE MAIN INGREDIENT OF THIS CLASSIC LEBANESE SALAD, TABBOULEH, IS PARSLEY, FLAVOURED WITH A HINT OF MINT AND TOSSED WITH A LITTLE FINE BULGUR SO THAT THE GRAINS RESEMBLE TINY GEMS IN A SEA OF GREEN. TABBOULEH IS ALSO A REFRESHING ACCOMPANIMENT TO GRILLED MEATS.

SERVES FOUR TO SIX

INGREDIENTS

- 65g/2½oz/½ cup fine bulgur
- juice of 2 lemons
- 1 large bunch flat leaf parsley (about 225g/8oz)
- handful of fresh mint leaves
- 2–3 tomatoes, skinned, seeded and finely diced
- 4 spring onions (scallions), trimmed and finely sliced
- 60ml/4 tbsp olive oil
- sea salt and ground black pepper
- 1 cos or romaine lettuce, trimmed and split into leaves, to serve

1 Rinse the bulgur in cold water and drain well. Place it in a bowl and pour over the lemon juice. Leave to soften for 10 minutes while you prepare the salad.

2 With the parsley tightly bunched, slice the leaves as finely as you can with a sharp knife. Transfer to a bowl.

3 Slice the mint leaves and add them to the bowl together with the tomatoes, spring onions and the soaked bulgur.

4 Pour in the oil, season with salt and pepper and toss the salad gently.

5 Serve immediately, so that the herbs do not get the chance to soften. Arrange the lettuce leaves around the salad and use them to scoop up mouthfuls of tabbouleh.

COOK'S TIP

The trick when preparing the parsley is to make sure it is sliced rather than chopped, with a very sharp knife, this means the herb stays dry and fresh rather than mushy, giving the salad its distinctive appearance and texture.

Energy 232kcal/965kJ; Protein 5.2g; Carbohydrate 34.6g, of which sugars 2.7g; Fat 8.4g, of which saturates 1.1g; Cholesterol 0mg; Calcium 51mg; Fibre 1.4g; Sodium 12mg.

OLIVE AND PEPPER SALAD

ALMOST EVERY HILLSIDE IN THE EASTERN MEDITERRANEAN IS DOTTED WITH OLIVE TREES, AND MOST VILLAGES HAVE A COMMUNAL OLIVE PRESS WHERE THE HARVEST CAN BE CRUSHED FOR ITS VALUABLE, FRUITY OIL. OLIVES APPEAR ON MOST MEZZE TABLES, MARINATED IN OIL AND HERBS OR SPICES, OR TOSSED WITH SUN-RIPENED RED PEPPERS IN THIS REFRESHING SALAD.

SERVES FOUR TO SIX

INGREDIENTS

- 2 long, red Mediterranean peppers, or red or orange (bell) peppers
- 30–45ml/2–3 tbsp Kalamata or other fleshy black olives
- 30–45ml/2–3 tbsp fleshy green olives
- 1 large tomato, skinned, seeded and diced
- 2 spring onions (scallions), trimmed and finely sliced
- 1 handful fresh mint leaves, roughly chopped
- 1 small bunch fresh coriander (cilantro), roughly chopped
- juice of 1 lemon
- 30ml/2 tbsp olive oil
- sea salt and ground black pepper

1 Place the peppers on a hot griddle, or directly over a gas flame, turning until the skin is evenly charred. Place in a plastic bag for a few minutes to sweat, then hold each one under cold running water and peel off the skin. Remove the stalks and seeds, dice the flesh and place in a bowl.

2 Pit the olives and slice them in half lengthways. Add the halves to the bowl with the chopped peppers.

3 Add the tomatoes, spring onions and herbs and pour in the oil and lemon juice. Season and toss well. Serve with warm pitta bread.

Energy 68kcal/283kJ; Protein 1.1g; Carbohydrate 4.6g, of which sugars 4.4g; Fat 5.2g, of which saturates 0.8g; Cholesterol 0mg; Calcium 30mg; Fibre 1.9g; Sodium 232mg.

CHICKPEA AND BULGUR SALAD WITH MINT

This is a traditional village salad, using ingredients that are readily available in the hills and valleys of the Middle East. The mixture is also used as a filling for vine leaves or peppers and aubergines (eggplants) when meat is scarce. To prepare it as a salad, the ingredients are simply bound with olive oil and lemon juice, then tossed with mint.

SERVES FOUR TO SIX

INGREDIENTS

- 150g/5oz/scant 1 cup fine bulgur, rinsed
- 400g/14oz can chickpeas, drained and rinsed
- 1 red onion, finely chopped
- 15–30ml/1–2 tbsp toasted sesame seeds
- 2–3 cloves garlic, crushed
- 60–75ml/4–5 tbsp olive oil
- juice of 1–2 lemons
- 1 bunch flat leaf parsley, finely chopped
- 1 large bunch mint, coarsely chopped
- sea salt and ground black pepper
- 5ml/1 tsp paprika, to garnish

COOK'S TIP

To toast sesame seeds, heat a frying pan, pour in enough seeds to just cover the bottom of the pan, then dry-fry over a low heat, stirring constantly, until the seeds turn golden brown. Remove from the pan immediately, and leave to cool. Alternatively, roast in a medium oven for a few minutes until golden brown.

1 Place the bulgur in a bowl and pour over boiling water to cover. Leave to soak for 10–15 minutes, until it has doubled in volume.

2 Meanwhile, place the chickpeas in a bowl with the onion, sesame seeds and garlic, and bind with the olive oil and lemon juice.

3 When cool enough to handle, squeeze the bulgur to remove any excess water and add it to the chickpeas.

4 Add the chopped parsley and mint to the bowl. Toss well, season with salt and pepper to taste, and sprinkle the paprika over the top before serving.

Energy 267kcal/1116kJ; Protein 8.6g; Carbohydrate 34.1g, of which sugars 3.3g; Fat 11.4g, of which saturates 1.4g; Cholesterol 0mg; Calcium 89mg; Fibre 4.1g; Sodium 153mg.

ORANGE, LEMON AND ONION SALAD

This Middle Eastern salad is often served with spicy dishes and grilled meats. Some versions omit the lemons, but this Syrian recipe is particularly refreshing. Herbs, such as parsley, coriander and mint are often added, and the Lebanese and Turks tend to add small, mild-tasting black olives.

SERVES FOUR

INGREDIENTS

- 3 sweet, juicy oranges, peeled with pith and pips (seeds) removed
- 1 juicy lemon, peeled with pith and pips (seeds) removed
- 1 red onion, finely sliced in rounds
- 8–12 kalamata olives
- 5ml/1 tsp cumin seeds, crushed
- sea salt
- 1 small bunch fresh mint and coriander (cilantro), finely chopped

1 Carefully slice the oranges and lemons into neat rounds on to a plate to catch the juice.

2 Place the orange slices into a bowl with the reserved juice and toss in the sliced onions.

VARIATION
Omit the olives, if you prefer.

3 Add the olives, the cumin seeds and salt to taste, and drizzle with olive oil.

4 Chill the salad in the refrigerator for about 30 minutes, then stir in the chopped herbs, before serving.

Energy 71kcal/298kJ; Protein 2g; Carbohydrate 14g, of which sugars 13g; Fat 1g, of which saturates 0g; Cholesterol 0mg; Calcium 82mg; Fibre 2.9 g; Sodium 310mg.

WHITE CABBAGE SALAD

THIS SIMPLE WHITE CABBAGE SALAD, SALATAT MALFOUF ABIAD, IS SERVED THROUGHOUT THE EASTERN MEDITERRANEAN REGION AND IS PARTICULARLY POPULAR IN KEBAB HOUSES AS AN APPETIZER, OR AS AN ACCOMPANIMENT TO KEBABS SERVED IN PITTA BREAD OR TO SOME OF THE HEAVIER MEAT DISHES. IN SOME REGIONS, THE WHITE CABBAGE IS PICKLED, THEN SERVED IN THE SAME WAY.

SERVES FOUR

INGREDIENTS

- 1 small white cabbage, trimmed and rinsed
- 30ml/2 tbsp olive oil
- juice of 1 lemon
- 1 clove garlic, crushed
- sea salt

1 Cut the cabbage into quarters and then slice each one into very thin strips. Place the strips in a large serving bowl and sprinkle with salt.

2 Whisk together the olive oil, lemon juice and garlic in a small bowl.

3 Pour the dressing over the cabbage and toss well. Leave the salad to sit for about 30 minutes and serve to whet the appetite, or as part of a mezze spread.

Energy 92kcal/381kJ; Protein 1g; Carbohydrate 5g, of which sugars 4g; Fat 8g, of which saturates 1g; Cholesterol 0mg; Calcium 44mg; Fibre 1.9 g; Sodium 104mg.

POTATO AND PEPPER SALAD WITH NIGELLA AND LIME

NIGELLA SEEDS ARE PRIMARILY EMPLOYED AS A FLAVOURING ON BREADS AND SAVOURY PASTRIES, BUT IN SOME PARTS OF THE MIDDLE EAST THEY ARE ADDED TO PICKLES AND SALADS.

SERVES FOUR

INGREDIENTS

- 8–12 medium new potatoes
- 45–60ml/3–4 tbsp olive oil
- 2 red onions, halved lengthways and finely sliced with the grain
- 2–3 cloves garlic, finely chopped
- 1 red chilli, seeded and finely sliced
- 10ml/2 tsp nigella seeds
- 5ml/1 tsp coriander seeds
- 5ml/1 tsp cumin seeds
- 5–10ml/1–2 tsp ground turmeric
- sea salt and ground black pepper
- juice of 1 lime
- 1 lime, cut into wedges, to serve

1 Wash the potatoes, place in a pot of water and boil until tender but still firm.

2 When the potatoes are cooked, drain and refresh under a running cold tap then peel off the skins. Cut them into bite size chunks.

3 Heat the oil in a pan and stir in the onions for 1–2 minutes to soften. Add the garlic, chilli and nigella seeds for 2–3 minutes.

4 Add the coriander, cumin seeds and the turmeric to the pan, then toss in the potato chunks, stir to coat with the seasoned mixture and cook to heat through. Add salt and pepper to taste.

5 Squeeze in the lime juice, then leave the mixture to cool in the pan before transferring it to a serving dish. Serve at room temperature with lime wedges to squeeze over it.

Energy 234kcal/976kJ; Protein3; Carbohydrate 22g, of which sugars 6g; Fat 16g, of which saturates 2g; Cholesterol 0mg; Calcium 49mg; Fibre 2.1 g; Sodium 114mg.

Egg and Onion Salad

This is a lovely egg dish, ideal for a snack or as part of the mezze table. In one simple dish it represents so many of the tastes particular to the Eastern Mediterranean – salty olives, toasted sesame seeds, tangy sumac, Middle Eastern pepper, and parsley.

SERVES FOUR

INGREDIENTS
- 4–6 eggs
- 1 red onion, halved lengthways and sliced
- 60ml/4 tbsp fleshy green olives, pitted and quartered
- 30ml/2 tbsp pine nuts, toasted
- 45ml/3 tbsp sesame seeds, toasted
- 10ml/2 tsp Middle Eastern red pepper, or 1 red chilli, seeded and finely chopped
- 10ml/2 tsp ground sumac
- 30–45ml/2–3 tbsp olive oil
- juice of 1 lemon
- 1–2 cloves garlic, crushed to a paste with salt
- 1 small bunch flat leaf parsley, finely chopped
- ground black pepper

1 Put the eggs into a pan of water and bring it to the boil for 4–5 minutes. Refresh the eggs under running cold water and shell them. Quarter them on a board.

2 Cut the peeled eggs into quarters and place into a bowl. Add the onion, olives, pine nuts, sesame seeds, Middle Eastern red pepper, and sumac.

3 In a small bowl, whisk the lemon juice and olive oil together with the garlic paste and seasoning and pour it over the eggs. Add the parsley.

4 Toss the salad lightly, so that the eggs don't break up, then garnish with a little sumac. Serve at room temperature with crusty bread.

Energy 308kcal/1272kJ; Protein 12g; Carbohydrate 4g, of which sugars 3g; Fat 27g, of which saturates 5g; Cholesterol 289mg; Calcium 129mg; Fibre 2.0 g; Sodium 769mg.

TOMATO SALAD WITH CHILLI AND CORIANDER

RIPE, JUICY TOMATOES ARE PILED HIGH IN THE MARKETS OF THE EASTERN MEDITERRANEAN, USED DAILY IN RAW SALADS AND COOKED DISHES. IN JORDAN THIS FIERY TOMATO SALAD IS A POPULAR MEZZE DISH AND IS DELICIOUS SERVED WITH GRILLED AND ROASTED MEATS AND FISH.

SERVES FOUR

INGREDIENTS

- 6 plump, fresh tomatoes
- 1 hot green chilli, seeded and finely sliced
- 2 cloves garlic, finely chopped
- 5ml/1 tsp ground fenugreek
- ½ tsp sugar
- 30ml/2 tbsp olive oil
- juice of ½ a lemon
- 1 bunch fresh coriander (cilantro) leaves, finely chopped
- sea salt

1 Prick the tomatoes with a fork, and place in a large bowl. Pour just-boiled water from the kettle over the tomatoes and leave until the skins start to peel.

2 Drain the tomatoes, and leave to cool. When they are cool enough to handle, peel off and discard the skin.

3 Cut the tomatoes in half, use a teaspoon to remove and discard the seeds, then chop the flesh finely, and place in a bowl.

4 Toss in the chilli and garlic along with the fenugreek and sugar. Season with salt and pepper, and add the olive oil and lemon juice.

5 Finally, toss in the chopped coriander and serve the salad straight away, with other mezze dishes.

Energy 94kcal/390kJ; Protein 1g; Carbohydrate 5g, of which sugars 5g; Fat 8g, of which saturates 1g; Cholesterol 0mg; Calcium 15mg; Fibre 1.3g; Sodium 111mg.

Soups, Breads and Hot Snacks

Soups in the Lebanon, Jordan and Syria are hearty and satisfying. They are enjoyed throughout the day, even for breakfast, and are sold on street corners as a warming snack during the winter months. Street vendors also sell a variety of freshly baked breads, an essential part of every meal, and delicious snacks, such as tasty little pastries introduced to the region by the Ottoman Turks.

Chicken and Saffron Broth with Noodles

The delicate soups of the region are served as an appetizer to a meal, whereas hearty soups made with vegetables, lentils, meat or grains may be served as a meal on their own. This soup falls into another category, a clear broth served as a palate cleanser.

SERVES SIX TO EIGHT

INGREDIENTS

For the stock

- 2 celery stalks, with leaves, roughly chopped
- 2 carrots, peeled and roughly chopped
- 1 onion, roughly chopped
- 1 lean, organic chicken, about 1.5kg/3¼lb, cleaned and trimmed
- 1 small bunch parsley, roughly chopped
- 6 peppercorns
- 6 allspice berries

For the broth

- 1 generous pinch of saffron fronds
- 115g/4oz/1 cup vermicelli, or other noodles, broken into pieces
- sea salt and ground black pepper
- 1 small bunch fresh parsley or mint, finely chopped, to garnish

COOK'S TIP

Chicken stock will remain clear if the water is simmered gently rather than boiled, but if it does become cloudy don't worry, the flavour is not impaired, and some say that the stock becomes more nutritious if it is boiled rather than simmered.

1 To make the stock, place all the chopped vegetables in a large pan. Put the chicken on top and add the parsley, peppercorns and allspice berries. Pour in enough water to cover.

2 Bring the water to the boil, then reduce the heat, cover the pan and simmer gently for about 1½ hours, until the chicken starts to fall off the bones.

3 Lift the chicken out of the pan and set aside. Strain the stock into a fresh pan and discard the vegetables and spices.

4 When the chicken is cool enough to handle, pull the meat off the carcass. Discard the bones and reserve the dark meat for another dish. Use your fingers to tear the breast meat into thin strips, cover and keep warm.

5 Reheat the broth and stir in the saffron fronds. Bring the broth to the boil and add the noodles. Reduce the heat and boil gently for about 10 minutes, until the noodles are cooked.

6 Add the chicken strips to the soup and heat through. Check the seasoning and add salt and pepper to taste. Pour the hot soup into individual bowls and sprinkle with parsley or mint.

Energy 260kcal/1088kJ; Protein 28.4g; Carbohydrate 11.3g, of which sugars 0g; Fat 11.3g, of which saturates 3.4g; Cholesterol 86mg; Calcium 17mg; Fibre 0g; Sodium 106mg.

Lamb and Wheat Soup

This traditional peasant soup, hreesi, is prepared with lamb or chicken, combined with wheat, cooked slowly until the consistency of porridge. It makes a substantial meal. In Lebanon, the Christian communities often prepare Hreesi for the Feast of the Assumption, while Muslims traditionally eat it to break their fast at Ramadan.

SERVES FOUR TO SIX

INGREDIENTS

- 900g/2lb lamb shanks
- 225g/8oz/1¼ cups wholegrain wheat, soaked in water overnight
- 10ml/2 tsp cumin seeds
- 30–45ml/2–3 tbsp ghee or butter
- 10ml/2 tsp ground cinnamon
- sea salt and ground black pepper

1 Place the lamb in a large pan and pour in enough water to cover. Bring the water to the boil and skim off any foam.

2 Drain the wheat and add it to the pan. Season with salt and lots of pepper, reduce the heat, cover and simmer for 1½–2 hours, until the meat is tender. Top up with extra water, if necessary.

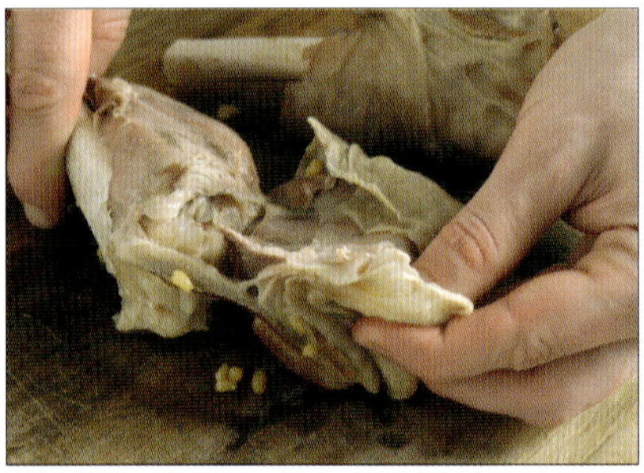

3 Lift out the lamb and remove the meat from the bones. Shred the meat into fine strands, using your fingers, or two forks, and return it to the pan.

4 Continue to simmer the meat with the wheat, beating the mixture with a wooden spoon until it has reached the consistency of thick porridge. Adjust the seasoning, if necessary, turn off the heat, and cover with a lid to keep warm.

5 Heat a small frying pan and dry fry the cumin seeds until they begin to release their fragrance – be careful not to let them scorch. Add the ghee or butter and allow it to melt, then stir in the cinnamon.

6 Ladle the steaming hreesi into warmed bowls and press the back of a spoon into the middle of each bowlful to make a hollow. Pour some of the spiced melted butter into each hollow and serve immediately.

COOK'S TIP

If you are unable to find lamb shanks, use the same weight of shoulder, cut into large chops with the bone left in.

Energy 364kcal/1516kJ; Protein 18.8g; Carbohydrate 29.2g, of which sugars 0g; Fat 19.4g, of which saturates 9.8g; Cholesterol 73mg; Calcium 25mg; Fibre 0g; Sodium 73mg.

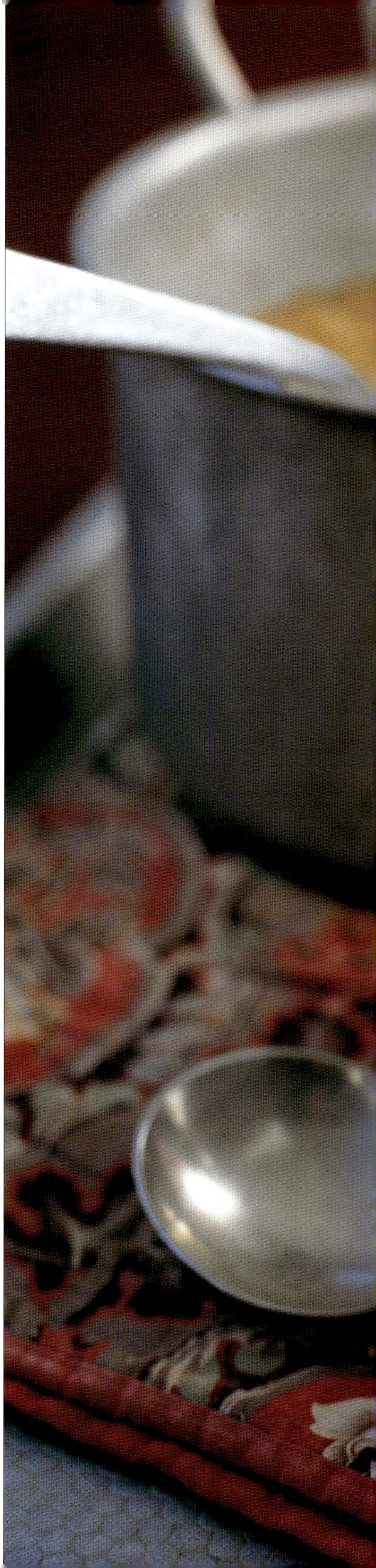

FISH SOUP WITH PEPPERS AND POTATOES

The fish soups of the Eastern Mediterranean are a legacy of all the seafaring civilizations, such as the Phoenicians, the ancient Greeks, and the Crusaders, which have left their stamp on certain coastal dishes. Whether you are in Latakia in Syria, Sidon in Lebanon, or Antakya in Turkey, the thick stew-like fish soups will consist of the day's catch combined with the season's vegetables, a sprinkling of spices and herbs, and is served with bread, often as a meal on its own.

SERVES FOUR TO SIX

INGREDIENTS

- 30–45ml/2–3 tbsp olive oil
- 1 onion, finely chopped
- 2 cloves garlic, finely chopped
- 1 red (bell) pepper and 1 green (bell) pepper, seeded and sliced
- 12 new potatoes, peeled and quartered
- 1 red or green chilli, seeded and sliced
- 10ml/2 tsp coriander seeds
- 5ml/1 tsp cumin seeds
- 1 pinch saffron threads
- 2 large tomatoes, skinned, seeded and sliced
- 15ml/1 tbsp tomato paste (purée)
- 5–10ml/1–2 tsp granulated (white) or palm sugar (jaggery)
- 850ml/1½ pints/3½ cups fish stock (or 600ml/1 pint/2½ cups stock and 300ml/½ pint/1¼ cups white wine)
- 12 prawns (shrimp), shelled and deveined
- 450g/1lb fillets of a firm-fleshed fish, such as red snapper, or sea bass, cut into bitesize chunks
- 1 small bunch flat leaf parsley, roughly chopped
- sea salt and ground black pepper
- 1 lemon, cut into wedges, to serve

1 Heat the oil in a large, heavy pan. Add the chopped onion, garlic, and red and green peppers to the pan and cook, stirring, until they soften.

2 Add the potatoes pieces to the pan with the chilli, coriander seeds, cumin seeds and saffron, and cook for 2–3 minutes more.

3 Add the sliced tomatoes to the pan, and stir in the tomato paste together with the sugar.

4 Pour the stock into the pan, and bring it to the boil. Reduce the heat and simmer for about 20 minutes, until the potatoes are tender. Season to taste with salt and pepper.

5 Add the prawns and fish. Simmer for a further 5 minutes, until the fish is just cooked. Stir in some of the parsley and garnish with the rest. Serve hot with the lemon wedges.

Energy 266kcal/1118kJ; Protein 26g; Carbohydrate 20g, of which sugars 9g; Fat 10g, of which saturates 2g; Cholesterol 125mg; Calcium 102mg; Fibre 2.5 g; Sodium 438mg.

BEDOUIN SPINACH AND LENTIL SOUP

THIS IS A TYPICAL BEDOUIN SOUP, TANGY AND LIGHT, EMPLOYING INGREDIENTS THAT THE NOMADIC PEOPLE CARRY WITH THEM, SUCH AS GRAINS, PULSES AND SIMPLE FLAVOURINGS. FOR THE POORER FAMILIES IN THE BEDOUIN CAMPS, THIS SOUP MIGHT CONSTITUTE A MAIN MEAL BUT, IN THE WEALTHIER HOUSEHOLDS AND RESTAURANTS SPECIALIZING IN BEDOUIN FOOD, IT IS OFTEN SERVED TO WHET THE APPETITE BEFORE A MEAL. IN JORDAN, THIS SOUP IS SOMETIMES MADE WITH MELOKHIA LEAVES, HERE IT IS SPICED WITH TAKLIA, A GARLICKY BUTTER THAT IS STIRRED IN AT THE END.

SERVES FOUR TO SIX

INGREDIENTS
- 30ml/2 tbsp olive oil
- 1 onion, finely sliced
- 2 cloves garlic, finely chopped
- 150g/5oz brown lentils, well rinsed and drained
- 850ml/1½ pints/3½ cups chicken or vegetable stock
- 300g/11oz spinach
- 1 small bunch fresh coriander (cilantro), a few leaves reserved for garnishing
- juice of 2 lemons
- sea salt and ground black pepper

For the taklia
- 2–3 cloves garlic, crushed to a paste with 2.5ml/½ tsp salt
- 30ml/2 tbsp butter, or ghee
- 5ml/1 tsp ground coriander

1 Heat the oil in a large heavy pan. Stir in the sliced onion and garlic until they begin to colour.

2 Stir the lentils into the soup for a minute, then pour in the stock and bring it to the boil.

3 Reduce the heat and simmer the soup gently for about 25 minutes, until the lentils are soft but not mushy. Stir in the lemon juice.

4 Add the spinach and coriander leaves to the pan. Season to taste, but do not add too much salt, as the taklia enough. Simmer for 10 minutes, until the spinach wilts. Meanwhile, prepare the taklia. Melt the butter or ghee in a small pan and add the crushed garlic.

5 When the garlic is light golden in colour, stir in the coriander for a minute, then turn off the heat.

6 Stir the taklia into the soup, garnish with the few remaining coriander leaves and ladle the soup into bowls.

Energy 188kcal/786kJ; Protein 8g; Carbohydrate 16g, of which sugars 3g; Fat 11g, of which saturates 3g; Cholesterol 11mg; Calcium 117mg; Fibre 3.7g; Sodium 661mg.

Creamy Red Lentil Soup with Cumin

Lentil and grain soups, often containing several ingredients together with chunks of meat or a mixture of vegetables, are common fare throughout the Middle East, but every so often you come across a much more simple, puréed soup, flavoured with a single ingredient such as mint or cumin, which is pleasantly refreshing.

SERVES FOUR

INGREDIENTS

- 225g/8oz/1 cup red lentils, rinsed and drained
- 30ml/2 tbsp olive oil
- 40g/1½oz butter
- 10ml/2 tsp cumin seeds
- 2 onions, chopped
- 1 litre/1¾ pints/4 cups chicken stock
- 5–10ml/1–2 tsp ground cumin
- sea salt and ground black pepper
- 1 lemon, cut into wedges, to serve
- 60ml/4 tbsp Greek (US strained plain) yogurt, to serve (optional)

1 Heat the oil and butter in a large, heavy pan and stir in the cumin seeds. Cook, stirring, until they emit a nutty aroma. Add the onion, and fry, stirring until it begins to turn golden brown.

2 Add the drained lentils to the onions, and stir to coat with oil.

3 Pour the stock into the pan and bring to the boil. Reduce the heat, cover the pan and simmer for about 30 minutes, topping up with water if necessary. Ladle the mixture into a food processor or blender and whizz to a paste.

4 Return the soup to the pan to reheat, season with salt and pepper and ladle it into individual bowls. Dust with a little ground cumin and serve with lemon wedges to squeeze over. Add a spoonful of yogurt to each bowl, if you like.

Energy 235kcal/991kJ; Protein 13g; Carbohydrate 28.4g, of which sugars 3.7g; Fat 8.9g, of which saturates 2.2g; Cholesterol 0mg; Calcium 66mg; Fibre 2.9g; Sodium 40mg.

CUCUMBER AND YOGURT SOUP

In Turkey and Syria, a popular dish of cucumber combined with yogurt and mint is often served as an accompaniment, whereas the Lebanese enjoy a similar combination in the form of a cold soup. Middle Eastern cooks believe that salting the cucumber before using in salads and soups makes it easier to digest; it also stops the soup being watery.

SERVES FOUR

INGREDIENTS

- 1 large cucumber, peeled, quartered lengthways and finely sliced
- 1 handful of fresh mint leaves
- 600ml/1 pint/2½ cups thick, creamy yogurt
- 2 cloves garlic, crushed
- 300ml/½ pint/1¼ cups water
- sea salt
- about 12 ice cubes, to serve

1 Place the cucumber slices on a plate and sprinkle them with salt. Leave to weep for 10–15 minutes, then gather the cucumber slices in your hands and squeeze gently to remove the salt and excess water. Meanwhile, chop the mint, reserving a few whole small leaves for garnishing.

2 In a bowl, beat the yogurt with the crushed garlic and chopped mint. Stir in the water to thin it down and then fold in the cucumber. Adjust the seasoning, cover and chill until completely cold for 1–2 hours.

3 When ready to serve, place 2 or 3 ice cubes in each bowl and ladle the chilled soup over them. Garnish with the reserved mint leaves.

Energy 77kcal/322kJ; Protein 6.9g; Carbohydrate 10.3g, of which sugars 10.1g; Fat 1.3g, of which saturates 0.6g; Cholesterol 2mg; Calcium 255mg; Fibre 0.3g; Sodium 106mg.

Fermented Yogurt and Bulgur Soup

This soup is flavoured with kishk, a powder made by soaking medium or coarse grain bulgur in milk or yogurt and leaving it to ferment before spreading it out in the sun to dry. It is used to thicken sauces and soups and is available in Middle Eastern stores.

SERVES FOUR

INGREDIENTS

- 15–30ml/1–2 tbsp olive oil
- 1 onion, finely chopped
- 2 cloves garlic, finely chopped
- 2 red chillies, seeded and sliced
- 5ml/1 tsp dried mint
- 115g/4oz kishk
- 850ml/1½ pints/3½ cups chicken stock
- sea salt and ground black pepper
- 1 handful fresh mint leaves, shredded, to garnish
- 1 lemon, cut into wedges, to serve

1 Heat the oil in a large heavy pan and fry the onion, garlic and chillies until they begin to colour. Stir in the dried mint and kishk and heat for 1 minute.

2 Pour in the stock and bring to the boil, stirring. Simmer for 10 minutes, stirring from time to time, until thick. Season, garnish with shredded mint, and serve hot with wedges of lemon.

Energy 164kcal/683kJ; Protein 4g; Carbohydrate 18g, of which sugars 4g; Fat 9g, of which saturates 1g; Cholesterol 2mg; Calcium 58mg; Fibre 0.6 g; Sodium 703mg.

Thick Mung Bean Soup

There are a variety of thick pulse and grain soups in Syria, Jordan and Lebanon, but this one is unusual. Mung beans are native to India and only grow in the south of Lebanon and the north of Syria. This hearty soup is a meal in itself.

SERVES FOUR

INGREDIENTS

- 30ml/2 tbsp olive oil
- 1 onion, finely chopped
- 2 cloves garlic, finely chopped
- 10ml/2 tsp cumin seeds
- 150g/5oz mung beans
- 850ml/1½ pints/3½ cups stock
- 25g/1oz medium, or long grain rice
- 15ml/1 tbsp oil and a little butter
- 1 onion, cut in half and sliced
- 1 orange, cut into segments

1 Heat the oil in a large pan, add the onion and garlic with the cumin seeds and fry for 2–3 minutes.

2 Add the mung beans and stock. Bring to a boil, reduce the heat and simmer for about 25 minutes, until the beans are soft. Stir the rice into the pan, simmer for 10 minutes, until the rice is cooked, and season.

3 Heat the oil with the butter in a pan and stir in the onion until it begins to turn a deep brown. Blend the soup until smooth, reheat, and serve, garnished with onions and with the orange wedges to squeeze into it.

Energy 296kcal/1224kJ; Protein 12g; Carbohydrate 32g, of which sugars 8g; Fat 14g, of which saturates 3g; Cholesterol 5mg; Calcium 64mg; Fibre 1.8g; Sodium 26mg.

BULGUR AND LAMB PATTIES

Both the Lebanese and the Syrians claim kibbeh – a mixture of bulgur, or rice, and chopped meat. There are numerous variations – with different spices, different fillings, fried or baked. This one uses fragrant lamb and bulgur wheat.

SERVES SIX

INGREDIENTS

- 225g/8oz/1¼ cups bulgur, rinsed and drained
- 450g/1lb lean lamb, cut into small chunks
- 2 onions, grated
- 5–10ml/1–2 tsp ground allspice
- 5–10ml/1–2 tsp paprika
- 10ml/2 tsp ground cumin
- 5–10ml/1–2 tsp salt
- 1 small bunch parsley, finely chopped
- sunflower oil, for frying
- ground black pepper
- 1–2 lemons, cut into wedges, to serve

1 Tip the bulgur into a bowl and pour in just enough boiling water to cover it. Cover the bowl with a clean dish towel and leave the bulgur for up to 20 minutes to swell.

2 Put the lamb into a food processor and blend to a paste. Turn it into a bowl and add the onion, spices and parsley, with salt and lots of pepper.

3 Squeeze any excess water from the bulgur and add it to the lamb (process it first for a smoother texture if you wish). Use your hands to mix everything together and knead well. Process the mixture again and return it to the bowl for further kneading.

4 With wet hands, divide the mixture into small balls and flatten each one in the palm of your hand. Heat enough oil for frying in a shallow pan and cook the patties in batches, about 3 minutes on each side, until nicely browned.

5 Drain the kibbeh on kitchen paper as you cook them, and then serve hot with lemon wedges to squeeze over them.

COOK'S TIP

Using wet hands to form the balls helps to prevent the mixture from sticking to them. You can freeze the kibbeh balls uncooked, and defrost and fry as needed.

Energy 407kcal/1694kJ; Protein 20.1g; Carbohydrate 35.9g, of which sugars 3.9g; Fat 20.9g, of which saturates 5.3g; Cholesterol 57mg; Calcium 65mg; Fibre 1.4g; Sodium 400mg.

CHICKEN WINGS WITH GARLIC AND SUMAC

THE AROMA OF CHICKEN GRILLING OVER CHARCOAL IS ALWAYS ENTICING, WHETHER IT IS IN A BUSY STREET MARKET OR IN A CLEARING IN THE COUNTRYSIDE. THESE CHICKEN WINGS ARE GREAT STREET AND PICNIC FOOD, BEST EATEN WITH YOUR FINGERS, STRAIGHT FROM THE GRILL OR BARBECUE.

SERVES FOUR TO SIX

INGREDIENTS
- 45–60ml/3–4 tbsp olive oil
- juice of 1 lemon
- 4 cloves garlic, crushed
- 15ml/1 tbsp ground sumac
- 16–20 chicken wings
- sea salt

1 In a bowl, mix together the olive oil, lemon juice, garlic and sumac.

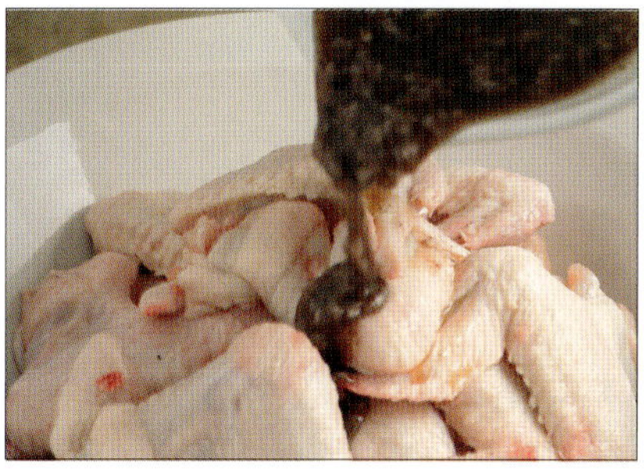

2 Place the chicken wings in a shallow dish and rub the marinade all over them. Cover the dish and leave to marinate in the refrigerator for 2 hours.

VARIATION
If you do not want to barbecue or grill the wings, you can roast them instead. Preheat the oven to 200°C/400°F/Gas 6, place the chicken wings in an ovenproof dish, brush with the marinade and roast them at the top of the oven, for 15–20 minutes until slightly charred.

3 Prepare the barbecue or preheat a conventional grill (broiler). Place the chicken wings in a single layer on the rack and cook for about 6–8 minutes on each side, basting them with the marinade while they cook.

4 When the wings are completely cooked, remove from the heat, sprinkle with salt and serve while still hot.

Energy 272kcal/1132kJ; Protein 23g; Carbohydrate 1.4g, of which sugars 0.1g; Fat 19.5g, of which saturates 4.7g; Cholesterol 98mg; Calcium 12mg; Fibre 0.1g; Sodium 68mg.

LEBANESE MEAT PASTRIES

LITTLE MEAT PASTRIES ARE POPULAR THROUGHOUT THE REGION, VARYING IN THE SPICES AND HERBS USED OR IN THE SHAPE OF THE PASTRY – WHICH MAY BE HALF-MOON, TRIANGULAR OR CIGAR-SHAPED. PERHAPS THE MOST COMMON OF ALL ARE THESE MEAT-FILLED ONES, SAMBOUSAK LAHMA, PREPARED FOR FEASTS.

SERVES SIX

INGREDIENTS

- 30ml/2 tbsp olive oil
- 1 onion, finely chopped
- 30ml/2 tbsp pine nuts
- 250g/9oz lean lamb, minced (ground)
- 10ml/2 tsp ground cinnamon
- 30ml/2 tbsp Greek (US strained plain) yogurt
- 1 small bunch flat leaf parsley, finely chopped
- plain (all-purpose) flour, for dusting
- 450g/1lb ready-made puff pastry
- sunflower oil, for frying
- sea salt and ground black pepper

1 Heat the oil in a heavy pan, stir in the onion and cook until transparent. Add the pine nuts and, just as they begin to colour, stir in the minced lamb. Cook for 4–5 minutes to brown the meat. Stir in the cinnamon and season well.

2 Transfer the mixture to a large bowl, and leave to cool, then beat in the strained yogurt and chopped parsley.

3 On a floured work surface, roll out the pastry thinly. Cut 10cm/4in rounds or squares, depending on whether you want moon-shaped or triangular pastries.

4 Place 10ml/2 tsp of the meat mixture on each piece of pastry, just off centre.

5 Dampen the edges with water and pinch together to seal. Create a pattern along the edge with a fork, if you like.

6 Heat enough oil in a pan and fry the pastries in batches for 5–6 minutes, until golden brown. Drain and serve warm or at room temperature.

Energy 555kcal/2308kJ; Protein 14.5g; Carbohydrate 34.8g, of which sugars 4.4g; Fat 41.5g, of which saturates 4.3g; Cholesterol 32mg; Calcium 76mg; Fibre 0.9g; Sodium 275mg.

CHEESE AND DILL PASTRIES

THESE LITTLE CHEESE PASTRIES, SAMBUSAK JIBNEH, ARE BEST SERVED HOT SO THAT THE CHEESE IS STILL SOFT AND LIGHT AND THE PASTRY CRISP. IDEAL FOR SNACKS, PARTIES OR A MEZZE SPREAD, THEY ARE REALLY VERSATILE, AS YOU CAN ADD ANY COMBINATION OF HERBS, CRUSHED OLIVES OR CHILLI PASTE. USING READY-PREPARED PUFF PASTRY MAKES THEM EXTREMELY EASY TO MAKE.

SERVES FOUR TO SIX

INGREDIENTS

- 225g/8oz feta cheese, rinsed and drained
- 225g/8oz mozzarella or halloumi cheese
- 1 small bunch fresh dill, chopped
- 2 eggs, lightly beaten
- flour, for dusting
- 450g/1lb ready-prepared puff pastry
- 2 egg yolks, mixed with a little oil or water, for brushing
- sea salt and ground black pepper

1 Preheat the oven to 200°C/400°F/ Gas 6. In a bowl, mash the feta with a fork. Grate the mozzarella or halloumi, or whizz to a paste in a blender or food processor, and add it to the feta.

2 Mix in the chopped dill and beaten eggs, season with salt and pepper and mix together. Set aside while you prepare the pastry.

3 Dust the work surface with flour and roll out the pastry thinly. Using a round pastry cutter, or the rim of a cup, cut out 10cm/4in rounds.

4 Gather up the pastry trimmings, re-roll and cut out further rounds. Dust the pastry circles lightly with flour and stack them as you cut them out.

5 Place 10ml/2 tsp of the cheese mixture just off centre on each pastry round. Lift the other side and bring it up over the filling until the edges touch each other to make a half-moon shape.

VARIATION

These make great picnic or lunch box food, but if serving cold use ricotta cheese with the feta, rather than halloumi or mozzarella, as it won't be tough when cooled.

6 Dampen the edges with a little water, pinch them together to seal, and use a fork to make a pattern around the edge.

7 Line several baking trays with baking parchment and arrange the pastries on them. Brush the top of each pastry with a little of the beaten egg yolk mixture and place the trays in the oven.

8 Bake for about 20 minutes, until the pastries are puffed up and golden brown. Serve immediately, while the cheese filling is warm.

Energy 526kcal/2192kJ; Protein 20.6g; Carbohydrate 30.5g, of which sugars 1.8g; Fat 37.4g, of which saturates 11.3g; Cholesterol 179mg; Calcium 352mg; Fibre 0.5g; Sodium 950mg.

SPINACH PASTRIES WITH PINE NUTS

Many varieties of these little pastries, sambousek lahme, are found throughout the eastern Mediterranean; in Lebanon, because they contain no meat, this spinach and pine nut version is often prepared by the Christian communities for Lent.

SERVES SIX

INGREDIENTS

- 500g/1¼lb fresh spinach, trimmed, washed and drained
- 30ml/2 tbsp olive oil, plus extra for brushing
- 15ml/1 tbsp butter
- 2 onions, chopped
- 45ml/3 tbsp pine nuts
- 15ml/1 tbsp ground sumac, or the juice of 1 lemon
- 5ml/1 tsp ground allspice
- 450g/1lb ready-made puff pastry
- sea salt and ground black pepper

1 Steam the spinach until wilted, then drain, refresh under running cold water and squeeze out the excess liquid with your hands. Chop the spinach coarsely. Preheat the oven to 180°C/350°F/Gas 4.

2 Heat the oil and butter in a heavy pan and stir in the onion to soften. Add the pine nuts and cook for 2–3 minutes until they begin to turn golden. Stir in the spinach, sumac or lemon juice and allspice, and season. Set aside to cool.

3 Roll out the pastry on a lightly floured surface and cut out as many 10cm/4in rounds as you can.

4 Spoon a little spinach mixture into the middle of each round. Pull up the sides to make a pyramid by pinching the edges with your fingertips.

5 Line several baking trays with baking parchment and place the pastries on them. Brush the tops with a little oil and bake the pastries for about 30 minutes, until golden brown.

Energy 441kcal/1834kJ; Protein 9g; Carbohydrate 36.8g, of which sugars 7.2g; Fat 30.4g, of which saturates 2.3g; Cholesterol 6mg; Calcium 212mg; Fibre 3.1g; Sodium 371mg.

Cheese Omelette with Peppers and Olives

This kind of thick omelette is often served as a snack, or cut into portions as a mezze dish. On street stalls, omelettes are often cooked in large, wide pans and divided up for customers. They may be spiked with chillies and some include local Lebanese sausages.

SERVES FOUR TO SIX

INGREDIENTS

- 30ml/2 tbsp olive oil
- 1 red onion, chopped
- 1 green or red (bell) pepper, chopped
- 1 red chilli, seeded and chopped
- 225g/8oz feta cheese, crumbled
- 12 black olives, pitted and halved
- 1 small bunch flat leaf parsley, chopped
- 1 small bunch mint leaves, chopped
- 6 eggs, lightly beaten with about 50ml/2fl oz/¼ cup milk
- ground black pepper

1 Heat the oil in a heavy non-stick pan and cook the onion, peppers and chilli until they begin to brown. Stir in the feta cheese, olives and herbs, and quickly add in the beaten eggs. Season with pepper.

2 Pull the egg mixture into the middle of the pan to help it spread and cook evenly. Reduce the heat, cover the pan with a lid, or a piece of foil, and let the omelette cook gently for 5–10 minutes until thick and solid.

3 At a street stall, the omelette would be served directly from the pan at this stage, but at home, you can drizzle a little extra oil over the top and brown it under a preheated grill (broiler), or in a hot oven, if you like.

4 When cooked through, cut the omelette into portions and serve hot or at room temperature.

Energy 303kcal/1252kJ; Protein 13.8g; Carbohydrate 5.5g, of which sugars 4.6g; Fat 25.4g, of which saturates 8.6g; Cholesterol 217mg; Calcium 230mg; Fibre 3.1g; Sodium 2304mg.

ARAB BREAD AND COURGETTE OMELETTE

Arab omelettes are similar to Spanish ones, packed with ingredients and flavour, and can be eaten hot or cold. This one contains bread for a more substantial snack.

SERVES FOUR TO SIX

INGREDIENTS

- 2 medium courgettes (zucchini)
- 30ml/2 tbsp olive oil
- 2–3 slices bread
- milk, for soaking
- 15–30ml/1–2 tbsp butter
- 1 onion, halved and sliced
- 1 small bunch fresh mint, chopped, a few leaves retained to garnish
- 6 eggs, beaten
- 2–3 slices bread
- sea salt and ground black pepper

1 Thinly slice the courgettes, place in a colander, and sprinkle with salt. Leave to stand for 15 minutes, rinse and dry.

2 Remove the crusts from the bread and soak the slices in a little milk.

3 Heat the oil with the butter in a heavy frying pan. Stir in the onions to soften, then add the courgettes. Fry until both the onions and courgettes are golden. Stir in the mint and set aside to cool.

4 Crack the eggs into a large bowl and beat them lightly. Squeeze the bread dry and add it to the eggs, crumbling it with your fingers. Beat well.

5 Add the cooled courgette and onion mixture to the beaten egg and bread. Season with salt and pepper.

6 Heat the rest of the butter in the frying pan. Tip the courgette and egg mixture into the pan, cover and cook gently until the eggs have set. Sprinkle a little finely chopped mint over the top, divide into portions and serve warm or at room temperature.

Energy 230kcal/958kJ; Protein 10g; Carbohydrate 12g, of which sugars 2g; Fat 16g, of which saturates 5g; Cholesterol 242mg; Calcium 77mg; Fibre 0.9 g; Sodium 276mg.

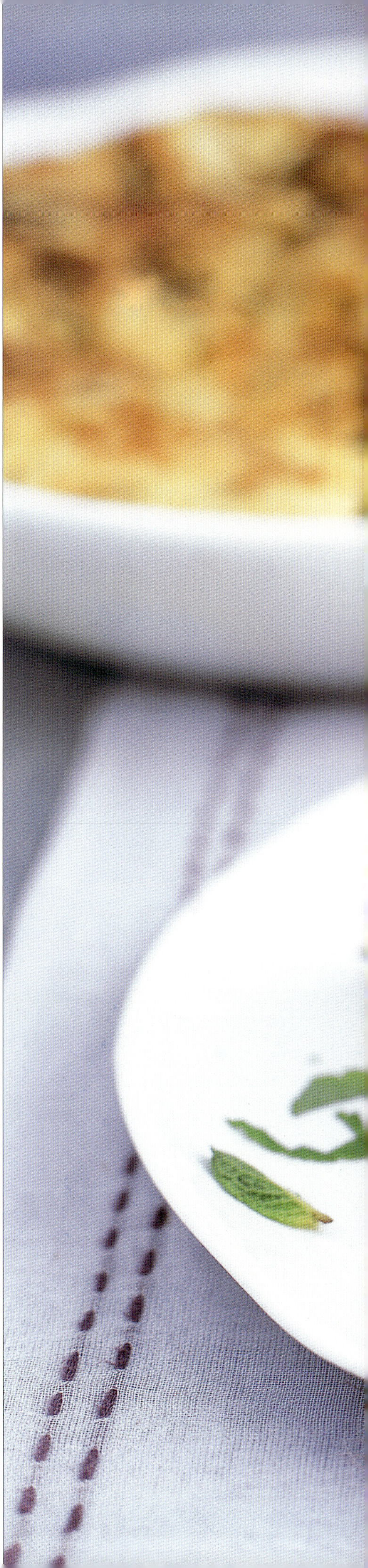

EGGS WITH GARLIC AND SUMAC

BOILED, FRIED OR SCRAMBLED WITH SPICY SAUSAGE OR TOMATOES, EGGS OFTEN FORM PART OF A QUICK SNACK, SERVED WITH BREAD. THIS PARTICULAR DISH IS VERY POPULAR IN THE STREETS AND AT BUS AND TRAIN STATIONS, AND IS OCCASIONALLY SERVED WITH GARLIC-FLAVOURED YOGURT, A GREAT FAVOURITE OF THE TURKS, OR A TAHINI OR NUT SAUCE.

SERVES THREE TO FOUR

INGREDIENTS

- 6 free-range eggs
- 30ml/2 tbsp olive oil
- a knob (pat) of butter
- 2–3 cloves garlic, crushed
- 5–10ml/1–2 tsp dried sumac
- 5ml/1 tsp dried mint
- sea salt
- garlic-spiced yogurt, to serve

1 Crack all the eggs into a large bowl, being very careful not to break any of the yolks as you do so.

2 Heat the oil in a heavy frying pan with the butter. Stir in the garlic and sumac and fry for 2–3 minutes.

3 Slip the eggs into the pan, moving the bowl so that each one falls into its own section of the pan.

4 Sprinkle the dried mint over the eggs and cover the pan with a lid. Reduce the heat and cook until the egg yolks are set to taste.

5 Sprinkle a little sea salt over the eggs and divide them into portions. Serve immediately with garlic-spiced yogurt and an extra pinch of sumac if you like.

Energy 220kcal/911kJ; Protein 12g; Carbohydrate 0g; Fat 20g, of which saturates 5g; Cholesterol 362mg; Calcium 65mg; Fibre 0.1 g; Sodium 243mg.

SYRIAN SAUSAGE ROLLS

Ready-prepared, cured sujuk hang in the markets of Syria, Jordan, Lebanon and Turkey, along with batons of cured beef, basterma. They are the Middle Eastern version of salami, but are invariably spicy and generally prepared with lamb. This Syrian recipe, however, is a homely version, baked in pastry, similar to a Western sausage roll.

SERVES SIX

INGREDIENTS
- 450g/1lb lean lamb, diced
- 2 cloves garlic, crushed
- 10ml/2 tsp Middle Eastern pepper
- 10ml/2 tsp ground cumin
- 5ml/1 tsp ground coriander
- 5ml/1 tsp ground allspice
- 5ml/1 tsp ground turmeric
- 5ml/1 tsp ground fenugreek
- 5ml/1 tsp olive oil
- sea salt
- freshly ground black pepper
- 500g ready-made puff pastry

1 Using a mortar and pestle, pound the meat with the spices, or whiz them together in a food processor. Bind with the olive oil to make a smooth paste, and season with salt and pepper.

2 On a lightly floured surface, roll the pastry into a long, thin rectangle. Place the meat in a sausage shape on one side and fold over to make a roll, or spread the meat in a thin layer, taking it right to the edges, and roll into a spiral.

3 Heat the oven to 200°C/400°F/Gas 6. Slice the pastry log or spiral into roughly 2.5cm/1in portions and place them on a lightly oiled baking sheet. Bake them in the oven for about 12 minutes, until golden brown and puffed up. Serve hot.

Energy 449kcal/1875kJ; Protein 20g; Carbohydrate 31g, of which sugars 1g; Fat 29g, of which saturates 3g; Cholesterol 56mg; Calcium 70mg; Fibre 0.0g; Sodium 378mg.

LITTLE SPICY LAMB PIZZAS

Variations of this minced lamb pizza, lahm bi ajeen, appear all over the Eastern Mediterranean, particularly in Syria and Turkey. The key flavourings include the Middle Eastern red pepper, also known as the Aleppo pepper, and sumac. This Syrian version employs a yogurt-based dough which can be used for a variety of little savoury breads.

SERVES THREE TO FOUR

INGREDIENTS

For the dough:

- 300g/11oz plain (all-purpose) flour
- 2.5ml/½ tsp sea salt
- 15ml/1 tbsp dried yeast
- 5ml/1 tsp sugar
- 50ml/2fl oz/¼ cup lukewarm water
- 150g/5oz plain, natural set yogurt
- 45ml/3 tbsp olive oil

For the topping

- 250g/9oz minced (ground) lamb, briefly processed
- 1 onion, finely chopped
- 1 large tomato, skinned and finely chopped
- 1 small bunch flat leaf parsley, finely chopped
- 10ml/2 tsp Middle Eastern pepper, or 1 red chilli, seeded and finely chopped
- 5ml/1 tsp ground allspice
- 5–10ml/1–2 tsp pomegranate molasses
- sea salt and ground black pepper
- olive oil, for brushing
- 5–10ml/1–2 tsp sumac, to serve

1 Sift the flour with the salt into a large bowl. Cream the yeast with the sugar and the water until it begins to froth.

2 In another bowl, beat the yogurt with the olive oil until it is light and creamy.

3 Make a well in the centre of the flour and pour in the creamed yeast and sugar mixture.

4 Add the yogurt mixture to the bowl. With your fingers, draw in the flour from the sides to make dough. Knead until you have a smooth, silky ball of dough.

5 Pour a few drops of oil in the base of the bowl and roll the ball of dough in it. Cover the bowl with a clean damp dish towel and leave the dough to prove for at least 2 hours, until doubled in size.

6 Meanwhile, place the minced lamb on a board with the onion, tomato and parsley and chop until it forms a paste.

7 Add the Middle Eastern pepper or chilli, allspice, pomegranate molasses and seasoning, and knead well.

8 Preheat the oven to 220°C/450°F/Gas 8. Punch the risen dough with your fist to knock the air out of it, then knead it lightly on a floured surface.

9 Divide the dough into roughly 12 portions and roll each one into a ball.

10 Flatten each ball in the palm of your hand and stretch it into a mini pizza shape. Place each round on a lightly oiled baking sheet.

11 Brush each dough round with a little olive oil and then spread a thin layer of the meat paste over the top.

12 Place the pizzas in the hot oven for about 5–10 minutes, until the base is lightly browned and crispy, and the meat is only just cooked. Sprinkle with sumac and serve immediately.

Energy 418kcal/1769kJ; Protein 23g; Carbohydrate 69g, of which sugars 11g; Fat 7g, of which saturates 3g; Cholesterol 50mg; Calcium 226mg; Fibre 3.3g; Sodium 231mg.

AUBERGINE WITH BASTERMA AND HALLOUMI

The air-dried beef fillet, basterma, cured in a garlic and fenugreek coating, appears on tables throughout Lebanon, Syria, Jordan and Turkey. Thin slices are often served as a mezze dish along with cubes of feta and olives. It is delicious sandwiched between slices of courgette or aubergine, fried and served hot as a mezze dish or a tasty snack, often accompanied by garlic-flavoured yogurt or a tahini sauce. The Armenians are said to be the best producers of basterma, which can be found in Middle Eastern and Turkish stores, along with blocks of delicious, salty halloumi cheese.

SERVES THREE TO FOUR

INGREDIENTS

- 2 large aubergines (eggplant)
- sea salt
- 115/4oz basterma, very finely sliced
- 115g/4oz halloumi, thinly sliced
- 1 handful fresh mint or basil leaves
- sea salt and ground black pepper
- 30–45ml/2–3 tbsp plain flour
- 30–45ml/2–3 tbsp breadcrumbs
- 5–10ml/1–2 tsp zahtar
- 2 eggs, lightly beaten
- sunflower oil, for frying
- 1 lemon, cut into wedges, to serve

1 Slice the aubergines into rounds, roughly 1.5cm /½ in thick, and discard the ends – you need 16 slices in total, to make 8 patties.

2 Sprinkle the slices with salt and leave them to weep for 15 minutes. Rinse the aubergine slices, pat dry, and place them on a wooden board or clean work surface.

3 Take one slice and place a slice of basterma on it, followed by a slice of halloumi, and topped with a mint or basil leaf. Season with a little salt and plenty of black pepper.

4 Place a similar-sized slice of aubergine on top, to create a sandwich.

5 Place the flour in a shallow dish. Dust each side with flour. Repeat with the remaining aubergine slices until you have at least 8 sandwiches.

6 In a shallow bowl, or on a plate, mix the breadcrumbs with a little seasoning and the zahtar. Beat the eggs in another bowl with a splash of water.

7 Place the bowl of beaten egg next to the bowl of breadcrumbs. Carefully, dip each aubergine sandwich into the egg and then coat it in the breadcrumbs. Let the patties stand for a few minutes to allow the breadcrumbs to adhere.

8 Heat enough oil for frying in a heavy frying pan. Gently, place the patties in the hot oil and fry them in batches on both sides until golden brown. Remove from the pan, and drain on kitchen paper as they are cooked.

9 Sprinkle with a little salt, and serve hot with wedges of lemon to squeeze over them. If you like, you can accompany the patties with a simple yogurt or tahini sauce.

Energy 358kcal/1501kJ; Protein 22g; Carbohydrate 25g, of which sugars 4g; Fat 19g, of which saturates 8g; Cholesterol 158mg; Calcium 302mg; Fibre 4.2g; Sodium 622mg.

BREAD WITH FETA AND FIGS

MANOUSHI BREAD DOUGH PRODUCES AN EXTREMELY VERSATILE FLAT BREAD, WHICH IS SIMILAR TO A SOFT, CHEWY PIZZA BASE. YOU WILL ENCOUNTER THESE LITTLE FLATBREADS ALL OVER SYRIA, JORDAN AND LEBANON WITH AN ASSORTMENT OF TOPPINGS, SERVED FOR BREAKFAST OR AS A SNACK AT ANY TIME OF DAY.

SERVES FOUR

INGREDIENTS

For the dough
- 350g/12oz plain (all-purpose) flour
- 1.5ml/½ tsp salt
- 5ml/1 tsp dried yeast
- 1.5ml/½ tsp sugar
- 200ml/7fl oz/scant 1 cup lukewarm water
- 15ml/1 tbsp olive oil

For the topping
- 225g/8oz feta, rinsed and crumbled
- 175g/6oz moist, dried figs, chopped
- 10ml/2 tsp zahtar

1 Sift the flour with the salt into a large bowl. In another bowl, cream the yeast with the sugar in a little of the warm water until it begins to froth.

2 Make a well in the centre of the flour and tip the creamed yeast into it. Add the rest of the water and, drawing the flour in from the sides, work the mixture into a sticky dough.

3 Add the olive oil and knead until the dough is smooth and elastic. Pour a few drops of oil in the base of the bowl and then roll the dough in it. Cover the bowl with a damp dish towel and prove for 2 hours, until it has doubled in size.

4 Punch the dough with your fist to knock out the air and transfer it to a floured surface. Divide into 12 and lightly flour. Cover with a clean dish towel and leave for 20 minutes.

5 Preheat the oven to 230°C/450°F/Gas 8. Take each portion and roll into a ball. Flatten the ball and stretch into a circle, roughly 12.5cm/5in in diameter. Place the circles of dough on a lightly greased baking tray and bake in the oven for 4–5 minutes, until golden brown and crisp.

6 While still hot, scatter the feta and figs over each one. Drizzle a little oil over the top and sprinkle with zahtar. Serve immediately while still warm.

Energy 568/2395kJ; Protein 19g; Carbohydrate 91g, of which sugars 24g; Fat 17g, of which saturates 8g; Cholesterol 39mg; Calcium 431mg; Fibre 5.7g; Sodium 986mg.

Pitta Bread

Plain flat breads come in various guises throughout the Middle East, some with hollow pockets and some without. They are delicious when freshly baked or griddled and drizzled in butter or honey, and ideal, toasted, for dipping or as the base for grilled meat dishes. This is the standard bread dough in Lebanon shaped to make various loaves.

SERVES SIX TO EIGHT

INGREDIENTS

- 7g/¼oz/2¼ tsp dried yeast
- 2.5ml/½ tsp sugar
- 300ml/½ pint/1¼ cups lukewarm water
- 450g/1lb/4 cups strong white bread flour, or a mixture of strong white and wholemeal (whole-wheat) flours
- 2.5ml/½ tsp salt
- a little sunflower oil

1 In a small bowl, dissolve the yeast with the sugar in a little of the water. Leave for about 15 minutes, until frothy.

2 Sift the flour and salt into a bowl. Make a well in the centre and pour in the yeast mixture and the rest of the water. Gradually draw the flour in and knead into a pliable dough.

3 Turn the dough on to a lightly floured surface and knead until smooth and elastic. Pour a drop of oil into the bowl and roll the dough in it to coat.

4 Cover the bowl with a damp cloth and leave to rise in a warm place for at least 2 hours, or overnight, until it has doubled in size.

5 Knock back (punch down) the dough and knead lightly. Divide into tangerine-sized balls and flatten with your hand.

6 Dust a clean cloth with flour and place the rounds of dough on it, leaving room to expand between them. Sprinkle with flour and lay another cloth on top. Leave to prove for 1–2 hours.

7 Preheat the oven to 230°C/450°F/Gas 8. Place several baking sheets in the oven to heat, then lightly oil them and place the bread rounds on them. Sprinkle the rounds with a little water and bake for 6–8 minutes – they should be lightly browned but not too firm, and slightly hollow inside.

8 Place the flat breads on a wire rack to cool a little before eating while warm, or wrap them in a clean, dry cloth to keep them soft for eating later.

Energy 207kcal/877kJ; Protein 5.4g; Carbohydrate 44.5g, of which sugars 0.9g; Fat 2g, of which saturates 0.3g; Cholesterol 0mg; Calcium 80mg; Fibre 1.8g; Sodium 677mg.

FLAT BREADS WITH ZAHTAR AND SUMAC

THESE SPICY LITTLE BREADS, MANAKAKEISH BIL ZAHTAR, FLAVOURED WITH THYME-SCENTED ZAHTAR, ARE VERY POPULAR TO EAT AS A SNACK IN THE STREETS OF BEIRUT AND AT NEIGHBOURHOOD BAKERIES, WHERE THEY ARE OFTEN CHOSEN FOR BREAKFAST. THEY ARE GREAT TO SERVE FRESHLY BAKED, EITHER AS A SNACK OR AS AN ACCOMPANIMENT TO A MEZZE SPREAD.

SERVES FOUR TO SIX

INGREDIENTS
- 7g/¼oz/2¼ tsp dried yeast
- 2.5ml/½ tsp sugar
- 300ml/½ pint/1¼ cups lukewarm water
- 450g/1lb/4 cups strong white (bread) flour, or a mixture of strong white and wholemeal (whole-wheat) flours
- 2.5ml/½ tsp salt
- 30–45ml/2–3 tbsp olive oil, plus extra for oiling
- 45–60ml/3–4 tbsp zahtar
- sea salt

1 In a small bowl, dissolve the yeast with the sugar in a little of the water and leave to cream for about 10 minutes, until it begins to froth.

2 Sift the flour with the salt into a bowl and make a well in the centre. Pour the creamed yeast into the well with the rest of the water and draw the flour in from the sides to form a dough.

3 Turn the dough on to a floured surface and knead for 10 minutes, until it is smooth and elastic. Pour a drop of oil into the base of the bowl, roll the dough in it and cover with a damp cloth. Leave to prove for about 2 hours, until it has doubled in size. Preheat the oven to 200°C/400°F/Gas 6.

4 In a small bowl, mix together the olive oil and the zahtar to make a paste.

5 Knock back (punch down) the dough, knead it lightly, then divide it into about 20 pieces. Knead each piece into a ball, flatten and stretch it, and smear it with some of the zahtar paste.

6 Place the breads on lightly greased baking trays and bake them in the hot oven for about 10 minutes, until slightly risen and golden brown.

7 Sprinkle a little sea salt over the flat breads and serve them warm on their own, or to accompany other dishes.

COOK'S TIP

You can use the ready-prepared spice mix, zahtar, which is available in Middle Eastern stores, or make your own mix by combining 45ml/3 tbsp dried thyme with 15ml/1 tbsp sumac and 15ml/1 tbsp toasted sesame seeds.

Energy 310kcal/1314kJ; Protein 8.2g; Carbohydrate 60.9g, of which sugars 1.1g; Fat 5.6g, of which saturates 0.8g; Cholesterol 0mg; Calcium 119mg; Fibre 2.3g; Sodium 169mg.

GRAINS AND PULSES

No Middle Eastern kitchen is complete without several types of grain. Wheat has been eaten since ancient times and is at the root of many classic dishes. Rice is a more recent introduction: although there are records of it being used in some medieval dishes, it was not until the Ottomans that it became widespread. Bulgur is a staple, as are lentils, beans and chickpeas, and there are few meals in Lebanon, Syria or Jordan that do not include them.

ROASTED GREEN WHEAT WITH PISTACHIOS

Also known as freek, frikkeh is immature wheat that has been roasted in the husk to produce grain with a nutty texture and a mild smoky flavour. The green grains are cooked like ordinary wheat grains and served on their own or as an accompaniment to a main dish. In Lebanon, a popular method of preparing frikkeh is to simmer a whole chicken or shoulder of lamb in water to produce a stock, which is then used for cooking the frikkeh. The grains and the poached meat are served together.

SERVES FOUR TO SIX

INGREDIENTS

- 30ml/2 tbsp ghee or 30ml/2 tbsp olive oil with a knob (pat) of butter
- 1 onion, finely sliced
- 2 cloves garlic, finely chopped
- 1–2 green chillies, seeded and finely sliced
- 115g/4oz/1 cup unsalted pistachios,
- 250g/9oz frikkeh, rinsed
- 900ml/1½ pints/3¾ cups well-flavoured chicken stock
- 30ml/2 tbsp pine nuts
- sea salt and ground black pepper
- Greek (US strained, plain) yogurt, to serve

COOK'S TIP

An ancient food in traditional Arab cuisine, frikkeh is highly nutritious, very high in fibre and with a low GI rating. It is now being produced commercially in other parts of the world as coarse grains as well as flakes, for use as a breakfast cereal, and milled into flour. Look for frikkeh in specialist Middle Eastern or health food stores.

1 Heat the ghee, or olive oil and butter mixture, in a heavy pan and stir in the sliced onion, garlic and green chillies. Cook until they begin to colour.

2 Halve the pistachios, and add to the pan. Fry for 1 minute, stirring.

3 Add the frikkeh to the pan, and stir it well to coat the grains in the butter.

4 Pour in enough stock to just cover the mixture, and bring it to the boil. Add salt and pepper to taste, reduce the heat and simmer for 15–20 minutes, until all the stock has been absorbed.

5 Turn off the heat, cover the pan with a clean dish towel, followed by the lid, and leave the grains to steam for a further 10 minutes.

6 Meanwhile, put the pine nuts in a frying pan and dry-roast them over medium heat, until golden brown. Remove from the heat and transfer them to a plate to cool and crisp.

7 Transfer the frikkeh to a warmed serving dish and sprinkle the pine nuts over the top.

8 Serve immediately, with a dollop of creamy yogurt, as an accompaniment to any roasted or barbecued meat or poultry dish.

Energy 342kcal/1420kJ; Protein 8.7g; Carbohydrate 36.2g, of which sugars 3.2g; Fat 18.6g, of which saturates 2.2g; Cholesterol 0mg; Calcium 49mg; Fibre 1.7g; Sodium 226mg.

BULGUR WITH LAMB AND CHICKPEAS

Throughout Lebanon, Syria, Jordan and Turkey, bulgur or cracked wheat is a staple ingredient. Bulgur is whole wheat, boiled until the grain is tender and the husk cracks open, then dried and ground, either coarsely or finely. There are many peasant dishes combining this much-loved grain with meat or chicken. Some recipes require the two ingredients to be cooked separately and then combined in a wide pan at the end; others call for both to be cooked together in the method of a pilaff. The Lebanese opt for the latter to produce this simple, hearty dish.

SERVES FOUR TO SIX

INGREDIENTS

- 30ml/2 tbsp ghee or 30ml/2 tbsp olive oil with a knob (pat) of butter
- 1 onion, finely chopped
- 5ml/1 tsp ground cumin
- 5ml/1 tsp ground fenugreek
- 200g/7oz lean lamb, cut into chunks
- 200g/7oz/1⅓ cups cooked chickpeas
- 250g/9oz/1½ cups coarse bulgur
- sea salt and ground black pepper
- 1 small bunch fresh coriander (cilantro), finely chopped, to garnish

1 Rinse and drain the bulgur. Heat the ghee, or olive oil and butter mixture, in a heavy pan and add the chopped onion. Cook, stirring, until the onion softens and begins to turn a golden brown colour.

2 Stir the ground cumin and fenugreek into the onions, and stir through until they release their aromas.

3 Toss the chunks of lamb into the pan and stir to coat the meat in the buttered onion and spices.

4 Add the chickpeas to the pan, stir to mix and cook for 1 minute, then add the bulgur.

5 Add about 900ml/1½ pints/3¾ cups water to the pan and bring it to the boil. Season with salt and pepper and stir gently. Reduce the heat and simmer for 20 minutes.

6 When all the water has been absorbed, turn off the heat, cover the pan with a clean dish towel, followed by the lid, and leave the bulgur to steam for a further 10 minutes.

7 Fork through gently, then transfer the bulgur and lamb mixture into a warmed serving dish and garnish with the chopped coriander. Serve immediately.

Energy 366kcal/1533kJ; Protein 18.5g; Carbohydrate 51.8g, of which sugars 2.7g; Fat 10.3g, of which saturates 2.5g; Cholesterol 25mg; Calcium 87mg; Fibre 4g; Sodium 46mg.

ARMENIAN JEWELLED BULGUR

IN SYRIA, JORDAN AND LEBANON, MANY OF THE SAVOURY DISHES COMBINED WITH FRUIT ARE ATTRIBUTED TO ANCIENT PERSIA. THERE ARE A VARIETY OF THESE PERSIAN RECIPES IN THE REGION, ALL OF WHICH ARE DELICIOUS SERVED WITH LEMON AND YOGURT.

SERVES FOUR TO SIX

INGREDIENTS

For the bulgur

- 30ml/2 tbsp olive oil with a knob (pat) of butter, or ghee
- 1 onion, finely chopped
- 5ml/1 tsp sugar
- 2–3 cardamom pods
- 225g/8oz medium or coarse bulgur, well rinsed and drained
- 450ml/¾ pint/scant 2 cups chicken stock, or water
- sea salt and ground black pepper

For the jewels

- 30ml/2 tbsp olive oil with a knob (pat) of butter
- 115g/4oz blanched almonds
- 100g/3½oz walnuts, roughly chopped
- 100g/3½oz apricots, thinly sliced
- 100g/3½oz figs, thinly sliced
- 50g/2oz sultanas (golden raisins)
- 5ml/1tsp ground cinnamon
- 15–30ml/2 tbsp pomegranate molasses

1 Melt the olive oil and butter, or ghee, in a heavy pan and stir in the onion with the sugar, until it turns golden. Add the cardamom pods and stir in the bulgur.

2 Pour the stock into the pan, season with salt and pepper and bring it to the boil. Reduce the heat and simmer for 10–12 minutes, until all the water has been absorbed.

3 Turn off the heat, cover the pan with a clean dish towel and put on the lid. Leave the bulgur to steam for a further 10 minutes.

4 Meanwhile, prepare the fruit and nuts. Heat the oil with the butter in a heavy pan and stir in the almonds and walnuts.

5 Once the nuts begin to brown, stir in the sliced apricots, figs and sultanas and cook for 1–2 minutes.

6 Transfer the bulgur to a serving dish, creating a mound. Spoon the nuts and fruit over the bulgur, dust with cinnamon, and drizzle the pomegranate molasses over the top.

7 Serve the bulgur hot with grilled meats and poultry. It can also be eaten on its own with dollops of thick, creamy (strained) yogurt, mixed with a little lemon juice.

Energy 577kcal/2401kJ; Protein 12g; Carbohydrate 56g, of which sugars 26g; Fat 35g, of which saturates 4g; Cholesterol 4mg; Calcium 161mg; Fibre 4.7g; Sodium 288mg.

Palestinian Rice with Chestnuts

Popular in Lebanon, Syria and Jordan, the makloub (maqlubi) dishes involve cooking the rice on top of layers of vegetables or meat and then inverting the cooking vessel on to a serving dish so that the moulded rice is on the bottom with a layer of vegetables or meat on top. The word makloub means 'turned over' in Arabic.

SERVES FOUR TO SIX

INGREDIENTS

- 450g/1lb medium or long grain rice
- 15–30ml/1–2 tbsp ghee
- 1 onion, halved and sliced
- 225g/8oz lean lamb, diced into bite size pieces
- 5ml/1 tsp ground cumin
- 5ml/1 tsp ground coriander
- 600ml/1pint/2½ cups water
- 225g/8oz cooked chestnuts, already shelled and halved
- sea salt and ground black pepper

1 Place the rice in a large bowl and cover with just-boiled water from the kettle. Leave the rice to soak for 10 minutes, then drain.

2 Heat the ghee in a heavy pan, add the onion and fry until golden.

3 Add the meat to the pan and brown it all over. Add the spices to the pan, pour in the water, and season with salt.

4 Bring the liquid to the boil, reduce the heat and simmer for about 30 minutes. When the meat is tender, drain it, reserving the stock. Season the stock to taste with salt and pepper.

5 Clean the pan or use another heavy pan with a lid. Brush a little oil in the base and around the sides.

6 Arrange the meat in a layer on the bottom of the pan, followed by a layer of chestnuts.

7 Cover the chestnuts with the soaked, drained rice then carefully pour the stock over the top.

8 Cover the pan with a lid, bring the liquid slowly to the boil, then reduce the heat and simmer for about 20 minutes. By this time the liquid will have been absorbed, and the rice should be almost done. Turn off the heat and leave, still covered, to stand for 10–15 minutes, until the rice is cooked.

9 To serve, use a palette knife or spatula to loosen all the way around the edges of the pan, then place a serving dish upside down over the top of the pan, and carefully, using both hands, invert the pan so that the serving dish is on the bottom. Gently ease the pan away, leaving a mould of rice with a layer of meat on top. Serve hot.

COOK'S TIP

You can buy chestnuts canned or dried, but the best way is probably vacuum packed, as they retain the best flavour and texture.

Energy 440kcal/1862kJ; Protein 14g; Carbohydrate 80g, of which sugars 4g; Fat 9g, of which saturates 4g; Cholesterol 35mg; Calcium 73mg; Fibre 2.2g; Sodium 100mg.

Bulgur with Courgettes, Mint and Dill

This delightful dish has the definite markings of Ottoman influence with the balancing of the 'cool' vegetable with the 'warm' herbs. Variations of this summery dish appear all over Syria, Jordan and Lebanon. With the fresh flavours of mint and dill, this is a great dish for a barbecue, or to serve with any grilled or roasted meat and fish.

SERVES FOUR TO SIX

INGREDIENTS

- 225g/8oz coarse bulgur, well rinsed and drained
- 30ml/2 tbsp ghee, or 30ml/2 tbsp olive oil with a knob (pat) of butter
- 1 onion, finely chopped
- 2–3 courgettes (zucchini), trimmed and diced
- a pinch of saffron threads
- 15ml/1 tbsp butter, or ghee
- 1 bunch dill fronds, chopped
- 1 bunch mint leaves, chopped
- sea salt and ground black pepper
- 1 lemon, cut into wedges, to serve

1 Transfer the bulgur into a bowl and pour over enough boiling water to cover by about 2cm/1in. Cover and leave to swell for about 15 minutes.

2 Heat the ghee or olive oil and butter in a heavy pan and stir in the onion, until it begins to turn golden brown. Add the courgettes with the saffron and sauté for 2–3 minutes, until the courgettes begin to turn golden.

3 Add the bulgur and mix thoroughly by tossing the ingredients lightly so you don't squash the courgettes. Season with salt and pepper. Toss in the dill and most of the mint. Serve hot, garnished with the rest of the mint, and with lemon wedges to squeeze over it.

Energy 216kcal/898kJ; Protein 5g; Carbohydrate 32g, of which sugars 8g; Fat 5g, of which saturates 19g; Cholesterol 19mg; Calcium 47mg; Fibre 0.8g; Sodium 85mg.

UPSIDE-DOWN RICE WITH AUBERGINE

LITERALLY TRANSLATED AS UPSIDE-DOWN, MAKLOUBEH DISHES ARE POPULAR IN THE EASTERN MEDITERRANEAN, WHERE DIFFERENT COMMUNITIES CLAIM A PARTICULAR VERSION AS THEIR OWN. IN LEBANON, THIS AUBERGINE RECIPE, MAKLOUBEH BAJINJAN, IS MUCH CHERISHED AND IS OFTEN PREPARED FOR SPECIAL OCCASIONS, SUCH AS BIRTHDAYS AND THE HOMECOMING OF A RELATIVE.

SERVES FOUR TO SIX

INGREDIENTS

- 4 medium aubergines (eggplants)
- sunflower oil for deep-frying
- 300g/11oz medium or long grain white rice, well rinsed
- sea salt and ground black pepper
- 30ml/2 tbsp olive oil
- 1 onion, finely chopped
- 250g/9oz minced (ground) lamb
- 5–10ml/1–2 tsp ground cinnamon
- 5ml/1 tsp ground allspice
- 30ml/1 tbsp blanched almonds and 30ml/1 tbsp pine nuts, for garnishing

1 Heat the oven to 180°C/350°F/Gas 4 Partially peel the aubergines, leaving stripes of skin, and cut lengthways into long, thin slices. Heat oil for deep-frying in a pan and fry the aubergine in batches. Drain and set aside.

2 Pour 850ml/1½ pints/3½ cups water into a pot and bring it to the boil. Add the rice and boil for 1-2 minutes. Season with salt and pepper, reduce the heat and simmer for 15–20 minutes, until the rice has absorbed the water.

3 Heat 15ml/1 tbsp olive oil in a frying pan. Add the onion and stir until it begins to colour.

4 Add the minced lamb and spices to the onion, and mix well. Stir the mixture over medium heat for about 10 minutes, until the meat is cooked and dry.

5 Line a lightly greased dome-shaped tin (pan), or oven-proof bowl, with most of the aubergine slices. Spoon some of the rice into the dome to fill it a third of the way up.

6 Season the lamb with salt and pepper, then spoon it on top of the rice. Then spoon the rest of the rice on top of the lamb. Place the the remaining aubergine slices on top of the rice to seal, and place the tin in the oven for 15–20 minutes.

7 Meanwhile, heat the remaining 15ml/1 tbsp olive oil in a small heavy-based pan and stir in the almonds for 1–2 minutes, until they begin to colour. Add the pine nuts. As soon as they begin to colour, transfer onto kitchen paper to drain and crisp.

8 Remove from the tin from the oven. Place a plate on top. Using oven gloves, hold the platewith one hand and invert the dish. Ease the tin off. Garnish the dome with the roasted nuts, and serve.

Energy 464kcal/1946kJ; Protein 15g; Carbohydrate 50g, of which sugars 6g; Fat 24g, of which saturates 4g; Cholesterol 31mg; Calcium 78mg; Fibre 4.8g; Sodium 102mg.

SAFFRON RICE WITH PINE NUTS

ALTHOUGH RELATIVELY NEW TO LEBANON, RICE NOW PLAYS A HUGE ROLE IN THE DIET, AND A DISH OF IT IN SOME FORM WILL APPEAR AT ALMOST EVERY MEAL. THIS RECIPE, TINTED GOLD WITH SAFFRON, IS IDEAL FOR SERVING WITH GRILLED FISH OR ROASTED MEAT OR POULTRY.

SERVES FOUR

INGREDIENTS

- 45ml/3 tbsp butter or ghee
- 225g/8oz/generous 1 cup long grain rice
- 1 pinch of saffron fronds
- 600ml/1 pint/2½ cups chicken stock or water
- 30ml/2 tbsp pine nuts
- sea salt and ground black pepper

1 Melt 30ml/2 tbsp of the butter or ghee in a heavy pan. Stir in the rice and saffron, making sure the grains are coated in butter. Pour in the stock, season with salt and pepper, and bring to the boil.

2 Reduce the heat and simmer for 15 minutes, until all the water has been absorbed, then turn off the heat and cover the pan with a clean dish towel, followed by the lid. Leave to steam for a further 10 minutes.

3 Meanwhile, melt the remaining butter in a frying pan. Stir in the pine nuts and cook until they turn golden. Drain them on kitchen paper.

4 Fluff up the rice with a fork and transfer to a warmed serving dish. Sprinkle the pine nuts over the top and serve it immediately.

COOK'S TIP

Saffron may be expensive, but it is worth it. The colour and gentle aroma it imparts is unique, and it is ideal for a mildly-flavoured dish such as this.

Energy 316kcal/1316kJ; Protein 5.5g; Carbohydrate 45.2g, of which sugars 0.3g; Fat 12.5g, of which saturates 5g; Cholesterol 20mg; Calcium 13mg; Fibre 0.2g; Sodium 246mg.

RICE AND MASTIC PARCELS

KHUBZ MARKOUK ARE FLAT, PAPER-THIN ROUNDS OF BREAD, SOMETIMES REFERRED TO IN LEBANON AND SYRIA AS MOUNTAIN BREAD. IT TAKES TIME AND SKILL TO PREPARE THE PAPER-THIN SHEETS USUALLY USED TO MAKE THESE LITTLE PARCELS, SO IT IS EASIER TO USE FILO PASTRY INSTEAD.

SERVES FOUR

INGREDIENTS

- 225g/8oz medium or long grain white rice
- sea salt
- 1–2 mastic crystals
- 5ml/1 tsp sugar
- 4–6 sheets of filo
- 25g/1oz butter or ghee
- sunflower oil, for frying
- 5–10ml/1–2 tsp sumac, or zahtar

1 Bring 600ml/1 pint/2½ cups of water to the boil with a pinch of salt. Toss in the rice and continue to boil the water for 2–3 minutes. Reduce the heat and simmer for about 10 minutes, until the water has been absorbed.

2 Turn off the heat, cover the pan with a clean dish towel, and put on the lid. Leave to stand for about 10 minutes so the steam completes the cooking.

3 Using a mortar and pestle, pound the mastic crystals together with the sugar to a powder. Stir the pulverized mastic into the rice.

4 Place the filo sheets on a flat surface and spoon portions of the rice into the middle of each one. Dot the rice with a little butter and fold the edges of the pastry up and over the rice to form a package, tucking the sides underneath.

5 Fry the parcels in the sunflower oil for 2–3 minutes each side, until crisp and golden brown. Sprinkle with sumac or zahtar and serve as a snack, or as an accompaniment to grilled food.

Energy 356kcal/1459kJ; Protein 5g; Carbohydrate 57g, of which sugars 2g; Fat 12g, of which saturates 4g; Cholesterol 13mg; Calcium 44mg; Fibre 0.5g; Sodium 139mg.

Brown Rice with Walnuts and Basterma

Many versions of this dish are prepared in the villages of Syria, Jordan and Lebanon. It is a wholesome dish that can be served on its own or as an accompaniment to grilled and roasted meats. Brown rice is often used for this recipe, but you can easily substitute it with bulgur.

SERVES FOUR TO SIX

INGREDIENTS

- 115g/4oz chickpeas, soaked overnight, or for at least 6 hours
- 15–30ml/1–2 tbsp ghee or olive oil with a knob (pat) of butter
- 2 onions, finely chopped
- 2 cloves garlic, finely chopped
- 1 red or green chilli, seeded and chopped
- 10ml/2 tsp cumin seeds
- 5–10ml/1–2 tsp sugar
- 5ml/1 tsp ground cinnamon
- 5ml/1 tsp ground allspice
- 5ml/1 tsp ground fenugreek
- 225g/8oz medium or long grain brown rice, well rinsed and drained
- 850ml/1½ pints/3½ cups chicken stock, or water
- 1 small bunch coriander, finely chopped
- a few mint leaves, finely chopped
- sea salt and ground black pepper

For serving

- 15ml/1 tbsp butter
- 4 slices basterma, cut into thin strips
- 30ml/2 tbsp walnuts, roughly chopped

1 Drain the chickpeas and put them in a pan with plenty of water. Bring the water to the boil, reduce the heat and simmer for about 45 minutes, until the chickpeas are tender but not too soft. Drain well and remove any loose skins.

2 Heat the ghee, or olive oil and butter, in a large pan or frying pan and stir in the onions, garlic, and chilli with the cumin seeds and sugar. When the onion begins to brown, stir in the spices.

3 Add the rice to the pan, stirring to coat the grains in the spices. Then add the chickpeas.

4 Pour in the stock or water, season with salt and pepper, and bring it to the boil. Reduce the heat and simmer for about 30 minutes, until the rice is cooked but still retains a bite. Stir in most of the herbs and transfer the mixture onto a serving dish.

5 Melt the butter in a frying pan and stir in the basterma for 1 minute. Add the walnuts and stir for another minute.

6 Spoon the walnuts over the rice and chickpeas. Garnish with the remaining herbs and serve hot.

Energy 337kcal/1418kJ; Protein 12g; Carbohydrate 46g, of which sugars 6g; Fat 13g, of which saturates 6g; Cholesterol 27mg; Calcium 73mg; Fibre 3.6g; Sodium 592mg.

LEBANESE COUSCOUS

ALTHOUGH COUSCOUS IS MOST CLOSELY ASSOCIATED WITH NORTH AFRICA, IT IS ALSO ENJOYED IN LEBANON, SYRIA AND JORDAN, WHERE IT IS CALLED MOGRABIYEH, MEANING 'FROM THE MAGHREB'.

SERVES SIX

INGREDIENTS
- 450g/1lb/2½ cups couscous, rinsed and drained
- 30ml/2 tbsp ghee, or 30ml/2 tbsp olive oil with a knob (pat) of butter
- 1 onion, finely chopped
- 2–3 cloves garlic, finely chopped
- 1 red or green chilli, seeded and very finely chopped
- 1 medium carrot, finely diced
- 5–10ml/1–2 tsp ground cinnamon
- 1 small bunch fresh coriander (cilantro), finely chopped
- sea salt and ground black pepper

For the stock
- 1 small organic chicken
- 2 onions, quartered
- 2 cinnamon sticks
- 4 cardamom pods
- 4 cloves
- 2 bay leaves

1 Place the chicken in a deep pan with the other stock ingredients and cover with water. Bring the water to the boil, reduce the heat and simmer for 1 hour, or until the chicken is tender.

2 Transfer the chicken to a plate. Strain the stock, return it to the pan and boil it over high heat for about 30 minutes, to reduce. Set aside.

3 Remove and discard the skin from the chicken and tear the flesh into thin strips, or cut it into bitesize chunks. Cover the chicken and keep warm.

4 Tip the couscous into a bowl and pour in about 500ml/17fl oz/2 cups boiled water. Stir in 5ml/1 tsp salt then cover with a clean dish towel. Leave for 10 minutes for the couscous to swell.

5 Meanwhile, heat the ghee or olive oil and butter in a frying pan and stir in the onions and garlic. Cook for a minute to soften, then add the chilli and carrot. Fry for 2–3 minutes, until softening.

6 Stir the cinnamon and half the coriander into the onion mixture, then add the couscous, forking through it to mix well and stop the grains from clumping together, until heated through.

7 Transfer the couscous into a warmed serving dish and arrange the shredded chicken on top. Season the reduced stock with salt and pepper, reheat if necessary, and spoon some of it over the chicken to moisten.

8 Garnish with the remaining coriander and serve with the rest of the stock in a bowl for spooning over portions.

Energy 376kcal/1574kJ; Protein 31.9g; Carbohydrate 44.6g, of which sugars 4g; Fat 8.8g, of which saturates 3.5g; Cholesterol 70mg; Calcium 49mg; Fibre 1.1g; Sodium 128mg.

BROWN BEANS WITH FETA AND PARSLEY

Traditionally a peasant dish, with its origins in ancient Egypt, this bean dish, known as 'foul medames', is a popular staple dish in Lebanon, Syria and Jordan. It is generally served with freshly baked bread for breakfast, or as part of a mezze spread.

SERVES FOUR TO SIX

INGREDIENTS

- 250g/9oz/1¼ cups dried brown beans, soaked overnight
- 30–45ml/2–3 tbsp olive oil
- 2 cloves garlic, crushed
- 5–10ml/1–2 tsp cumin seeds, dry roasted and crushed
- juice of 1 lemon
- sea salt and ground black pepper

To serve

- 1–2 red onions, halved lengthways, and halved again crossways
- 1 bunch of flat leaf parsley, chopped
- 225/8oz feta cheese

1 Drain the beans and place them in a deep pan. Cover with water, bring to the boil, reduce the heat and simmer for 1 hour, until the beans are tender.

2 When the beans are almost cooked, prepare the accompaniments. Finely slice the onions on the grain and place in a bowl. Place the chopped parsley in another bowl.

3 Using your fingers, roughly crumble the feta cheese into a third small serving bowl.

4 Drain the beans and, while they are still warm, transfer them into a large serving bowl and add the olive oil, garlic and cumin. Squeeze in the lemon juice, season with salt and pepper, and mix.

5 Serve the warm beans immediately, accompanied by the bowls of red onions, feta and parsley, to which everyone helps themselves.

Energy 200kcal/846kJ; Protein 13.6g; Carbohydrate 27.3g, of which sugars 1.5g; Fat 4.8g, of which saturates 0.7g; Cholesterol 0mg; Calcium 65mg; Fibre 9.4g; Sodium 12mg.

Butter Bean Stew

As beans are nourishing and readily available, there are times when a stew like this may constitute the main meal of the day. Some include meat or root vegetables, but this version simply contains beans. Serve with a dollop of yogurt and bread.

SERVES FOUR TO SIX

INGREDIENTS

- 450g/1lb/2½ cups dried butter (lima) beans, soaked overnight, then drained
- 30ml/2 tbsp ghee, or 30ml/2 tbsp olive oil with a knob (pat) of butter
- 2 onions, finely chopped
- 4–6 cloves garlic, crushed
- 10ml/2 tsp sugar
- 10ml/2 tsp cumin seeds
- 10ml/2 tsp coriander seeds
- 1 large cinnamon stick
- 2 x 400g/14oz cans chopped tomatoes
- 1 small bunch fresh coriander (cilantro), coarsely chopped
- sea salt and ground black pepper

1 Place the beans in a pan of water. Bring to the boil, reduce the heat and simmer for 45 minutes, until tender. Drain and remove any loose skins.

2 Heat the oil and butter in a heavy pan and cook the onions, garlic and sugar for 2–3 minutes. Add the spices.

3 Add the beans and tomatoes to the pan and cook over medium heat for about 20 minutes. Season and stir in half the coriander.

4 Transfer to a bowl, removing the cinnamon. Garnish with coriander and serve with bread, or with a meat dish.

Energy 295kcal/1251kJ; Protein 18.8g; Carbohydrate 45.4g, of which sugars 11.5g; Fat 5.7g, of which saturates 0.9g; Cholesterol 0mg; Calcium 108mg; Fibre 14.1g; Sodium 29mg.

Peasant Beans and Bulgur with Cabbage

This recipe, makhlout, can be prepared as a vegetarian dish or served with sautéed lamb tossed through it. For this version, you can use any type of canned beans or chickpeas, rinsed and drained, or dried beans, soaked overnight and then simmered in plenty of water for about 40 minutes (25 minutes for haricot beans). In Syria and Jordan, makhlout is served with yogurt and a tomato salad, or with steamed cabbage leaves.

SERVES FOUR TO SIX

INGREDIENTS

- 115g/4oz/1 cup brown lentils, rinsed and drained
- 115g/4oz bulgur, rinsed and drained
- 15–30ml/1–2 tbsp ghee, or olive oil with a knob of butter
- 2 onions, finely chopped
- 2–3 cloves garlic, finely chopped
- 10ml/2 tsp cumin seeds
- 10ml/2 tsp coriander seeds
- 1 small handful dried sage leaves, crumbled
- 115g/4oz cooked kidney beans, canned or dried, soaked and cooked
- 115g/4oz cooked haricot (navy), or soya, beans, canned or dried, soaked and cooked
- 115g/4oz cooked chickpeas, canned or dried, soaked and cooked
- 5ml/1 tsp paprika
- 12 cabbage leaves, trimmed
- sea salt and ground black pepper
- garlic-spiced Greek (US strained, plain) yogurt or tahini sauce, to serve

1 Put the lentils into a pan of boiling water, reduce the heat and simmer for about 20 minutes, until they are tender. Drain and refresh immediately under running cold water.

2 Tip the bulgur into a bowl and pour in just enough boiling water to cover the grains by about 1cm/½ in. Cover and leave to swell for about 15 minutes.

3 Heat the ghee or olive oil and butter in a frying pan, and stir in the onion and garlic with the spices and sage leaves. Once the onions begin to brown, add the beans and cook for 2 minutes.

4 Add the bulgur and stir until all the grains and pulses are heated through. Season with salt and pepper, and dust with paprika. Keep warm.

5 Steam the trimmed cabbage leaves until wilting but not too soft. Drain and pat dry with kitchen paper.

6 Spoon portions of the mixture into the middle of each of the steamed cabbage leaves, then fold the edges in to wrap them up. Serve immediately with garlic-spiced yogurt or tahini sauce. You can keep them warm in the oven for a while.

Energy 261kcal/1097kJ; Protein 13g; Carbohydrate 40g, of which sugars 5g; Fat 7g, of which saturates 3g; Cholesterol 14mg; Calcium 104mg; Fibre 5.8g; Sodium 78mg.

WHITE BEAN PURÉE WITH FETA AND OLIVES

TRADITIONALLY THIS DISH IS PREPARED WITH THE DRIED WHITE BROAD (FAVA) BEANS, BUT HARICOT (NAVY) AND BUTTER (LIMA) BEANS ARE GOOD SUBSTITUTES. THROUGHOUT THE EASTERN MEDITERRANEAN, THERE ARE VARIATIONS OF THIS BROAD BEAN PURÉE, SUCH AS THE COLD MEZZE DISH, FAVA, WHICH IS MUCH SOUGHT AFTER IN LEBANON AND TURKEY. THIS RECIPE IS FOR A WARM BEAN PURÉE THAT MAKES A DELICIOUS ACCOMPANIMENT TO ANY VEGETABLE OR MEAT DISH.

SERVES FOUR TO SIX

INGREDIENTS

- 30–45ml/3–4 tbsp olive oil
- 1 onion, finely chopped
- 225g/8oz dried white beans, soaked in plenty of water overnight and drained
- 850ml/1½ pints/3½ cups chicken stock, or water
- 2 cloves garlic, crushed to a paste with a little salt
- juice of 1 lemon
- 115g/4oz feta cheese, crumbled
- 30ml/2 tbsp green or black olives, stoned and chopped
- sea salt and ground black pepper
- 5ml/1 tsp paprika, to serve

1 Heat 15–30ml/1–2 tbsp olive oil in a heavy pan. Stir in the onion and, when it begins to colour, add the beans. Pour in the stock and bring to the boil. Reduce the heat and simmer for about 40 minutes, until the beans are tender.

2 Drain the beans and remove any loose skins. Transfer them into an electric blender, or crush through a sieve (strainer) with a fork. Combine the crushed beans with the garlic paste, the remaining olive oil, and the lemon juice.

3 Spoon the purée into a pan and heat it through. Fold most of the feta and olives into the purée, season to taste, and transfer to a bowl. Garnish with the rest of the olives, dust with paprika, and serve immediately.

Energy 195kcal/810kJ; Protein 6g; Carbohydrate 9g, of which sugars 2g; Fat 15g, of which saturates 4g; Cholesterol 13mg; Calcium 105mg; Fibre 2.8g; Sodium 881mg.

CHICKPEAS WITH TOASTED BREAD AND YOGURT

A number of popular dishes fall into the category known as fatta, an Arabic term denoting the breaking of toasted flat bread into pieces to provide a bed for the other ingredients. This simple dish of chickpeas is popular street food.

SERVES FOUR

INGREDIENTS

- 225g/8oz/1¼ cups chickpeas, soaked overnight
- 600ml/1 pint/2½ cups Greek (US strained plain) yogurt
- 2–3 cloves garlic, crushed
- 4 pitta breads
- 5–10ml/1–2 tsp dried mint
- 5ml/1 tsp paprika
- 15ml/1 tbsp butter
- 30ml/2 tbsp pine nuts
- sea salt and ground black pepper

1 Drain the chickpeas and transfer them to a pot. Cover with plenty of water and bring it to the boil.

2 Reduce the heat and simmer the chickpeas for 1 hour, until tender. Drain, reserving the cooking liquid.

3 Toast the pitta breads, then break up into bitesize pieces and arrange them on a serving dish.

4 Spread the chickpeas over the bread and moisten with a few tablespoons of the cooking liquid.

5 Beat the yogurt with the garlic and season with salt and pepper. Spoon the yogurt generously on top of the chickpeas and sprinkle with the dried mint and paprika.

6 Quickly melt the butter in a frying pan and fry the pine nuts, stirring constantly, until they turn golden. Sprinkle them over the top of the yogurt and chickpeas and serve immediately.

COOK'S TIP

Use canned chickpeas if you wish.

Energy 354kcal/1489kJ; Protein 21.5g; Carbohydrate 41.1g, of which sugars 13.1g; Fat 13g, of which saturates 3.4g; Cholesterol 11mg; Calcium 380mg; Fibre 6.5g; Sodium 175mg.

LENTILS AND RICE WITH CRISPY ONIONS

THIS IS AN ANCIENT CLASSIC AND A GREAT FAVOURITE IN LEBANON. KNOWN AS 'MOUJADARA' IT IS OFTEN SERVED DURING LENT AMONG THE CHRISTIAN COMMUNITIES, WHEREAS FOR MUSLIMS IT IS AN ESSENTIAL PART OF THE MAIN MEAL SERVED TO BREAK THE FAST DURING RAMADAN.

SERVES FOUR TO SIX

INGREDIENTS

- 225g/8oz/1¼ cups brown lentils, well rinsed
- 45–60ml/3–4 tbsp ghee or olive oil
- 2 onions, finely chopped
- 5ml/1 tsp sugar
- 5ml/1 tsp ground coriander
- 5ml/1 tsp ground cumin
- 225g/8oz/generous 1 cup long grain rice, well rinsed
- sea salt and ground black pepper
- 5ml/1 tsp ground cinnamon, to garnish

For the crispy onions

- sunflower oil for deep-frying
- 2 onions, halved lengthways and sliced with the grain

1 Boil the lentils in a pan of water for 10–15 minutes, until tender but firm. Drain and refresh under cold water.

2 Heat the oil or ghee in a heavy pan and cook the onions with the sugar for 3–4 minutes, until they begin to turn golden. Add the spices and cook for 1–2 minutes, then add the lentils and rice, tossing to coat the grains in the spicy onion mixture.

3 Add water to just cover the lentils and rice, and bring to the boil. Reduce the heat and simmer gently for about 15 minutes, until the water has been absorbed. Turn off the heat, cover the pan with a clean dish towel, followed by the lid, and leave the rice and lentils to steam for a further 10 minutes.

4 Meanwhile, prepare the crispy onions. Heat the oil in a deep frying pan and fry the onions until brown and crisp, then drain on kitchen paper. Transfer the rice to a serving dish, season and fluff up with a fork. Sprinkle with cinnamon and spoon the onions on top. Serve immediately with yogurt, or with any meat, poultry or fish dish.

Energy 411kcal/1717kJ; Protein 13.7g; Carbohydrate 58.3g, of which sugars 7g; Fat 14.3g, of which saturates 1.8g; Cholesterol 0mg; Calcium 68mg; Fibre 5g; Sodium 9mg.

GREEN LENTILS WITH BULGUR

This dish, 'imjadra', is similar to moujadara *(see page 137)**, and is one of Lebanon's lesser known countryside specialities. It combines lentils with a grain to produce a wholesome dish that can be served on its own, or with any meat, poultry or fish dish.*

SERVES FOUR TO SIX

INGREDIENTS

- 225g/8oz/1¼ cups green lentils, rinsed
- 30ml/2 tbsp ghee, or olive oil with a knob (pat) of butter
- 2 onions, finely chopped
- 5–10ml/1–2 tsp cumin seeds
- 225g/8oz/1¼ cups coarse bulgur, rinsed
- 900ml/1½ pints/3¾ cups stock
- sea salt and ground black pepper
- 15ml/1 tbsp ghee or butter, to serve
- mint and parsley, to garnish

1 Bring a pan of water to the boil, add the lentils and cook for about 15 minutes, until they are tender but not soft or mushy. Drain and refresh.

2 Heat the ghee in a heavy pan, stir in the onions and cook until they begin to colour. Add the cumin seeds and stir in the bulgur, coating it in the ghee. Add in the lentils and pour in the stock.

3 Season to taste with salt and pepper and bring to the boil. Reduce the heat and simmer for 15 minutes.

4 Turn off the heat and place a clean dish towel over the pan, followed by the lid. Leave to steam for 10 minutes.

5 Meanwhile, melt the butter in a small pan. Transfer the rice and lentils into a serving dish, pour the melted butter over the top and garnish with the mint and parsley leaves.

Energy 306kcal/1284kJ; Protein 13.8g; Carbohydrate 52.8g, of which sugars 4.2g; Fat 5.4g, of which saturates 0.6g; Cholesterol 0mg; Calcium 63mg; Fibre 4.3g; Sodium 9mg.

LENTILS WITH ONIONS, PARSLEY AND MINT

LENTILS HAVE FORMED PART OF THE DAILY DIET OF THE EASTERN MEDITERRANEAN SINCE ANCIENT TIMES. HOT OR COLD, THEY CAN BE SERVED AS PART OF A MEZZE SPREAD OR ON THEIR OWN. THIS RECIPE, POPULAR IN SYRIA AND LEBANON, IS PREPARED IN A SIMILAR WAY TO TABBOULEH.

SERVES FOUR

INGREDIENTS
- 225g/8oz/1¼ cups brown lentils
- 2 cloves garlic
- 45–60ml/3–4 tbsp olive oil
- juice of 1 lemon
- 2–3 spring onions (scallions), trimmed and finely chopped
- 1 bunch flat leaf parsley, chopped
- sea salt and ground black pepper
- lemon wedges, to serve

1 Put the lentils in a pan with plenty of water and bring it to the boil. Reduce the heat and simmer for about 25 minutes, until the lentils are tender but still retain a bite to them.

2 Rinse and drain the lentils and put in a bowl. Crush the garlic with the salt to make a paste and stir it into the lentils.

3 Add the olive oil, lemon juice, pepper and salt to taste, and toss to mix well.

4 Stir the spring onions and parsley into the lentils and serve while the lentils are still warm as a hot mezze, with lemon wedges to squeeze over it. It is also a great accompaniment to grilled and roasted meat and poultry dishes.

Energy 308kcal/1293kJ; Protein 14g; Carbohydrate 29g, of which sugars 2g; Fat 16g, of which saturates 2g; Cholesterol 0mg; Calcium 59mg; Fibre 5.4g; Sodium 107mg.

FISH AND SHELLFISH

The region's recipes rarely specify a particular type of fish, as people would use whatever was available, so most firm-fleshed fish are interchangeable in soups, kibbeh and stews, and are ideal for barbecuing and baking. The most common way to cook fish is to grill it over charcoal and serve it with a tahini sauce and lemon wedges. Fish is rarely served with dairy products, as there is a widespread belief that this combination renders fish harmful.

JORDANIAN FISH STEW WITH TAMARIND

Variations of this sour, spicy stew can be found in Jordan, Egypt and the Arabian Gulf. The flavours echo the history of trade between the Arabs and the Indians, as turmeric and fenugreek play an important role. Dried tamarind pulp is available in Middle Eastern stores. The dish can be prepared with fish steaks or large prawns.

SERVES FOUR TO SIX

INGREDIENTS

- 115g/4oz/1 cup dried tamarind pulp, soaked in 350ml/12fl oz/1½ cups water for 20 minutes
- 1kg/2¼lb fish steaks, such as sea bream, grouper, sea bass
- 15–30ml/1–2 tbsp olive oil
- 1 onion, halved and sliced
- 4 cloves garlic, chopped
- 5ml/1 tsp cumin seeds
- 10ml/2 tsp ground turmeric
- 5ml/1 tsp ground fenugreek
- 2.5ml/½ tsp chilli powder
- roughly 12 small new potatoes, peeled and left whole
- 1 x 400g/14oz can of plum tomatoes, drained of juice
- 5ml/1 tsp palm sugar (jaggery)
- sea salt and ground black pepper
- 1 bunch coriander (cilantro), chopped

1 Squeeze the tamarind pulp in your hand to separate the pulp from the seeds and stalks, then strain the pulp through a sieve (strainer). Reserve the strained pulp and liquid.

COOK'S TIP

You should be able to find palm sugar (jaggery) in Middle Eastern stores. If not, replace it with the same amount of white or demerara (raw) sugar.

2 Heat the oil in a heavy pan and sear the fish steaks for 1–2 minutes on each side, then transfer them to a plate. Stir the onion, chilli, garlic and cumin seeds into the pan and cook until they begin to colour. Add the spices to the pan, then toss in the potatoes and cook for 2–3 minutes. Stir in the tomatoes and add the sugar.

3 Pour the tamarind water into the pan and bring the liquid to the boil. Reduce the heat, cover the pan, and simmer gently for about 15 minutes, until the potatoes are tender.

4 When the potatoes are cooked, season with salt and pepper to taste, then slip in the seared fish steaks. Cover the pan again and cook gently for about 10 minutes, until the fish is cooked. Stir half the coriander into the stew and garnish with the rest. Serve hot with a rice pilaff or bread.

Energy 317kcal/1337kJ; Protein 32g; Carbohydrate 26g, of which sugars 5g; Fat10g, of which saturates 1g; Cholesterol 63mg; Calcium 103mg; Fibre 1.2g; Sodium 291mg.

SAFFRON FISH STEW WITH COUSCOUS

THIS IS A PERFECT ONE-POT MEAL FOR A BUSY WEEKDAY SUPPER. IT TAKES LESS THAN HALF AN HOUR TO PREPARE, AND CAN BE EATEN ON ITS OWN OR WITH SOME STEAMED GREENS. USE WHATEVER FIRM WHITE-FLESHED FISH IS AVAILABLE FOR THIS SAFFRON-FLAVOURED STEW. YOU CAN USE MEDIUM OR GIANT COUSCOUS FOR THIS DISH.

SERVES FOUR TO SIX

INGREDIENTS

- 115g/4oz/1 cup couscous, washed and drained
- 30–45ml/2–3 tbsp olive oil
- 1 onion, finely chopped
- 2 leeks, trimmed and finely chopped
- 2–3 cloves garlic, finely chopped
- 5ml/1 tsp cumin seeds
- a pinch saffron threads
- a few sprigs fresh thyme
- 1 small bunch fresh sage leaves, chopped
- 5ml/1 tsp Middle Eastern red pepper
- 1 x 400g/14oz can of plum tomatoes, drained of juice
- 600ml/1 pint/2½ cups fish stock
- sea salt and ground black pepper
- 4 fish fillets, such as sea bass, haddock, or trout, cut into bite size chunks
- 1 small bunch fresh coriander (cilantro), roughly chopped, to garnish

1 Tip the couscous into a bowl and pour in just enough warm water to cover. Leave for 15 minutes to swell and double in volume.

2 Heat the oil in a heavy pan and stir in the onion, leeks and garlic, cook for 2-3 minutes, until they begin to colour.

COOK'S TIP

Check the fish for bones and remove with tweezers. Bones are difficult to spot when the fish is in a stew like this.

3 Add the cumin, saffron, thyme, sage and red pepper to the pan, and stir in the tomatoes. Pour in the stock and bring the liquid to the boil. Reduce the heat and simmer for 15 minutes, then season and stir in the couscous.

4 Add the fish chunks to the pan and cook gently for 4–5 minutes, until the fish is just cooked.

5 Sprinkle the chopped coriander over the top and serve in warm bowls.

Energy 348kcal/1449kJ; Protein 22g; Carbohydrate 15g, of which sugars 4g; Fat 23g, of which saturates 3g; Cholesterol 80mg; Calcium 166mg; Fibre 1.2g; Sodium 443mg.

Fish Baked in a Tahini Sauce

Tahini is employed in many dishes in the eastern Mediterranean. Mixed with a fruit molasses, such as grape or date, it can be served as a sweet or savoury dip for bread and blended with lemon juice, garlic and a little water it is used as a dressing for numerous salads or as a sauce for grilled and baked dishes, such as this one.

SERVES FOUR TO SIX

INGREDIENTS

- 300ml/½ pint/1¼ cups tahini (light or dark)
- 150ml/½ pint/¾ cup lemon juice
- 150ml/½ pint/¾ cup water
- 2 cloves garlic crushed
- sea salt and ground black pepper
- 15–30ml/1–2 tbsp olive oil
- 2 onions, halved and sliced
- 5–10ml/1–2 tsp cumin seeds
- 500g/1¼lb fish fillets, such as sea bass, haddock or trout, cut in half
- 1 bunch flat leaf parsley, finely chopped, to garnish

1 Preheat the oven to 160°C/325°F/Gas 3 In a bowl, beat the tahini with the lemon juice and water to form a smooth, creamy sauce – it will thicken with the lemon juice at first but then thin down with the water. Beat in the garlic and season to taste.

2 Heat the oil in a heavy frying pan and sauté the onions with the cumin seeds, until they begin to turn golden brown.

3 Spread half of the onion mixture in the base of an oven-proof dish, lay the fish fillets on top, then spread the rest of the onion mixture over the fish. Pour the tahini sauce over the fish and place it in the oven for 25–30 minutes, until the fish is cooked.

4 Sprinkle the dish with the chopped parsley, and serve immediately with a salad and chunks of bread to mop up the sauce.

Energy 437kcal/1810kJ; Protein 25g; Carbohydrate 5g, of which sugars 3g; Fat 35g, of which saturates 5g; Cholesterol 38mg; Calcium 374mg; Fibre 4.9g; Sodium 129mg.

FRIED RED MULLET WITH PITTA BREAD

Red mullet is regarded as a fish of distinction in Lebanon. Splendidly pink and succulent, the fresh fish are caught daily and invariably grilled or fried. If red mullet is not available, you can use sea bass or red snapper instead. In this classic dish the fried fish is covered with crisp, golden strips of pitta bread and served with a tahini sauce.

SERVES FOUR

INGREDIENTS

- 4 red mullet, about 250g/9oz each, gutted, scaled and cleaned
- 15–30ml/1–2 tbsp plain (all-purpose) flour
- 2 pitta breads
- olive, sunflower, or groundnut (peanut) oil for frying
- sea salt and ground black pepper
- 1 small bunch flat leaf parsley, coarsely chopped, to garnish
- 1 lemon, cut into quarters, to serve

For the tahini sauce

- 1–2 cloves garlic
- 150ml/¼ pint/⅔ cup smooth tahini
- juice of 1 lemon
- juice of 1 small orange

1 First prepare the tahini sauce. Pound the garlic cloves in a mortar and pestle with a little salt, until you have a paste.

2 Beat the tahini in a bowl with the lemon and orange juices, until thick and smooth. Beat in the garlic paste, and season to taste. Set aside.

3 Rinse the mullet under cold running water and pat dry inside and out with kitchen paper. Using a sharp knife, slash each fish with three diagonal cuts on each side. Sprinkle with salt and pepper and toss them in flour so that they are lightly coated. Cut the pitta bread into strips.

4 Heat enough oil for frying in a heavy pan and cook the fish, two at a time, for about 3 minutes on each side, until they are crisp and golden. Drain on kitchen paper and keep warm.

5 Toss the strips of pitta in the same oil, until they too are crisp and golden, and drain them on kitchen paper.

6 Arrange the fish on a serving dish, drizzle a little tahini sauce over them, garnish with the parsley, and sprinkle the pitta strips over the top.

7 Serve immediately, with lemon wedges to squeeze over them and the rest of the tahini sauce.

Energy 556kcal/2318kJ; Protein 35.1g; Carbohydrate 23.9g, of which sugars 1.2g; Fat 36.2g, of which saturates 4.4g; Cholesterol 0mg; Calcium 386mg; Fibre 4.2g; Sodium 329mg.

FISH SAUTÉED WITH ALMONDS

There are variations of this simple dish throughout the eastern Mediterranean, sometimes substituting almonds with walnuts or pine nuts. This dish takes just minutes to prepare and, served with fresh bread and a salad, makes a very quick and easy meal. Trout, sea bass, and sole are all delicious cooked in this way.

SERVES FOUR

INGREDIENTS
- 30ml/2tbsp olive oil
- 50g/2oz/1 cup blanched almonds, halved
- 15g/½oz/1 tbsp butter
- 2 cloves garlic, finely sliced
- 4 large fish fillets, divided in half
- 5–10ml/1–2 tsp sumac
- sea salt
- 1 lemon, cut into wedges, to serve

1 Heat the oil in a heavy pan and stir in the almonds, until they turn golden. Remove them from the oil with a slotted spoon and set aside.

2 Add the butter to the same pan and stir in the garlic.

COOK'S TIP

To blanch almonds that still have their skins, simply place in a heatproof bowl and cover with just-boiled water. Once the water has cooled, the almonds can be squeezed easily out of their skins. Cut in half with a sharp knife or leave whole.

3 Add the fish fillets to the pan and sauté for 2–3 minutes on each side. Return the almonds to the pan and sprinkle with salt and the sumac. Serve immediately with the lemon wedges.

Energy 298kcal/1245kJ; Protein 37g; Carbohydrate 1g, of which sugars 1g; Fat 16g, of which saturates 2g; Cholesterol 86mg; Calcium 58mg; Fibre 1.0g; Sodium 214mg.

Poached Fish with Rice and Pine Nuts

Originally a simple dish prepared by fishermen out at sea, this recipe has become more sophisticated and now ranks as a Lebanese classic. It is served every day in restaurants in coastal areas, but in homes it is prepared as a special dish to honour guests.

SERVES FOUR TO SIX

INGREDIENTS

- 30–45ml/2–3 tbsp olive oil
- 2 onions, finely sliced
- 1 firm-fleshed fish, such as sea bass or trout (about 900g/2lb), scaled, gutted and cleaned
- 1 bunch flat leaf parsley
- 2–3 bay leaves
- 1 cinnamon stick
- 6 black peppercorns
- 250g/9oz/1¼ cups long grain rice, well rinsed and drained
- 5–10ml/1–2 tsp ground cumin
- 5–10ml/1–2 tsp ground cinnamon, plus extra for dusting
- 30ml/2 tbsp pine nuts
- sea salt
- 1 lemon, cut into wedges, to serve

COOK'S TIP

If you don't have a pan large enough to poach the fish whole, cut it into two or three pieces to fit, or transfer the fish and stock to a roasting pan and bake in the oven.

1 Heat the oil in a heavy pan and fry the onions for 5–10 minutes, until dark brown. Turn off the heat and set aside.

2 Rub the fish with salt inside and out. Place the parsley leaves in the base of a pan, lay the fish on top and add the bay leaves, cinnamon stick and black peppercorns. Pour in enough water to just cover, and bring to the boil. Reduce the heat and simmer gently for about 5 minutes.

3 Transfer the fish to a board and leave it to cool a little, remove the skin, take the flesh off the bone and break it into bitesize pieces. Cover with foil.

4 Return the skin, head and bones to the cooking liquid and bring to the boil. Reduce the heat and bubble for 15–20 minutes, to reduce by half. Strain the stock, return it to the pan and bring it to the boil again.

5 Add the browned onions to the stock, and simmer for 10–15 minutes more.

6 With a slotted spoon, lift the onions out and press through a sieve (strainer) back into the pot.

7 Stir the stock well and add seasoning to taste. Return to the boil, add the rice, cumin and cinnamon and simmer for 10 minutes, until the rice has absorbed the stock.

8 Turn off the heat, cover the pan with a clean dish towel, followed by the lid, and leave to stand for 10 minutes to finish cooking.

9 Dry-roast the pine nuts in a pan over a medium heat until golden.

10 Transfer the rice to a serving dish, stir some of the fish into it and place the rest on top. Sprinkle the roasted pine nuts on top, dust with cinnamon and serve with lemon wedges.

Energy 385kcal/1611kJ; Protein 28.3g; Carbohydrate 40.6g, of which sugars 4.9g; Fat 12.2g, of which saturates 1.8g; Cholesterol 96mg; Calcium 68mg; Fibre 1.3g; Sodium 90mg.

Charcoal-Grilled Trout with Lemon

The traditional method of cooking fish in the eastern Mediterranean is over charcoal or wood embers. Whether it is sea or freshwater fish, the flesh is always tasty and juicy cooked this way. If you don't want to use a barbecue you can use a griddle instead.

SERVES FOUR

INGREDIENTS

- juice of 2 lemons
- 4 cloves garlic, crushed
- 4 small trout (about 300g/11oz each), gutted and cleaned
- 10ml/2 tsp zahtar
- sea salt
- ground pink peppercorns
- 1 lemon, cut into wedges, to serve

1 Using a sharp knife, score the flesh of the fish diagonally three times on each side. Rub a little salt and pink pepper into the fish, inside and out.

2 Prepare the barbecue or preheat a ridged griddle. In a bowl, mix together the lemon juice and crushed garlic.

3 Brush one side of the fish with the lemon juice and place it, lemon juice-side down, on an oiled rack set over the glowing coals. Cook for around 4 minutes, then turn the fish over.

VARIATION

Small whole sea bass can also be used instead of trout in this recipe.

4 Brush lemon juice on the other side and cook for 4 minutes more. Transfer to a serving dish. Sprinkle the zahtar over the top and serve with lemon wedges to squeeze over them.

Energy 279kcal/1176kJ; Protein 47.3g; Carbohydrate 1.7g, of which sugars 0.1g; Fat 9.4g, of which saturates 2.2g; Cholesterol 192mg; Calcium 78mg; Fibre 0.2g; Sodium 175mg.

BAKED FISH WITH BAY, ORANGES AND LIMES

UNTIL RECENTLY MANY HOUSEHOLDS IN LEBANON LACKED OVENS. INSTEAD, ONCE A WEEK OR SO A FRESHLY CAUGHT FISH MIGHT BE TAKEN ALONG TO THE COMMUNAL NEIGHBOURHOOD OVEN TO BE BAKED SIMPLY, AS IN THIS RECIPE. SERVE THE FISH WITH A SALAD OR TAHINI SAUCE.

SERVES FOUR

INGREDIENTS

- 1 sea bass or grouper (weighing about 900g/2lb), gutted and cleaned
- 2–3 bay leaves
- 1 small orange, finely sliced
- 1 lime, finely sliced
- 15ml/1 tbsp butter
- sea salt and ground black pepper

For the marinade

- juice of 2 oranges
- juice of 2 limes
- 30ml/2 tbsp olive oil
- 1 clove garlic, crushed

1 Whisk together all the ingredients for the marinade. Place the fish in a dish and pour the marinade over it. Cover and chill for 1–2 hours. Preheat the oven to 180°C/350°F/Gas 4.

2 Transfer the fish to an ovenproof dish and spoon the marinade over it. Tuck the bay leaves under it and arrange several slices of orange and lime alternately along the inside, and on top, of the fish.

3 Cover the dish with foil and bake for 15 minutes. Remove the foil, dot the fish with butter and bake uncovered for a further 10 minutes. Serve immediately.

Energy 257kcal/1078kJ; Protein 35g; Carbohydrate 1.1g, of which sugars 1.1g; Fat 12.6g, of which saturates 4g; Cholesterol 153mg; Calcium 56mg; Fibre 0g; Sodium 160mg.

Roasted Fish with Chillies and Walnuts

This simple dish is a favourite along the coast of Lebanon, particularly around Tripoli. Traditionally, dogfish is used, but any firm-fleshed white fish, such as sea bass or snapper, is ideal. Topped with a spicy tahini sauce, this dish is spectacular when garnished with jewel-like fresh pomegranate seeds.

SERVES FOUR

INGREDIENTS

- 2 x 900g/2lb firm-fleshed fish, gutted and cleaned
- 60ml/4 tbsp olive oil
- 2 onions, finely chopped
- 1 green (bell) pepper, very finely chopped
- 1–2 red chillies, seeded and very finely chopped
- 115g/4oz walnuts, finely chopped
- 15–30ml/1–2 tbsp pomegranate molasses
- 1 small bunch of fresh coriander (cilantro), finely chopped
- 1 small bunch of flat leaf parsley, finely chopped
- sea salt and ground black pepper

For the sauce

- 60ml/4 tbsp tahini
- juice of 1 lemon
- juice of 1 orange
- 15ml/1 tbsp olive oil
- 2 cloves garlic, finely chopped
- 1–2 red chillies, seeded and finely chopped
- sea salt and ground black pepper
- seeds of half a pomegranate, with pith removed, to garnish

1 Preheat the oven to 200°C/400°F/ Gas 6. With a sharp knife, make three or four diagonal slits on each side of the fish. Rub the cavity with salt and pepper, cover and chill for 30 minutes.

2 Meanwhile, prepare the filling. Heat 30ml/2 tbsp olive oil in a heavy pan and fry the onions, pepper, and chillies until lightly browned. Stir in the walnuts and pomegranate molasses, and add half the coriander and parsley. Season to taste and leave the filling to cool.

3 Fill the fish with the stuffing and secure the opening with a wooden skewer or cocktail sticks (toothpicks).

4 Place the fish in an oiled baking dish and pour over the remaining oil. Bake in the preheated oven for about 30 minutes.

5 For the tahini sauce, heat the olive oil in a small pan and stir in the garlic and chillies, until they begin to colour.

6 In a bowl, beat the tahini with the lemon and orange juice, until the mixture is smooth and creamy. Add the garlic and chilli mixture, beat to mix, then return to the pan and warm the sauce through. Season with salt and pepper and keep warm.

7 Transfer the cooked fish to a serving dish and drizzle some of the sauce over the top. Garnish with the pomegranate seeds and serve immediately, with the rest of the sauce served separately.

COOK'S TIP

You can use freshwater trout for this recipe as well as the usual firm white-fleshed sea bass, red mullet or snapper.

Energy 772kcal/3223kJ; Protein 78.8g; Carbohydrate 13.1g, of which sugars 10.3g; Fat 45.3g, of which saturates 6.5g; Cholesterol 288mg; Calcium 292mg; Fibre 4.9g; Sodium 276mg.

SPICY FISH WITH DRIED LIME

This dish is particular to the cooking of the Arabian Gulf, Egypt and Jordan. Both sweet and sour limes grow in this region but the sour ones, limun baladi, are dried whole and used in cooking to impart a earthy, tangy flavour to stews. Whole dried limes and powdered lime are available in Middle Eastern stores.

SERVES FOUR

INGREDIENTS
- 500g/1lb 2oz fish steaks
- 15–30ml/1–2 tbsp turmeric
- 15ml/1 tbsp ground coriander
- 15–30ml/1–2 tbsp ghee, or butter
- 2 onions, finely sliced
- 1 green chilli, seeded and sliced
- 25g/1oz fresh ginger, peeled and grated
- 2 cloves garlic, finely chopped
- 2 pieces of cinnamon bark
- 2 dried limes
- 5–10ml/1–2 tsp palm sugar (jaggery), or sugar
- 400g/14oz can chopped tomatoes
- sea salt and ground black pepper

1 Mix the turmeric and coriander in a dish and press the fish steaks into the spices so they are coated on both sides.

2 Heat the ghee in a heavy pan and brown the fish on both sides. Transfer the steaks from the pan to a plate.

3 Add the onion to the ghee and stir-fry for a few minutes. Just as it begins to soften, add in the chilli, ginger, garlic and cinnamon bark and cook for a further 1–2 minutes.

4 Pierce the dried limes twice with a skewer and add them to the pan.

5 Add the sugar and the chopped tomatoes to the pan and pour in roughly 150ml/ 1/4 pint/2/3 cup water on top. Bring the liquid to the boil then reduce the heat and simmer gently for about 15 minutes.

6 When the sauce has reduced and thickened, season the mixture with salt and pepper and place the fish steaks back in the pan.

7 Cover the pan and simmer for about 8–10 minutes, until the fish is just cooked through.

8 Serve the fish straight from the pan, accompanied by a rice pilaff or chunks of bread.

Energy 227kcal/950kJ; Protein26; Carbohydrate 13g, of which sugars 10g; Fat 9g, of which saturates 5g; Cholesterol 79mg; Calcium 75mg; Fibre 1.8g; Sodium 218mg.

GRILLED FISH IN DATE COATING

In this Bedouin recipe the coating of puréed dates seals the fish and keeps it moist while cooking, and also imparts a delicious fruity flavour to the fish. Originally it would have been cooked by simply impaling the fish on a stick through its mouth and setting it above glowing coals. If you do not want to use a barbecue, use a grill (broiler) or oven.

SERVES FOUR

INGREDIENTS
- 225g/8oz moist pitted dates
- 1 onion, finely chopped
- 2 cloves garlic, crushed
- 5ml/1 tsp ground turmeric
- 5ml/1 tsp baharat spice mixture
- 1 large trout, or 4 small ones, gutted and cleaned
- sea salt
- lemon wedges, to serve

1 Put the dates in an electric blender with a tablespoon or two of water to form a smooth paste – if your dates are not moist they will need to be soaked in water for several hours first.

2 In a small bowl, mix the onion, garlic, turmeric, and the baharat spice mixture. Rub the mixture around the inside of the fish, sprinkle with salt and lay a sprig of parsley in the cavity too.

3 Seal the cavity with a thin stick, or skewer, by weaving the edges together.

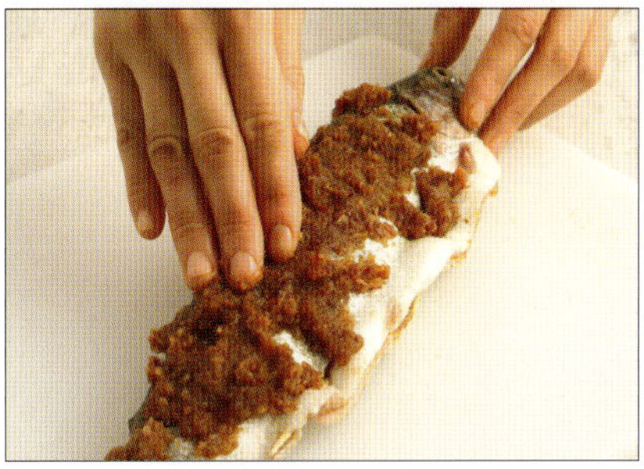

4 If roasting, preheat the oven to 180°C/350°F/Gas 4. Make sure the skin of the fish is dry, then rub the sticky date paste over it. Leave the fish to sit for 10–15 minutes, so that the paste firms up. If grilling, turn the grill (broiler) on.

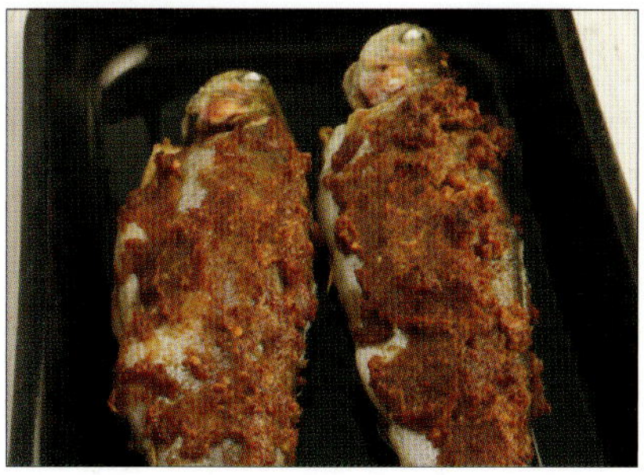

5 Place the fish in a roasting pan or on a rack. Grill for 6–8 minutes on each side, or bake for 15–20 minutes in a hot oven. Serve the fish while hot, with lemon wedges, a crisp salad and some bread.

Energy 335kcal/1415kJ; Protein 32g; Carbohydrate 41g, of which sugars 40g; Fat 6g, of which saturates 0g; Cholesterol 0mg; Calcium 55mg; Fibre 2.8g; Sodium 190mg.

FRIED SARDINES WITH LEMON

THIS SIMPLE DISH IS GENERALLY MADE WITH SARDINES OR SPRATS. OFTEN THE FISH ARE DIPPED IN FLOUR AND FRIED WHOLE BESIDE THE MOORED FISHING BOATS. LOCALS POP THEM WHOLE INTO THEIR MOUTHS, BUT GUTTED AND STEEPED IN LEMON JUICE OR BEER THE FISH ARE EVEN MORE DELICIOUS.

SERVES FOUR

INGREDIENTS

- 450g/1lb fresh small sardines, gutted and cleaned
- 300ml/½ pint/1¼ cups beer (optional)
- 60–75ml/4–5 tbsp chickpea or plain (all-purpose) flour
- olive or sunflower oil, for deep-frying
- sea salt and ground black pepper
- 2 lemons, halved, to serve

1 If you are marinating the fish, place them in a shallow dish and pour the beer over them. Cover and chill for 1–2 hours, then drain and pat dry.

2 Rub the fish with a little salt and pepper and dip them in the flour until lightly coated. Heat enough oil for deep-frying in a heavy pan.

3 Fry the fish in batches for 5–6 minutes, until crisp and golden. Drain them on kitchen paper and serve hot, with lemon halves to squeeze over.

COOK'S TIP

Frying the fish until deep golden means that the bones are crispy and edible.

Energy 358kcal/1488kJ; Protein 18.7g; Carbohydrate 11.7g, of which sugars 0.2g; Fat 26.5g, of which saturates 4.4g; Cholesterol 0mg; Calcium 107mg; Fibre 0.5g; Sodium 96mg.

FISH WITH TOMATO AND POMEGRANATE SAUCE

This is a tasty method of cooking any firm-fleshed fish, such as sea bass, red snapper, grouper and trout. The pomegranate molasses, often used in Middle Eastern cooking for savoury dishes, adds a tangy, sour note to the sauce and enriches the colour.

SERVES FOUR

INGREDIENTS

- 900g/2lb firm-fleshed fish fillets
- 45–60ml/3–4 tbsp olive oil
- juice of 1 lemon
- 2–3 cloves garlic, finely chopped
- 4 tomatoes, skinned, seeded, and chopped
- 15ml/1 tbsp pomegranate molasses
- 10ml/2 tsp sugar
- sea salt and ground black pepper
- 1 small bunch fresh parsley, finely chopped, to garnish

1 Preheat the oven to 180°C/350°F/Gas 4. Arrange the fish in an ovenproof dish, and rub with salt and pepper.

2 Pour 30ml/2 tbsp olive oil and the lemon juice over the fish. Cover with foil and bake for about 25 minutes, until the fish is cooked.

COOK'S TIP

Pomegranate molasses, sometimes sold as pomegranate syrup, is available from Middle Eastern stores and some delicatessens and supermarkets.

3 Meanwhile, heat the rest of the oil in a heavy frying pan. Fry the garlic until it begins to colour, then add the tomatoes. Cook for 5 minutes, then stir in the pomegranate molasses with the sugar. Reduce the heat and cook gently until the sauce thickens. Season with salt and pepper. Keep warm.

4 Arrange the fish on a serving dish, spoon the sauce over and around the fish and sprinkle with the parsley.

Energy 284kcal/1192kJ; Protein 41.7g; Carbohydrate 6.9g, of which sugars 6.9g; Fat 10.1g, of which saturates 1.5g; Cholesterol 104mg; Calcium 28mg; Fibre 0.8g; Sodium 149mg.

FISH KIBBEH WITH ONION FILLING

This kibbeh is traditionally prepared in the coastal towns to mark special events. Among the Christian communities it is a dish that most families prepare for Lent. Any firm-fleshed fish, including haddock and cod, can be used for this recipe. The kibbeh can also be served as a mezze dish if you mould the mixture into tiny bitesize balls.

SERVES FOUR

INGREDIENTS

For the filling

- 15–30ml/1–2 tbsp olive oil
- 2 onions, finely chopped
- 5ml/1 tsp ground cinnamon
- grated rind of half orange
- sea salt and ground black pepper

For the kibbeh

- 175g/6oz/1 cup fine bulgur, well rinsed and drained
- 1 onion, finely chopped
- 450g/1lb boneless fish fillets
- 5–10ml/1–2 tsp ground turmeric
- 1 small bunch fresh coriander (cilantro), finely chopped
- flour, for dusting
- sunflower oil, for frying
- 1 lemon, cut into wedges, to serve

1 First prepare the filling. Heat the oil in a small frying pan, stir in the onions and cook until they soften and begin to colour. Add the cinnamon and orange rind, stir through to mix together and season with salt and pepper. Set aside.

2 Place the bulgur in a bowl and pour over enough boiling water to just cover. Place a clean dish towel over the bowl and leave the bulgur to stand for about 10 minutes, until it has absorbed the water and expanded.

3 Squeeze the bulgur to drain off any excess water and place it in a blender or food processor with the chopped onion, fish fillets, turmeric and coriander. Whizz the mixture to a paste and season with salt and pepper.

4 With wet hands, take a small portion of the kibbeh mixture and mould it into the shape of an egg.

5 Hollow out the egg with a finger and fill the cavity with a little of the onion mixture. Pinch the edges of the kibbeh together to seal in the filling and form an egg shape once more. Repeat with the rest of the mixture.

6 Heat enough oil for shallow-frying in a heavy pan. Roll the kibbeh lightly in flour and fry them in batches until golden brown. Drain them on kitchen paper and serve hot with wedges of lemon to squeeze over them.

Energy 453kcal/1884kJ; Protein 29.7g; Carbohydrate 22.8g, of which sugars 11.5g; Fat 27.7g, of which saturates 9.7g; Cholesterol 93mg; Calcium 231mg; Fibre 1.1g; Sodium 178mg.

Tangy Prawn and Pepper Kebabs

A popular dish prepared in the fishing villages, these kebabs are simple and satisfying, served as here with rice and salad. Generally, they are prepared with green pepper in Lebanon, but variations are made with tomato and onion throughout the region.

SERVES FOUR

INGREDIENTS

- 15ml/1 tbsp pomegranate molasses
- 15ml/1 tbsp olive oil
- juice of 1 lemon
- 2 cloves garlic, crushed
- 10ml/2 tsp sugar
- 16 raw king prawns (jumbo shrimp), shelled and deveined
- 2 green (bell) peppers, cut into bitesize chunks
- sea salt

1 In a large bowl, mix together the pomegranate molasses, olive oil, lemon juice, garlic and sugar. Season the mixture with salt.

2 Add the prawns to the mixture, and toss gently, making sure they are all well coated with the marinade. Cover the dish and chill for 1–2 hours.

3 Prepare the barbecue, if using, or preheat a griddle or grill (broiler). Thread the prawns on to four skewers, alternating with the pepper pieces.

4 Grill the kebabs for 2–3 minutes on each side, basting with any leftover marinade. Serve immediately.

Energy 102kcal/427kJ; Protein 9.7g; Carbohydrate 8.6g, of which sugars 8.3g; Fat 3.4g, of which saturates 0.5g; Cholesterol 98mg; Calcium 48mg; Fibre 1.4g; Sodium 109mg.

SAUTÉED PRAWNS WITH CORIANDER AND LIME

THERE ARE MANY VERSIONS OF THIS DISH THROUGHOUT THE EASTERN MEDITERRANEAN, BUT THIS RECIPE IS VERY POPULAR IN THE PICTURESQUE FISHING VILLAGES UP THE COAST FROM BEIRUT, USING JUST-CAUGHT SEAFOOD AND SERVED WITH FRESHLY BAKED BREAD.

SERVES THREE TO FOUR

INGREDIENTS
- 1 lime
- 30–45ml/2–3 tbsp olive oil
- 2–3 cloves garlic
- 15–16 raw king prawns (jumbo shrimp), peeled to the tails and deveined
- 1 small bunch fresh coriander (cilantro), roughly chopped
- sea salt

1 Grate the lime skin, or use a zester to cut strips all the way around. Cut the lime in half and set aside.

2 Using a mortar and pestle, or a large-bladed knife, crush the garlic with a little salt. Heat the oil in a heavy pan, add the crushed garlic and cook, stirring constantly, until it just begins to turn a golden brown.

3 Add the lime rind to the garlic, add in the prawns, and stir-fry until they begin to turn pink.

4 Add the lime juice and coriander and season with salt, and let the liquid sizzle before removing from the heat. Eat immediately with your fingers.

Energy 106kcal/442kJ; Protein 11.8g; Carbohydrate 1.2g, of which sugars 0.4g; Fat 6.1g, of which saturates 0.9g; Cholesterol 122mg; Calcium 75mg; Fibre 0.8g; Sodium 123mg.

Spicy Grilled Squid

The coastal resorts of Syria and Lebanon are full of cafés and seaside restaurants specializing in delicious grilled seafood dishes. Prawns and squid are often grilled in spicy marinades or sautéed with garlic and herbs. To roast the spices, simply toss them in a heavy-based skillet over medium heat, until they darken and emit a nutty aroma.

SERVES FOUR

INGREDIENTS

- 8 baby squid, cleaned, heads, backbone and innards removed, and rinsed
- olive oil, for brushing
- a few sprigs fresh flat leaf parsley, roughly chopped, to garnish
- 1 lemon, cut into wedges, to serve

For the marinade

- 10ml/2 tsp cumin seeds, roasted
- 5ml/1 tsp coriander seeds, roasted
- 5ml/1 tsp black peppercorns
- 2–3 cloves garlic, crushed
- zest of 1 lemon
- 15ml/1 tbsp dried sage leaves, crumbled
- 30–45ml/2–3 tbsp olive oil
- sea salt

1 In a mortar and pestle, pound the roasted cumin and coriander seeds with the peppercorns. Beat in the crushed garlic, salt, lemon zest and sage leaves. Bind with the olive oil.

2 Rinse the squid under cold running water and pat dry with kitchen paper. Sever the tentacles just above the eyes, so that the top of the head and the tentacles are joined together.

3 Using a sharp knife, score the sacs in a criss-cross pattern and rub them and the tentacles with the spicy marinade. Leave to marinate for 30 minutes.

4 Heat a griddle pan and brush with a little oil. Place the sacs and tentacles on the griddle and cook for a minute on each side. Sprinkle the parsley over the squid and serve immediately with lemon wedges to squeeze over them.

Energy 510kcal/873kJ; Protein 16g; Carbohydrate 2g, of which sugars 0g; Fat 16g, of which saturates 2g; Cholesterol 225mg; Calcium 43mg; Fibre 0.2g; Sodium 211mg.

PRAWN KEBABS WITH PEPPER AND TOMATO

One of the most popular ways to enjoy the succulent jumbo prawns that are caught off the coast of Syria, Turkey and Lebanon is to thread them on to skewers with peppers and tomatoes, rather like a shish kebab. In some of the coastal restaurants, scallops and lobster tails are also prepared this way.

SERVES FOUR

INGREDIENTS
- 16 king prawns (jumbo shrimp)
- juice of 2 lemons
- 4 cloves garlic, crushed
- 5ml/1 tsp ground cumin
- 5ml/1 tsp paprika
- 8–12 cherry tomatoes
- 1 green (bell) pepper, cut into bite-sized squares
- sea salt
- 1 lemon, cut into wedges, to serve

1 Shell the prawns down to the tail, leaving a little bit of shell at the end.

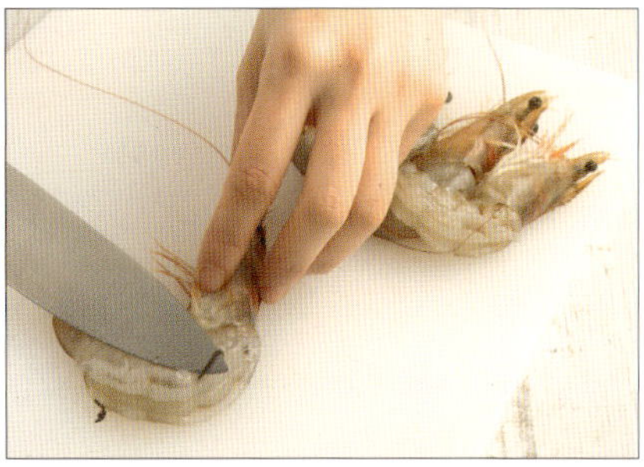

2 Remove the veins and put them into a shallow dish. Mix together the lemon juice, garlic, cumin, paprika and a little salt and rub it into the prawns. Leave to marinate for 30 minutes.

3 Light the charcoal grill. Thread the prawns on to metal skewers, alternating with the tomatoes and green peppers, until all the ingredients are used up.

4 Place the kebabs on an oiled rack over the glowing coals and cook them for 2–3 minutes on each side, basting with any of the left-over marinade, until the prawns are tender and the tomatoes and peppers are lightly browned. Serve with lemon to squeeze over them.

COOK'S TIP
You can also grill (broil) these kebabs under high heat.

Energy 82kcal/348kJ; Protein 15g; Carbohydrate 4g, of which sugars 3g; Fat 1g, of which saturates 0g; Cholesterol 156mg; Calcium 80mg; Fibre 1.2g; Sodium 259mg.

MEAT AND POULTRY

Throughout the history of the eastern Mediterranean the preferred meat has traditionally been mutton or lamb. The most highly prized breed is the Awassi, as it produces excellent meat and the fat stored in its tail is much sought after as a pungent cooking fat, aliya, which lends its flavour to many dishes. The addition of beef and veal to the diet is relatively recent. Traditionally, cows and oxen were valued solely for their milk and labour in the fields but nowadays beef is often substituted for lamb.

Fried Meat Patties with Parsley

These beef patties are the Lebanese and Syrian answer to burgers. Often cooked by street vendors or at family barbecues, they are delicious served with spicy potatoes, or baba ghanoush. You can make them larger, if you prefer, and serve them wrapped in flat bread.

SERVES FOUR TO SIX

INGREDIENTS

- 450g/1lb lean minced (ground) beef
- 1 onion, finely chopped
- 1 large bunch flat leaf parsley, finely chopped
- 1 small bunch mint leaves, finely chopped
- 5ml/1 tsp ground cinnamon
- 5ml/1 tsp ground allspice
- sea salt
- freshly ground black pepper
- 15–30ml/1–2 tbsp flour
- 15–30ml/1–2 tbsp olive oil
- Spicy Potatoes with Coriander, (see page 204), to serve

1 Place the minced beef in a bowl. Add the onions, herbs (reserve some parsley for garnishing) and spices and season. Using your hands, knead the mixture to a smooth paste and slap it down into the bowl to knock out the air.

2 Take apricot-sized portions of the mixture in your hands and shape them into balls. Place each ball in the palm of your hand and flatten it until it resembles a burger – if the mixture is sticky, dampen your fingers with water.

3 Place the patties in a shallow dish or on a board or a clean surface and lightly coat them with plain flour.

4 Heat the oil in heavy pan, or smear a little of the oil over a ridged griddle pan, and cook the patties for 2–3 minutes on each side. Sprinkle with the reserved chopped parsley and serve hot with the spicy potatoes.

Energy 176kcal/736kJ; Protein 18g; Carbohydrate 7g, of which sugars 2g; Fat 8g, of which saturates 2g; Cholesterol 44mg; Calcium 42mg; Fibre 0.8g; Sodium 50mg.

MEATBALLS WITH CHERRIES AND CINNAMON

Prepared with sour cherries, this medieval Arab dish is traditionally served on toasted flat bread. You can use sweet cherries instead but add the juice of a lemon to create a tangy sauce. Variations of this dish can be found throughout the region.

SERVES SIX

INGREDIENTS
- 450g/1lb lean minced (ground) lamb
- 10ml/2 tsp ground cinnamon
- 5ml/1 tsp ground cumin
- 5ml/1 tsp ground allspice
- sea salt and ground black pepper
- sunflower oil for frying
- 1 small bunch flat leaf parsley
- 1 small bunch coriander (cilantro)

For the sauce
- 15–30ml/1–2 tbsp ghee, or ordinary butter
- 225g/8oz fresh sour cherries, pitted
- 15ml/1 tsp sugar
- 2 pieces cinnamon bark

1 Put the lamb into a bowl and add the spices and seasoning. Knead thoroughly with your fingers, slapping it down into the base of the bowl to knock out the air. Take apricot-sized pieces of the mixture and mould into small balls.

2 Heat up enough sunflower oil to cover the base of a pan and fry the meatballs in it, until they are nicely browned. Drain the meatballs on kitchen paper.

3 Melt the ghee, or butter, in a heavy pan and stir in the cherries and cinnamon bark for 1–2 minutes. Add roughly 125ml/4fl oz water to the pan, stir in the sugar, and let it bubble up.

4 Add the meatballs to the pan, cover, reduce the heat and cook gently for about 15 minutes.

5 Lift the meatballs on to a serving dish, or on to portions of toasted flat bread. Boil up the sauce, check the seasoning then spoon over the meatballs. Garnish with parsley and coriander and serve.

Energy 225kcal/935kJ; Protein 16g; Carbohydrate 5g, of which sugars 0g; Fat 16g, of which saturates 7g; Cholesterol 70mg; Calcium 43mg; Fibre 0.1g; Sodium 122mg.

BAKED KIBBEH WITH ONIONS AND PINE NUTS

There are numerous versions of kibbeh, which is one of Lebanon's treasured national dishes. Here, the kibbeh mixture is baked and topped with onions and pine nuts. In Turkey a similar dish is prepared by Armenians, who cover it with a tomato sauce.

SERVES FOUR TO SIX

INGREDIENTS

- 450g/1lb/2 cups finely minced (ground) lean lamb
- 1 onion, grated
- 10ml/2 tsp ground cinnamon
- 5ml/1 tsp ground cumin
- 5ml/1 tsp ground allspice
- 115g/4oz/⅔ cup fine bulgur, well rinsed and drained
- 30ml/2 tbsp olive oil, or melted ghee
- sea salt and ground black pepper

For the topping

- 30–45ml/2–3 tbsp olive oil
- 2–3 onions, halved and sliced with the grain
- 30–45ml/2–3 tbsp pine nuts
- 5ml/1 tsp ground cinnamon
- 15ml/1 tbsp pomegranate molasses
- sea salt and ground black pepper
- 15–30ml/1–2 tbsp light tahini and small bunch of fresh parsley, finely chopped, to serve

1 Preheat the oven to 180°C/350°F/Gas 4 and grease a shallow ovenproof dish, such as a gratin dish or small roasting pan, with oil or butter.

2 In a bowl, use a wooden spoon or your fists to pound the lamb with the onion and spices. Season with plenty of salt and pepper and knead well so the air is punched out.

3 Add the bulgur to the lamb, and knead again for about 10 minutes, until the mixture is thoroughly mixed and has a paste-like consistency. Alternatively, you can place the mixture in a blender or food processor and whizz to a paste.

4 Turn the mixture into the greased dish and spread it evenly. Flatten the top with your knuckles and spread the oil or ghee over the surface.

5 Using a sharp knife, cut the mixture into wedges or diamond shapes and bake in the oven for about 30 minutes, until nicely browned.

6 Meanwhile, make the topping. Heat the oil in a frying pan and cook the onions until they begin to brown.

7 Add the pine nuts and stir until they turn golden. Add the cinnamon and pomegranate molasses, and season with salt and pepper.

8 When the kibbeh is ready, spread the onion mixture over the top and return it to the oven for 5 minutes.

9 Lift the portions on to a serving plate and drizzle tahini over each one or serve separately for people to add their own. Garnish with the parsley and serve while still warm.

COOK'S TIP

You can prepare this in advance and freeze it, after cutting and before it is baked, at step 5. Defrost completely before continuing the recipe at step 6.

Energy 399kcal/1659kJ; Protein 20.6g; Carbohydrate 30.4g, of which sugars 9.6g; Fat 22.4g, of which saturates 5.4g; Cholesterol 57mg; Calcium 69mg; Fibre 2.5g; Sodium 73mg.

Roasted Leg of Lamb with Rice

A simple roasted leg of lamb is a classic dish enjoyed throughout the region. Traditionally, the lamb would often be cooked in this way in the communal village oven.

SERVES SIX

INGREDIENTS
- 1kg/2¼lb leg of lamb
- 2 carrots, peeled and chopped
- 1 red (bell) pepper, chopped
- 6 cloves garlic, peeled and crushed
- 30–45ml/2–3 tbsp olive oil
- a little red wine
- sea salt and ground black pepper

For the rice
- 15ml/1 tbsp olive oil plus a knob (pat) of butter
- 1 onion, finely chopped
- 30ml/2 tbsp pine nuts
- 10ml/2 tsp ground cinnamon
- 100g/3¾oz/½cup lean minced (ground) lamb
- 250g/9oz/1¼ cups long grain rice, well rinsed and drained

1 Preheat the oven to 200°C/400°F/Gas 6. Rub the lamb with salt and pepper and place it in a roasting pan. Arrange the vegetables and garlic around the lamb and drizzle the oil over them all. Pour in about 300ml/½ pint/1¼ cups water, cover with foil and place the dish in the oven for about 50 minutes.

2 Meanwhile, prepare the rice. Heat the olive oil with the butter in a heavy pan and cook the onions until they begin to colour. Stir in the pine nuts, then add the cinnamon and the minced lamb. Cook over a medium heat for 2–3 minutes, then stir in the rice, coating the grains in the oil.

3 Add 500ml/17fl oz/generous 2 cups water to the pan, season with salt and pepper, and bring to the boil. Reduce the heat and simmer for 15 minutes, until the water has been absorbed.

4 Turn off the heat, cover the pan with a clean dish towel, followed by the lid, and leave the rice to stand and steam for 10–15 minutes.

5 Take the lamb out of the oven and remove the foil. Baste, then return to the oven, uncovered, for a further 15 minutes. Remove from the oven, and leave to rest.

6 Sieve (strain) the vegetables and juices, or whizz in a blender or food processor with a dash of wine, to make the gravy. Reheat and transfer to a serving jug (pitcher).

7 Spoon some rice on to a serving dish. Place the lamb on top of the rice and spoon the rest of the rice around it. Carve and serve with the gravy.

Energy 555kcal/2312kJ; Protein 33.1g; Carbohydrate 39.6g, of which sugars 4.9g; Fat 26.8g, of which saturates 8.9g; Cholesterol 115mg; Calcium 36mg; Fibre 1.3g; Sodium 113mg.

BAKED LAMB AND POTATO PIE

This warm, nourishing dish, 'kaleb batata', is prepared in homes throughout Lebanon. Enjoyed by the young and the elderly, it is in essence a glorified shepherd's pie, although the meat filling is sandwiched between two layers of potato. It can be prepared with lamb or beef and is delicious served with a salad.

SERVES FOUR TO SIX

INGREDIENTS

- 1kg/2¼lb potatoes, scrubbed and halved
- 300ml/½ pint/1¼ cups milk
- 100g/3¾oz butter
- 1 pinch of freshly grated nutmeg
- 30ml/2 tbsp olive oil
- 2 onions, finely chopped
- 15–30ml/1–2 tbsp pine nuts
- 5–10ml/1–2 tsp ground cinnamon
- 5ml/1 tsp ground allspice
- 450g/1lb/2 cups lean minced (ground) lamb
- 30ml/2 tbsp white breadcrumbs
- 30ml/2 tbsp finely grated Parmesan
- sea salt and ground black pepper

1 Preheat the oven to 180°C/350°F/Gas 4. Place the potatoes in a deep pan and cover with plenty of water. Bring the water to the boil and cook the potatoes for 15–20 minutes, or until they are tender. Drain and refresh under cold running water and peel off the skins.

2 Return the peeled potatoes to the pan and mash with a potato masher or a fork. Add the milk and butter and beat the mashed potatoes over the heat, until they are light and fluffy.

3 Season to taste with grated nutmeg and salt and pepper, cover the pan and set aside.

4 To prepare the filling, heat the olive oil in a heavy-based pan and cook the onions until they begin to colour. Stir in the pine nuts until they begin to colour then add the cinnamon and allspice.

5 Add the minced lamb and cook for 3–4 minutes. Season to taste.

6 Lightly grease an ovenproof dish and spread a layer of the potato mixture in the base.

7 Spread the meat filling over the top of the layer of potato and then top with another layer of potato, smoothing to the edges.

8 In a small bowl, mix together the breadcrumbs and grated Parmesan. Sprinkle them over the top of the pie.

9 Place the dish in the oven and bake for 30–40 minutes, until the top is nicely browned. Serve immediately with a salad or vegetable side dish.

COOK'S TIP

Depending on variety, the potatoes may absorb more butter and milk: add enough to make the mash taste creamy and light. This pie can be assembled in advance then stored in the refrigerator for up to 2 days, ready for baking. Increase the cooking time by 10 minutes if cooking from chilled.

Energy 548kcal/2289kJ; Protein 23.3g; Carbohydrate 39.6g, of which sugars 8.7g; Fat 34.2g, of which saturates 16.1g; Cholesterol 104mg; Calcium 174mg; Fibre 2.8g; Sodium 318mg.

MEAT AND BULGUR BALLS IN YOGURT

This is a popular dish in the cooler months of the year in Syria and Lebanon as it is warming and nourishing – Middle Eastern comfort food. Kibbeh prepared with lamb or vegetables can be served this way. Kibbeh are traditionally pounded by hand, which is a laborious task; many modern cooks prefer to use a food processor to make things easier.

SERVES SIX

INGREDIENTS

- 225g/8oz fine bulgur, well rinsed and squeezed dry
- 1 onion, cut into quarters
- 225g/8oz lean lamb, diced
- 10ml/2 tsp ground cinnamon
- 5ml/1 tsp ground allspice
- 5ml/1 tsp paprika
- sea salt and ground black pepper
- 600ml/1 pint/2½ cups Greek (US strained plain) yogurt
- 7.5ml/½ tbsp cornflour (cornstarch), slaked to a paste with a little water
- 15ml/1 tbsp butter, or ghee
- 1–2 cloves garlic, crushed
- 1 small handful dried mint leaves, crushed

1 Place the bulgur in a large bowl. Put the onion into the food processor, whizz to a purée, and add it to the bulgur. Process the lamb in batches in the food processor and add the puréed meat to the bulgur. Add the spices and the seasoning to the meat and bulgur mixture and mix well.

2 Blend the mixture in batches, combining it with spoonfuls of cold water to ease the process, or pound it with your fist until smooth. Knead the blended mixture once more in the bowl, if using a processor, then cover and chill in the refrigerator.

3 Meanwhile beat the yogurt until it is smooth and pour it into a heavy pan. Beat in the slaked cornflour with a little salt and gently heat the yogurt, stirring all the time, until it is almost at scalding point – don't let it boil as it will curdle. Reduce the heat and simmer for about 5 minutes, until it is thick.

4 Take portions of the kibbeh mixture in your fingers and mould them into ovals. Gently place them in the yogurt sauce, cover, and simmer gently for about 20 minutes, until the kibbeh are cooked.

5 Melt the butter in a pan and stir in the crushed garlic and mint until the garlic begins to brown. Drizzle the flavoured butter over the kibbeh in the yogurt sauce and serve immediately.

Energy 308kcal/1290kJ; Protein 17g; Carbohydrate 41g, of which sugars 9g; Fat 9g, of which saturates 4g; Cholesterol 44mg; Calcium 240mg; Fibre 0.4g; Sodium 192mg.

LAMB KEBABS WITH CHICKPEA PURÉE

There are so many types of kebab in the Eastern Mediterranean that you could spend a week trying them all. These spicy lamb kebabs are particularly popular in Syria and among the Palestinian communities in Jordan. A metal skewer with a wide blade is the most practical utensil for these kebabs, as the meat is pressed on to the skewer.

SERVES FOUR TO SIX

INGREDIENTS

For the kebabs:

- 450g/1lb minced (ground) lamb
- 1 onion, grated
- 10ml/2 tsp flaked red chillies, or hot paprika
- 10ml/2 tsp ground cumin
- 5ml/1 tsp ground coriander
- 5ml/1 tsp salt
- 1 small bunch flat-leaf parsley, finely chopped
- 1 small bunch coriander, finely chopped
- sea salt and ground black pepper

For the chickpea purée:

- 2 x 400g/14oz cans of prepared chickpeas, drained and well rinsed
- 100ml/3½fl oz/scant ½ cup olive oil
- juice of 2 lemons
- 5ml/1 tsp cumin seeds
- 2 cloves crushed garlic
- 30ml/2 tbsp thick yogurt
- 50g/2oz butter, melted

1 Heat the oven to 180°C/350°F/Gas 4 and prepare the charcoal grill, if using. Mix the minced lamb and onion with the spices and herbs and knead well in the bowl to knock out the air.

2 Take a piece of the mixture in your fingers and mould it tightly on to the kebab skewer like a thin sheath on a sword. Repeat with the rest of the mixture, then cover the kebabs and set aside until the grill is ready.

3 Prepare the chickpea purée. Whizz the chickpeas with the olive oil, lemon juice, cumin seeds, and garlic in an electric food processor, until smooth. Season to taste, then transfer the mixture into an ovenproof dish. Pour over the melted butter and bake the purée in the oven for about 20 minutes.

4 Grill the kebabs for 3–4 minutes each side over the hot charcoal, or turn the oven up to 200°C/400°F/Gas 6 and bake for 20 minutes. When cooked through, slide the kebabs off the skewer and serve with the hot chickpea purée.

Energy 448kcal/1866kJ; Protein 24g; Carbohydrate 20g, of which sugars 4g; Fat 31g, of which saturates 9g; Cholesterol 71mg; Calcium 106mg; Fibre 4.5g; Sodium 507mg.

Lamb Shanks with Winter Vegetables

This classic winter dish, 'shakriya', has variations in Jordan, Lebanon and Syria where it is also referred to as 'laban imoo'. Veal shanks are often used instead of the lamb, but either way it is delicious served on its own, or with chunks of bread.

SERVES FOUR

INGREDIENTS

- 60–75ml/4–5 tbsp olive oil
- 10ml/2 tsp cumin seeds
- 2 pieces cinnamon bark
- 12 shallots, peeled and left whole
- 3–4 sticks celery, cut into slices
- 2 carrots, peeled and cut into bite size pieces
- 4 cloves garlic, finely chopped
- 400g/14oz can cooked chickpeas, well rinsed and drained
- 400g/14oz can chopped tomatoes
- 30ml/2 tbsp plain (all-purpose) flour
- 15ml/1 tbsp ground ginger
- 15ml/1 tbsp ground cinnamon
- 4 lamb shanks
- 600ml/1 pint/2½ cups chicken stock, or stock and white wine
- 600ml/1 pint/2½ cups Greek (US strained plain) yogurt
- 7.5ml/½ tbsp cornflour (cornstarch), slaked to a paste with a little water
- 1 small bunch mint leaves, chopped
- the zest of 1 lemon
- sea salt and ground black pepper

VARIATION
You can bake this dish in the oven at 180°C/350°F/Gas 4 for the same time.

1 Heat half the oil in a heavy pan and stir in the cumin seeds and cinnamon bark. Add the shallots, celery, carrots and garlic for 2–3 minutes until they soften and begin to colour.

2 Stir the chickpeas and tomatoes into the pan, season well with salt and pepper, and set aside while you prepare the lamb shanks.

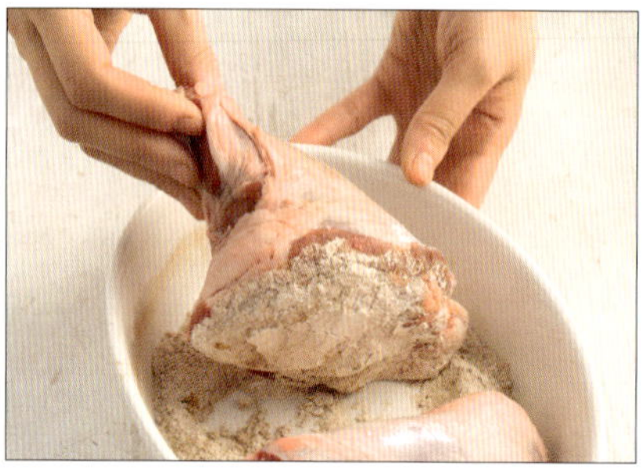

3 On a wooden board, or a clean surface, mix together the flour with the cinnamon and ginger and lightly coat the lamb shanks with it.

4 Heat the rest of the oil in a heavy pan and brown the lamb shanks.

5 Transfer the browned lamb shanks to the pan, on top of the vegetables.

6 Pour the stock over the lamb, and bring slowly to the boil. Reduce the heat to low, cover with a lid or a double layer of foil, and cook for about 1–1½ hours.

7 Meanwhile, prepare the yogurt. Beat the yogurt until it is smooth and transfer it to a heavy pan. Beat in the slaked corn flour with a little salt and gently heat the yogurt, stirring all the time in one direction, until it almost reaches scalding point – don't let it boil as it will curdle – then reduce the heat and simmer uncovered for 5–10 minutes, until it is thick.

8 When the meat is cooked, and coming away from the bones, carefully stir in the yogurt. Return the to the heat and simmer gently, uncovered, for about 15 minutes. Check the seasoning.

9 Mix the chopped mint and lemon zest together and sprinkle it over the lamb shanks before serving hot with a plain or saffron pilaff.

Energy 620kcal/2591kJ; Protein 40g; Carbohydrate 39g, of which sugars 18g; Fat 35g, of which saturates 10g; Cholesterol 109mg; Calcium 430mg; Fibre 4.3g; Sodium 543mg.

Spicy Meat Dumplings with Yogurt

Some cooks say this dish, 'shish barak', is of Armenian origin, while others believe it developed from an Anatolian dish during the Ottoman Empire. It is regarded as a classic in Lebanon, where it is served in homes and classy restaurants alike. You can replace the spices in the recipe with sabaa baharat, the Lebanese spice mix.

SERVES SIX

INGREDIENTS

- 6 sheets of filo pastry, cut in half
- 30ml/2 tbsp butter, melted
- 5ml/1 tsp rice flour or cornflour (cornstarch), slaked with 10ml/ 2 tsp water
- 1 litre/1¾ pints/4 cups Greek (US strained plain) yogurt
- 5ml/1 tsp dried oregano
- 5ml/1 tsp dried mint
- sea salt and ground black pepper

For the filling

- 30ml/2 tbsp olive oil
- 2 onions, finely chopped
- 1 red chilli, seeded and finely chopped
- 30ml/2 tbsp pine nuts
- 10ml/2 tsp ground cinnamon
- 5ml/1 tsp ground allspice
- 5ml/1 tsp paprika
- 450g/1lb/2 cups lean minced (ground) lamb
- 15ml/1 tbsp pomegranate molasses
- sea salt and ground black pepper

1 Heat the oil in a heavy pan and cook the onions and chilli until they begin to brown. Stir in the pine nuts and cook for a minute, then add the cinnamon, allspice and paprika.

2 Add the lamb to the pan fry for 2–3 minutes to brown, and season well. Stir in the pomegranate molasses and cook for a minute, then turn off the heat and leave to cool. Preheat the oven to 180°C/ 350°F/Gas 4.

3 Place the halved sheets of filo in a stack on a clean surface and keep covered. Brush the first sheet with a little melted butter then spoon some of the filling in a line along one of the long edges, stopping about 1cm/½in from each end.

4 Roll up the pastry into a long finger, tucking in the edges as you roll, then curl it into a tight coil. Repeat with the remaining filo sheets and filling to make 12 coils.

5 Place the filled coils on a lightly greased baking tray and bake them in the oven for about 15 minutes, until the pastry is a light golden brown but not fully cooked.

COOK'S TIP

For a slightly different end result, and a crispy texture, you could increase the baking time by 5–10 minutes until the pastry is fully cooked and crispy golden brown. Serve the sauce separately for people to help themselves.

6 Meanwhile, beat the rice flour and water mixture into the yogurt, and pour the mixture into a wide heavy pan. Stir over a medium heat until the yogurt is at scalding point, then season with salt and pepper and stir in the oregano.

7 Take the filled pastry coils out of the oven and carefully place them in the yogurt. Cook over a gentle heat for 10 minutes. Sprinkle the mint over the top and serve.

Energy 454kcal/1898kJ; Protein 27.2g; Carbohydrate 33.7g, of which sugars 15.8g; Fat 24.8g, of which saturates 9.3g; Cholesterol 88mg; Calcium 381mg; Fibre 1.4g; Sodium 237mg.

PASHA'S MEATBALLS IN TOMATO SAUCE

This famous dish of meatballs cooked in a tomato sauce and served with rice is said to have been one of the favourite dishes of Dawood Pasha, the first governor of Mount Lebanon appointed by the Ottomans in 1860. The recipe calls for the meat to be cooked in sheep's tail fat, but ghee, or olive oil with butter, is a good substitute.

SERVES FOUR

INGREDIENTS

For the meatballs

- 450g/1lb/2 cups lean minced (ground) lamb
- 5–10ml/1–2 tsp ground cinnamon
- 5ml/1 tsp ground allspice
- sunflower oil, for frying
- plain (all-purpose) flour, for coating
- sea salt and ground black pepper
- 1 lemon, cut into wedges, to serve
- steamed rice, to serve

For the sauce

- 15ml/1 tbsp ghee, or 15ml/1 tbsp olive oil with a knob (pat) of butter
- 2 onions, halved lengthways, cut in half crossways, and sliced with the grain
- 30ml/2 tbsp pine nuts
- 5ml/1 tsp ground cinnamon
- 400g/14oz can chopped tomatoes
- 10ml/2 tsp sugar
- sea salt and ground black pepper

1 In a bowl, mix together the minced lamb, cinnamon and allspice and season with about 2.5ml/½ tsp salt and a good grinding of black pepper.

2 Knead the mixture well with your hands then, with wet hands, mould it into small balls about the size of large cherries.

3 Heat enough sunflower oil for frying in a heavy pan. Roll the meatballs in a little flour and drop them into the oil. Fry for 4–5 minutes, turning, until they are nicely browned all over. Lift the meatballs out of the oil with a slotted spoon and drain them on kitchen paper.

4 To make the sauce, heat the ghee or olive oil and butter in a heavy pan and sauté the onion over a medium heat for 3–4 minutes, until golden brown. Stir in the pine nuts and cook until they begin to colour, then add the cinnamon, followed by the tomatoes and sugar.

5 Simmer the sauce, uncovered, for about 20 minutes, until it has reduced and thickened, and season with salt and pepper.

6 Place the meatballs in the sauce and heat through for 10 minutes. Serve hot with rice and lemon wedges.

Energy 485kcal/2014kJ; Protein 25.4g; Carbohydrate 18.1g, of which sugars 11.7g; Fat 35.2g, of which saturates 10.9g; Cholesterol 95mg; Calcium 66mg; Fibre 2.7g; Sodium 119mg.

LAMB STEW WITH PLUMS

A number of medieval dishes incorporating meat and fruit are still popular in Lebanon, Jordan and Syria. The most common include lamb or chicken that is stewed with apricots, prunes, quinces and plums. They are usually served with a buttery pilaff that may contain a hint of saffron or herbs.

SERVES FOUR TO SIX

INGREDIENTS

- 30ml/2 tbsp ghee, or 30ml/2 tbsp olive oil with a knob (pat) of butter
- 2 onions, finely chopped
- 2–3 cloves garlic, finely chopped
- 5ml/1 tsp cumin seeds
- 5ml/1 tsp coriander seeds
- 500g/1¼lb lean lamb, cut into cubes
- plain (all-purpose) flour, for coating
- 400ml/14fl oz/1⅔ cups chicken stock
- 350g/12oz plums, stoned (pitted) and quartered
- sea salt and ground black pepper
- 1 small bunch fresh mint leaves, finely shredded, to garnish
- plain pilaff, to serve

1 Heat the ghee in a heavy pan and cook the onions until they begin to colour, then add the garlic, cumin and coriander seeds.

2 Coat the lamb in flour, then add to the pan to brown. Pour in the stock, bring to the boil, reduce the heat, cover the pan and simmer for about 40 minutes.

3 When the meat is tender, add the plums to the stew and season with salt and pepper. Cover the pan again and simmer for a further 20 minutes, until the plums are soft.

4 Transfer the stew to a warmed serving dish, garnish with the shredded mint, and serve with a plain, buttery pilaff.

Energy 262kcal/1092kJ; Protein 18.4g; Carbohydrate 14.3g, of which sugars 9.6g; Fat 15g, of which saturates 6.7g; Cholesterol 63mg; Calcium 44mg; Fibre 2.1g; Sodium 212mg.

Dervish's Beads

During the Ottoman period, dervish lodges were founded throughout the Eastern Mediterranean, resulting in the spread of dishes attributed to the order. Traditionally, the components of this dish are cooked separately then assembled in layers afterwards, but modern cooks opt for the simpler method of cooking the layers together.

SERVES FOUR TO SIX

INGREDIENTS

- 60–75ml/4–5 tbsp olive oil
- 12–15 pearl (baby) onions, peeled
- 15ml/1 tbsp butter
- 5–6 potatoes, boiled and sliced
- 450g/1lb lean lamb fillet, thinly sliced
- 1 aubergine (eggplant), thinly sliced
- 1 green and 1 red (bell) pepper, thinly sliced
- 5–6 tomatoes, thinly sliced
- 15ml/1 tbsp tomato purée (paste)
- 5–10ml/1–2 tsp oregano
- 10ml/2 tsp cane sugar
- 5–10ml/1–2 tsp ground cinnamon
- sea salt and ground black pepper

1 Preheat the oven to 180°C/350°F/Gas 4. Heat 30ml/2 tbsp of the oil in a heavy pan.

2 Add the onions to the pan and fry until golden. Drain on kitchen paper.

3 Lightly butter an ovenproof dish and spread a layer of sliced potatoes over the base.

4 Lay the slices of lamb fillet on top, then the onions, followed by a layer of aubergine, a layer of peppers, and a final layer of tomatoes.

5 Mix the remaining olive oil with the tomato purée, 150ml/¼ pint/⅔ cup water, oregano and plenty of salt and pepper and pour it over the dish. Dot the tomatoes with butter and sprinkle with the sugar and cinnamon.

6 Cover with foil and bake for 45 minutes, then remove the foil and return the dish to the oven for a further 15–20 minutes, until browned.

Energy 365kcal/1527kJ; Protein 18.7g; Carbohydrate 27.7g, of which sugars 13.2g; Fat 20.8g, of which saturates 6.8g; Cholesterol 63mg; Calcium 45mg; Fibre 4.2g; Sodium 111mg.

STUFFED BREAST OF LAMB WITH APRICOTS

THE TRADITIONAL FESTIVE DISH OF THE BEDOUIN IS 'MANSAF', MEANING 'BIG DISH' WHICH IS EXACTLY WHAT IT IS – A HUGE TRAY, LINED WITH FLATBREAD COVERED WITH A LAYER OF RICE, ON TOP OF WHICH A WHOLE SPIT-ROASTED LAMB OR KID SITS. ALTHOUGH THIS IS JORDAN'S NATIONAL DISH, IT IS TOO BIG TO PREPARE AT HOME. THIS VARIATION, HOWEVER, 'DALA MAHSHI' USES BREAST OF LAMB AND IS PREPARED IN JORDAN AND SYRIA TO CELEBRATE EID EL KURBAN, THE RELIGIOUS FEAST MARKING THE NEAR-SACRIFICE OF ISAAC.

SERVES FOUR TO SIX

INGREDIENTS

- 1 large breast of lamb, chined and with a pouch cut between the skin and the ribs, rinsed and patted dry
- sunflower oil, for rubbing
- 175g/6oz dried apricots, soaked overnight in just enough water to cover
- 15–30ml/1–2 tbsp sugar
- sea salt and ground black pepper

For the stuffing

- 30ml/2 tbsp ghee, or olive oil with a knob (pat) of butter
- 1 onion, finely chopped
- 5–10ml/1–2 tsp turmeric
- 5ml/1 tsp ground cumin
- 125g/4¼oz minced (ground) beef
- 1 small bunch flat leaf parsley, finely chopped
- 250g/9oz long grain rice, washed and drained
- 115g/4oz pine nuts
- 115g/4oz unsalted pistachios, chopped

1 Preheat the oven to 200°C/400°F/Gas 6.

2 To make the stuffing, melt the ghee in a frying pan and cook the onion until it colours. Stir in the turmeric, cumin and beef and cook until it begins to brown.

3 Add the parsley and rice to the pan and pour in 200ml/7fl oz/scant 1 cup water. Season with salt and pepper and bring the liquid to the boil. Reduce the heat and simmer for about 15 minutes until the water has been absorbed.

4 Remove the pan from the heat, stir in the nuts and leave to cool.

5 When the filling is cool, stuff the breast pouches of the lamb. If there is any left over it can be served with the meat afterwards. Rub the joints with a little oil and then place the breasts into the oven for about 1 hour, until the meat is well browned and tender.

6 Meanwhile, prepare the apricots. Transfer the apricots and their soaking water to a pan and bring the liquid to the boil. Reduce the heat, stir in the sugar, and simmer partially covered until the apricots are soft.

7 Just before serving, spoon off any excess fat from the roasting dish and baste the meat. Turn the oven up to 220°C/450°F/Gas 8 and pour the apricots over the lamb. Return to the to the oven and glaze for 5 minutes.

8 Allow the lamb to rest for 10 minutes, then slice and serve it with a green salad and any leftover rice filling.

Energy 704kcal/2947kJ; Protein 31g; Carbohydrate 58g, of which sugars 21g; Fat 41g, of which saturates 11g; Cholesterol 90mg; Calcium 91mg; Fibre 4.1g; Sodium 244mg.

Roasted Onions Stuffed with Lamb

Lebanese markets display a variety of onions: some for salads or pickles, others for stews and kebabs, and yet others that are ideal for stripping into layers and stuffing, as in this recipe. Large golden or red onions are suitable for this dish, which can be served as an appetizer, as an accompaniment to grilled or roasted meats, or on its own with a salad. The preparation for this dish takes a while but the end result is worth the time.

SERVES FOUR TO SIX

INGREDIENTS

- 2–3 large onions
- 250g/9oz/generous 1 cup lean minced (ground) lamb
- 90g/3½oz/½ cup long grain rice, rinsed and drained
- 15ml/1 tbsp tomato paste (purée)
- 10ml/2 tsp ground cinnamon
- 5ml/1 tsp ground allspice
- 5ml/1 tsp ground cumin
- 5ml/1 tsp ground coriander
- 1 small bunch fresh parsley, finely chopped
- 30–45ml/2–3 tbsp olive oil
- 15–30ml/1–2 tbsp white wine or cider vinegar
- 5–10ml/1–2 tsp sugar
- 15ml/1 tbsp butter
- sea salt and ground black pepper
- 1 lemon, cut into wedges, to serve

1 Bring a pan of water to the boil. Make a cut down one side of each of the onions, cutting into the centre from top to bottom; this enables the layers to divide while cooking.

2 Cook the onions in the boiling water for about 10 minutes, until they soften and the layers begin to separate. Drain and refresh the onions under cold running water and carefully detach the layers.

3 In a bowl, pound the meat thoroughly with your hands. Add the rice, tomato purée, spices, parsley (reserving a little) and seasoning, and knead well to mix.

4 Spread out the separated onion layers and place a spoonful of the meat mixture inside each one.

5 Roll them up loosely, leaving room for the rice to expand as it cooks, and tuck in any open ends. Preheat the oven to 200°C/400°F/Gas 6.

6 Pack the stuffed onion layers close together in a heavy pan and pour over the olive oil, vinegar and sugar. Cover and cook the onions over a medium heat for about 25 minutes, until the meat and rice are cooked.

7 Dot the stuffed onions with a little butter and place in the oven, uncovered, for 15–20 minutes, until they are nicely browned on top and slightly caramelized. Garnish with the reserved parsley and serve hot with wedges of lemon.

COOK'S TIP

The Lebanese spice mix, sabaa baharat, a combination of pepper, cinnamon, coriander, cumin, paprika, cloves and nutmeg, is often used in this dish.

Energy 263kcal/1094kJ; Protein 12.2g; Carbohydrate 29g, of which sugars 11.4g; Fat 11.4g, of which saturates 4.1g; Cholesterol 37mg; Calcium 59mg; Fibre 2.4g; Sodium 67mg.

STUFFED ARTICHOKE BOTTOMS

WHEN GLOBE ARTICHOKES ARE IN SEASON, YOU WILL FIND THIS DISH BEING PREPARED IN HOMES THROUGHOUT THE EASTERN MEDITERRANEAN REGION. TASTY AND IMPRESSIVE LOOKING, IT IS QUITE TIME-CONSUMING TO PREPARE IF USING FRESH ARTICHOKES AND COOKING FOR MORE THAN TWO PEOPLE, BUT YOU CAN MAKE LIFE A LOT EASIER BY BUYING FROZEN PREPARED ARTICHOKE BOTTOMS, WHICH ARE AVAILABLE IN MIDDLE EASTERN STORES AND SOME SUPERMARKETS.

SERVES FOUR

INGREDIENTS

- 30ml/2 tbsp olive oil
- 2 medium onions, finely chopped
- 15–30ml/1–2 tbsp pine nuts
- 350g/12oz/1½ cups lean minced (ground) lamb
- 5ml/1 tsp ground cinnamon
- 2.5ml/½ tsp ground allspice
- 4–6 fresh or frozen artichoke bottoms
- juice of 1 lemon
- 200ml/7fl oz/scant 1 cup water
- 15ml/1 tbsp plain (all-purpose) flour
- sea salt and ground black pepper
- 1 lemon, cut into wedges, to serve

1 Preheat the oven to 180°C/350°F/Gas 4. Heat the oil in a heavy pan and cook the onions for 2–3 minutes until they begin to colour.

2 Stir in the pine nuts, reserving a few for garnishing, and cook for 1–2 minutes until they turn golden.

VARIATION

This tasty lamb mixture can also be used to stuff peppers and courgettes.

3 Add the lamb and spices to the pan, and fry until the meat begins to brown. Season with salt and pepper.

4 Place the artichoke bottoms, side by side, in a shallow ovenproof dish. Using a spoon, fill the artichokes with the meat mixture.

5 Combine the lemon juice and water in a bowl and stir in the flour, making sure it is thoroughly blended.

6 Pour the flour, water and lemon juice mixture over and around the artichokes.

7 Cover the dish with foil and place it in the oven for 25–30 minutes, until the artichokes are tender. Meanwhile, heat a frying pan and dry roast the reserved pine nuts until golden brown.

8 Remove the artichokes from the oven and transfer to a warmed serving dish. Sprinkle the roasted pine nuts over the top of the artichokes and serve with wedges of lemon to squeeze over them.

COOK'S TIP

Fresh artichokes should be treated like flowers and kept on their stems in water until ready to use. To prepare them for this dish, pull off the outer leaves, cut off the stalks and slice away the purple choke, the small leaves and any hard bits. Remove any fibres with the edge of a spoon and rub the artichoke bottoms with a mixture of lemon juice and salt to prevent them from discolouring.

Energy 277kcal/1153kJ; Protein 19.7g; Carbohydrate 14.3g, of which sugars 7.3g; Fat 16.1g, of which saturates 5.4g; Cholesterol 67mg; Calcium 61mg; Fibre 2.2g; Sodium 96mg.

Lamb and Vegetable Stew

This traditional dish is reputed to have been a favourite of the Prophet Muhammad. The vinegar acts as a preservative, enabling the dish to last for a number of days. It is fairly delicate and is usually eaten with chunks of bread to mop up the juices.

SERVES FOUR TO SIX

INGREDIENTS

- 450g/1lb lean boneless lamb, cut into bitesize chunks
- about 12 small shallots or pearl (baby) onions, peeled and left whole
- about 8 cloves garlic, peeled
- 2 cinnamon sticks
- 5ml/1 tsp fennel seeds
- 5ml/1 tsp cumin seeds
- 6 peppercorns
- 45–60ml/3–4 tbsp white wine or cider vinegar
- 2 courgettes (zucchini), cut into bitesize chunks
- 2 medium aubergines (eggplants), cut into bitesize chunks
- 10ml/2 tsp dried mint
- sea salt

1 Place the meat in a deep pan with the shallots, garlic, cinnamon, fennel and cumin seeds and the peppercorns.

2 Add water to cover and bring to the boil, skimming off any foam. Reduce the heat, cover and simmer for 35–40 minutes, until the meat is tender. Season with salt and stir in the vinegar.

3 Add the courgettes and aubergines to the pan and bring the liquid back to the boil. Reduce the heat, cover the pan and simmer for a further 10 minutes, until the vegetables are tender.

4 Transfer the stew to a serving dish, sprinkle the mint over the top and serve immediately with some flat bread.

Energy 182kcal/758kJ; Protein 17.5g; Carbohydrate 7.5g, of which sugars 5.3g; Fat 9.4g, of which saturates 4.1g; Cholesterol 57mg; Calcium 46mg; Fibre 2.6g; Sodium 69mg.

Sautéed Liver with Pomegranate Syrup

Generally, lamb's or calf's liver, is used in the eastern Mediterranean as it is very tender and ox liver has too strong a flavour. Sautéed or grilled, it is often served as a mezze dish or it is served as one of a variety of meat courses at a restaurant or a family feast.

SERVES FOUR

INGREDIENTS

- 450g/1lb lamb's liver, cut into bite size pieces
- 30ml/2 tbsp olive oil
- 2 red onions, halved and thinly sliced
- 2–3 cloves garlic, finely chopped
- 5ml/1 tsp ground cinnamon
- 2.5ml/½ tsp ground allspice
- sea salt and ground black pepper
- juice of 1 lemon
- 5–10ml/1–2 tsp pomegranate syrup

1 Heat the oil in a heavy-based pan and stir in the sliced onions and garlic. Once the onions begin to colour, toss in the liver for 2-3 minutes, until browned.

2 Stir in the spices and seasoning and add the lemon juice. Drizzle the pomegranate syrup over the liver and serve immediately from the pan.

Energy 257kcal/1074kJ; Protein 24g; Carbohydrate 8g, of which sugars 6g; Fat 15g, of which saturates 3g; Cholesterol 484mg; Calcium 46mg; Fibre 1.2g; Sodium 185mg.

BRAISED RABBIT WITH AUBERGINES

THERE WAS A TIME WHEN THE AREA REFERRED TO AS GREATER SYRIA WAS A HUNTER'S PARADISE. WILD BOAR, GAZELLE, HARE, PORCUPINE, QUAIL, PARTRIDGE AND PHEASANT AS WELL AS RABBIT WERE AMONG THE POPULAR CHOICES FOR THE POT. ALTHOUGH THERE IS STILL PLENTY OF GAME IN LEBANON, JORDAN AND SYRIA, IT IS REALLY ONLY A FEATURE OF THE VILLAGE MENU.

SERVES FOUR

INGREDIENTS

- 1 rabbit, roughly 1kg/3lb, jointed
- 15–30ml/1–2 tbsp plain flour
- 30ml/2 tbsp ghee or olive oil plus a knob (pat) of butter
- 10ml/2tsp coriander seeds
- 5ml/1 tsp cumin seeds
- 1 red chilli, seeded and chopped
- 2 onions, halved and sliced
- 2–3 cloves garlic, chopped
- 2 aubergines (eggplants)
- 400g/14oz can chopped tomatoes
- 10–15ml/2–3 tbsp pomegranate molasses
- sea salt and ground black pepper
- 1 bunch parsley, chopped

1 Toss the rabbit joints in the flour so that they lightly coated. Cut the aubergines into bite size pieces.

2 Heat the oil and butter in a heavy pan and brown the rabbit joints.

3 Lift the rabbit pieces out of the pan and set aside. Stir the coriander and cumin seeds into the oil along with the chilli, onions and garlic.

4 Once the onions begin to colour, add the aubergines to the pan and cook, stirring, until they are lightly browned.

5 Add the tomatoes, pomegranate molasses, and sugar to the pan. Cover, and bring gently to simmering point. Season with salt and pepper to taste.

6 Return the rabbit joints to the pan, cover, and cook gently for about 25 minutes, until the aubergines are tender, but not mushy, and the rabbit is tender. You may need to add a splash of water or white wine to keep the dish moist as it cooks.

7 Sprinkle with the parsley and serve hot with a pilaff or a loaf of rustic bread.

Energy 414kcal/1738kJ; Protein 38g; Carbohydrate 25g, of which sugars 14g; Fat 19g, of which saturates 6g; Cholesterol 85mg; Calcium 125mg; Fibre 5.7g; Sodium 264mg.

SPICY PIGEONS WITH OLIVES

PIGEONS USED TO BE EATEN FREQUENTLY ALL OVER THE EASTERN MEDITERRANEAN BUT NOW THEY ARE MOST COMMONLY FOUND IN JORDAN AND NEIGHBOURING EGYPT, WHERE SOME FAMILIES RAISE THE BIRDS FOR THE POT, AND STREET VENDORS GRILL THEM WITH LEMON JUICE AND HERBS. WILD WOOD PIGEONS ARE BEST FOR THIS RECIPE AND CAN BE PREPARED FOR YOU BY A BUTCHER.

SERVES FOUR

INGREDIENTS

- 15ml/1 tbsp tomato purée (paste)
- 10ml/2 tsp sugar
- 5ml/1 tsp paprika
- 5ml/1 tsp ground cinnamon
- 5ml/1 tsp ground cumin
- 5ml/1 tsp ground coriander
- 2.5ml/½ tsp ground cloves
- a grating of nutmeg
- 30ml/2 tbsp ghee or olive oil plus a knob (pat) of butter
- 4 fresh wood pigeons, prepared, cleaned and left whole
- 2 bay leaves
- juice of 1 lemon
- 45ml/3 tbsp green olives
- sea salt and ground black pepper

1 In a bowl, mix the tomato purée with the sugar and spices and put aside.

2 Heat the ghee, or olive oil and butter, in a wide shallow pan and add the pigeons, breast side down. Brown the meat and lift the pigeons out of the pan and on to a board or plate.

3 Add the bay leaves, spicy tomato paste, and lemon juice to the pan, together with 300ml/½ pint/1¼ cups water. Place the pigeons back in the pan, reduce the heat, cover the pan and simmer gently for about 1 hour, until the pigeon meat is tender.

4 Add the olives, season to taste and simmer with the lid off for a further 15 minutes. Serve hot with chunks of bread to mop up the sauce.

Energy 313kcal/1308kJ; Protein 34g; Carbohydrate 4g, of which sugars 4g; Fat 19g, of which saturates 5g; Cholesterol 21mg; Calcium 76mg; Fibre 0.5g; Sodium 501mg.

AROMATIC CHICKEN ON PITTA BREAD

The shawarma dishes of Lebanon are the equivalent of the Turkish döner kebab and are favourite street food. This chicken version, 'shawarma dajaj', is marinated in a delicious, aromatic combination of spices and served in pitta bread with a tahini sauce, tomatoes and pickles. At home, you can bake the chicken in the oven or cook it under a grill.

SERVES FOUR

INGREDIENTS
- 4 chicken breasts
- sea salt and ground black pepper
- 4 pitta breads, tahini sauce and pickled vegetables, to serve

For the marinade
- 30–45ml/2–3 tbsp olive oil
- juice of 2–3 lemons
- 10ml/2 tsp white wine or cider vinegar
- 2 cloves garlic, crushed
- 1 cinnamon stick, broken into pieces
- grated rind of ½ orange
- 4–6 cardamom pods, crushed

1 Mix together the ingredients for the marinade and toss the chicken breasts in the mixture, then cover and leave in the refrigerator for at least 6 hours.

2 Preheat the oven to 180°C/350°F/Gas 4. Put the chicken in an ovenproof dish, and bake for 20 minutes, basting with the marinade.

3 When cooked, lift the chicken out, shred, and return to the dish with any remaining marinade, season and return to the oven for 10 minutes.

4 Warm the pitta breads in the oven for 5 minutes. Serve the chicken with the pitta, accompanied by a tahini sauce and pickled vegetables.

Energy 408kcal/1726kJ; Protein 40.2g; Carbohydrate 44.7g, of which sugars 1.8g; Fat 8.9g, of which saturates 2.1g; Cholesterol 65mg; Calcium 90mg; Fibre 1.7g; Sodium 499mg.

PALESTINIAN CHICKEN WITH SUMAC

PARTICULARLY POPULAR IN JORDAN, WHERE THERE IS A HUGE PALESTINIAN COMMUNITY, THIS IS TRADITIONALLY A PEASANT DISH BASED ON A THICK SPONGY BREAD CALLED TABUN. THIS TANGY DISH IS IN FACT SIMILAR TO THE FATTA DISHES OF LEBANON AND SYRIA FOR WHICH PITTA BREAD CAN BE USED. IT CAN BE SERVED AS PART OF A MEAL, OR ON ITS OWN AS A SNACK.

SERVES FOUR

INGREDIENTS

- 30ml/2 tbsp ghee, or olive oil with a knob (pat) of butter
- 2 onions, sliced
- 2–3 cloves garlic, crushed
- 450g/1lb boned chicken breasts, cut into thin strips
- 10–15ml/2–3 tsp sumac
- 5ml/2 tsp ground cinnamon
- 2.5ml/½ tsp ground allspice
- juice of 1 lemon
- sea salt and ground black pepper
- 1 small bunch flat leaf parsley, roughly chopped
- 4 pitta breads, halved to form 8 pockets, parsley sprigs, and Greek (US strained plain) yogurt, to serve

1 Melt the ghee or olive oil and butter in a pan and stir in the onions. When they begin to soften, stir in the garlic and fry until the onions turn golden brown. Add the chicken to the pan with the sumac and stir-fry for 2-3 minutes. Season with salt and pepper. Preheat the oven to 180°C/350°F/Gas 4.

2 Add the cinnamon, allspice and lemon juice to the pan and cook for 6–10 minutes, until the chicken is done.

3 Fill the pitta pouches with the chicken and place on a baking sheet. Put in the oven for about 5 minutes, then serve with parsley and a dollop of yogurt.

Energy 457kcal/1927kJ; Protein 39g; Carbohydrate 53g, of which sugars 11g; Fat 12g, of which saturates 7g; Cholesterol 106mg; Calcium 272mg; Fibre 3.1g; Sodium 549mg.

CHICKEN STEW WITH MARINATED ONIONS

THE LEAVES OF THE MELOKHIA PLANT, ALSO KNOWN AS 'JEW'S MALLOW', ARE AN ACQUIRED TASTE, BUT THE SYRIANS AND JORDANIANS LOVE EATING THEM AS A VEGETABLE. THIS DISH COULD BE DESCRIBED AS A MIDDLE EASTERN 'COQ AU VIN' AS IT IS HALF SOUP, HALF STEW. SERVE WITH BREAD OR RICE.

2 Crush the dried melokhia leaves with your hand and place them in a bowl. Pour over just enough boiling water to cover and leave them to soak until they have doubled in bulk.

3 Place the chicken in a deep pot and cover with the water. Add the onions, carrots, garlic, cloves, cardamom pods and seasoning.

4 Bring the water in the pot to the boil then reduce the heat, cover, and simmer for about 25 minutes. Stir in the melokhia leaves and simmer, uncovered, for a further 25 minutes.

5 Lift the chicken out of the pot and check the seasoning of the stock. If it lacks flavour, boil rapidly for 10 minutes to reduce. Skin the chicken, cut it into joints, and return to the stock.

6 Serve the chicken in shallow bowls, spooning the carrots and melokhia leaves over it. Top each bowl with a spoonful of the marinated onions and pomegranate seeds, and serve with plenty of bread.

SERVES FOUR

INGREDIENTS

For serving
- 225g/8oz dried melokhia (mallow) leaves
- 1 chicken, approximately 1kg/2lb in weight
- 1.2 litres/2 pints/5 cups water
- 2 onions, quartered
- 2 carrots, peeled and each cut into 3
- 2 cloves garlic, smashed in their skins
- 4–5 cloves
- 3–4 cardamom pods
- sea salt and ground black pepper

For the marinated onions
- 2 onions, halved and sliced
- seeds of half a pomegranate
- 30ml/2 tbsp white wine vinegar

1 Place the onions and pomegranate seeds in a bowl and toss in the vinegar. Cover and set aside to marinate.

COOK'S TIP

Melokhia leaves are generally sold fresh where they are grown, but elsewhere packets of dried leaves are available.

Energy 342kcal/1441kJ; Protein 50g; Carbohydrate 21g, of which sugars 16g; Fat 7g, of which saturates 2g; Cholesterol 180mg; Calcium 133mg; Fibre 6.3g; Sodium 276mg.

ALEPPO QUAIL WITH WALNUTS AND LEMON

THE AROMA OF GRILLING CHICKEN OR QUAIL IN THE STREETS OF ALEPPO LEADS IRRESISTIBLY TO THE STREET VENDOR OR STALL WHERE THE BIRDS ARE ROASTING ON SPITS. CHARGRILLED QUAILS ARE POPULAR IN LEBANON AND JORDAN TOO, HUNTED EN ROUTE TO AFRICA.

SERVES FOUR

INGREDIENTS

- 8 quail, cleaned and split down the backbone
- 2 cloves garlic, crushed to a creamy paste with a little salt
- 50g/2oz walnuts, lightly toasted and chopped
- zest and juice of 1 lemon
- 5–10ml/1–2 tsp Middle Eastern red pepper
- 1 small bunch mint leaves, finely chopped
- 1 small bunch fresh coriander (cilantro), finely chopped
- 60ml/4 tbsp olive oil
- sea salt and ground black pepper
- 1 lemon, cut into wedges to serve

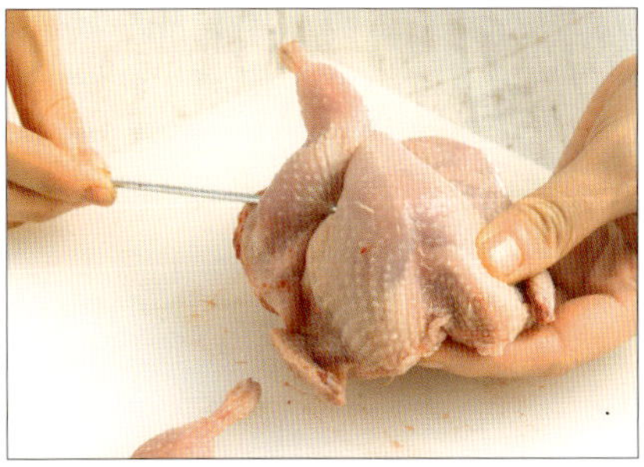

1 Lay the quail flat on a clean surface and pierce a wooden or metal skewer right through them, from one side to the other, to keep them flat.

2 In a bowl, mix the garlic paste with the walnuts, lemon zest and juice, Middle Eastern pepper and the herbs. Bind with the olive oil and season well.

3 Rub the walnut and lemon mixture all over both sides of the quail and leave them to marinate in a cool place for at least 1 hour. Meanwhile, prepare the charcoal grill.

4 When the barbecue is glowing, place the quail, skin-side down, on an oiled rack set over it. Grill the quail for 2–3 minutes each side, until the skin is crisp and the juices run clear when pricked with a skewer. Serve with lemon wedges to squeeze over them.

COOKS TIP

To grill the birds they need to be 'butterflied' first. Do this by splitting them down the backbone with a sharp knife, then laying them skin-side up and pressing down hard to flatten. If you don't have a charcoal grill, cook the quail on a griddle or grill (broiler).

Energy 418kcal/1735kJ; Protein 32g; Carbohydrate 2g, of which sugars 1g; Fat 32g, of which saturates 3g; Cholesterol 1mg; Calcium 59mg; Fibre 0.5g; Sodium 194mg.

ROASTED STUFFED TURKEY WITH THYME

Among the Christian communities of Lebanon, turkey is the traditional centrepiece for the Christmas meal. Around this time, live turkeys are shepherded through the markets and busy neighbourhoods, reminding cooks to begin their preparations.

SERVES FOUR TO SIX

INGREDIENTS

- 1 medium turkey, approximately 2.25–2.5kg/5–5½lb
- 115g/4oz/1½ cup butter, softened
- 6–8 sprigs of fresh thyme
- sea salt and ground black pepper

For the stuffing

- 30ml/2 tbsp olive oil plus a knob (pat) of butter
- 2 onions, finely chopped
- 30ml/2 tbsp pine nuts
- 30ml/2 tbsp blanched almonds, chopped
- 30ml/2 tbsp currants
- 225g/8oz/1 cup lean minced (ground) lamb
- 10–15ml/2–3 tsp ground cinnamon
- 250g/9oz/1¼ cups short grain rice
- 500ml/17fl oz/generous 2 cups chicken stock
- sea salt and ground black pepper

1 Preheat the oven to 200°C/400°F/ Gas 6. To make the stuffing, heat the oil with the butter in a heavy pan and cook the onions until they begin to colour.

2 Add the pine nuts, almonds and currants to the onions, and stir until the nuts begin to brown and the currants plump up.

3 Add the minced lamb and the cinnamon to the stuffing mixture, and stir until browned. Stir in the rice, coating it with the oil.

4 Pour the chicken stock into the pan, stir well, season with salt and pepper and bring to the boil. Reduce the heat and simmer gently for about 15 minutes, until the liquid has been absorbed. Remove from the heat.

5 Season the turkey inside and out with salt and pepper. Stuff the cavity with the rice mixture and secure the opening with a skewer.

6 Rub the skin of the turkey with the butter and place it breast side up in a roasting pan. Arrange half the sprigs of thyme around the turkey, place in the hot oven, and roast for about 30 minutes.

7 Reduce the heat to 180°C/350°F/ Gas 4. Baste the turkey with the cooking juices and pour about 250ml/8fl oz/1 cup water into the dish. Roast for a further 1½–2 hours, or until the juices run clear when the thigh is pierced with a skewer.

8 Transfer the turkey to a serving platter and garnish with fresh sprigs of thyme. Cover with foil to keep it warm and leave it to rest for 15 minutes before carving.

9 Reduce the cooking juices over a medium heat, skimming off the fat, and season to taste. Pour the juices into a jug (pitcher) and serve with the turkey.

Energy 761kcal/3174kJ; Protein 63.9g; Carbohydrate 43.4g, of which sugars 7.6g; Fat 36.9g, of which saturates 12.5g; Cholesterol 235mg; Calcium 68mg; Fibre 1.5g; Sodium 272mg.

VEGETABLES, FRUIT AND PRESERVES

Vegetables have featured in the cooking of the region since ancient times, but attained glory in the medieval period, influenced by the cuisine of Persia. Numerous dishes were dedicated to vegetables alone, and they were held in such high esteem that they became the focus of Arab sayings such as 'A table without vegetables is like an old man devoid of wisdom.' The Ottomans built on this by introducing vegetables from the New World such as corn, potatoes, peppers and, most importantly, tomatoes and chillies.

POTATO KIBBEH STUFFED WITH SPINACH

THE MUCH-LOVED KIBBEH OF JORDAN, SYRIA AND LEBANON ARE EATEN AT FESTIVALS, FEASTS, AND FAMILY CELEBRATIONS. THESE POTATO KIBBEH ARE OFTEN STUFFED WITH MINCED LAMB, CHEESE, OR SAUTÉED SPINACH AND SERVED AS A MEZZE DISH OR AN ACCOMPANIMENT TO GRILLED MEATS.

SERVES FOUR TO SIX

INGREDIENTS

For the kibbeh

- 175g/6oz fine or medium bulgur
- 500g/1/4 lb potatoes, cooked
- 25g/1oz plain (all purpose) flour
- 5ml/1 tsp allspice
- 5ml/1 tsp ground cumin
- 5ml/1 tsp ground coriander
- sea salt and ground black pepper

For the filling

- 15ml/1 tbsp olive oil
- 1 onion, finely chopped
- 30ml/2 tbsp pine nuts
- 250g/9oz spinach, steamed and finely chopped
- 115/4oz feta, crumbled
- a pinch of nutmeg
- sunflower oil for frying
- 1 lemon, cut into wedges, to serve

1 Pour the bulgur into a bowl and pour in enough boiling water to just cover. Leave to swell for 10 minutes. Use your hands to squeeze out any excess water.

2 Put the cooked potatoes and bulgur in a bowl and mash together. Add the flour, spices and seasoning, and knead until smooth. Cover the bowl and chill for 30 minutes before using.

3 To prepare the filling, heat the oil and stir in the onion until it softens. Add the pine nuts and sauté for 1–2 minutes, until the pine nuts and the onion are golden brown. Toss in the spinach with the nutmeg and heat it through. Toss in the crumbled feta and season to taste, as the feta is often quite salty.

4 Take an apricot-sized lump of kibbeh in your hand. Roll it into a smooth ball then, using your finger, hollow out the middle to create a hollow shell.

5 Fill the shell with a teaspoon of the filling, then pinch the edges together and smooth it over with a dampened finger to create a sealed mini torpedo, or a round ball. If not cooking them immediately, cover with plastic film and keep in the refrigerator.

6 Heat enough oil in a wide, shallow pan for frying. Cook the kibbeh in batches until golden brown all over. Drain them on kitchen paper.

7 Serve hot with wedges of lemon and a dollop of yogurt, if you like.

Energy 345kcal/1441kJ; Protein 10g; Carbohydrate42, of which sugars 3g; Fat 16g, of which saturates 4g; Cholesterol 13mg; Calcium 180mg; Fibre 2.8g; Sodium 411mg.

POTATOES WITH WALNUTS AND ROSE PETALS

HEAVILY SCENTED WITH CUMIN, THIS IS A DELICIOUS WAY TO PREPARE POTATOES. THERE ARE VARIATIONS OF THIS DISH, KNOWN AS 'KAMMOUNEH', THROUGHOUT THE REGION, A HAZELNUT VERSION IN THE BLACK SEA REGION, AND A MORE FIERY VERSION IN PARTS OF SYRIA AND JORDAN.

SERVES THREE TO FOUR

INGREDIENTS

- 750g/1½ lb new potatoes
- 30–45ml/2–3 tbsp olive oil
- 5ml/1 tsp sea salt

For the kammouneh

- 10–15ml/2–3 tsp cumin seeds
- 1 red onion, finely chopped
- 30–45ml/2–3 tbsp walnuts, finely chopped
- 1 red chilli, seeded and finely chopped
- 1 small bunch fresh basil leaves, finely shredded
- 1 small bunch fresh mint leaves, finely shredded
- 15ml/1 tbsp dried rose petals
- juice of 1 lemon

1 Boil the potatoes in their skins, until tender but not too soft. Drain, refresh under running cold water and peel off the skins. Transfer them to a bowl and toss in the olive oil and salt.

2 Roast the cumin seeds in a heavy pan, until they give off a nutty aroma. Using a mortar and pestle, grind them a little to release the flavour, then add the walnuts and grind a little more. Add the onion, chilli, herbs and most of the dried rose petals and pound lightly to combine the ingredients, but don't pound to a paste.

3 Bind the mixture with the lemon juice and spoon it over the potatoes while they are still warm. Toss well and garnish with rose petals.

COOK'S TIP

Dried rose petals are available in Middle Eastern stores, but you need to make sure they are the edible kind.

Energy 337kcal/1406kJ; Protein 6g; Carbohydrate 5g, of which sugars 34g; Fat 21g, of which saturates 3g; Cholesterol 0mg; Calcium 66mg; Fibre 2.9g; Sodium 124mg.

SPICY POTATOES WITH CORIANDER

THE SPICES IN THIS POPULAR POTATO DISH VARY ACROSS LEBANON, SYRIA AND JORDAN, BUT THE RECIPES INVARIABLY INCLUDE CHILLIES AND CUMIN. THE DISH CAN BE EATEN AT ROOM TEMPERATURE AS PART OF A MEZZE SPREAD, BUT IS ALSO OFTEN SERVED HOT AS AN ACCOMPANIMENT TO GRILLED (BROILED) AND ROASTED MEAT AND FISH.

SERVES FOUR

INGREDIENTS

- 350g/12oz new potatoes
- 60ml/4 tbsp ghee, or olive oil with a generous knob of butter
- 3–4 cloves garlic, finely chopped
- 2 red chillies, seeded and chopped
- 5–10ml/1–2 tsp cumin seeds
- 1 bunch fresh coriander (cilantro), finely chopped
- sea salt and ground black pepper
- 1 lemon, cut into wedges, to serve

COOK'S TIP

If the dish is to be eaten at room temperature it is preferable to cook the potatoes in olive oil, but ghee is often used instead when the potatoes are to be served hot.

1 Steam the potatoes with their skins on for about 10 minutes, until cooked but still firm. Drain and refresh under cold running water. Peel off the skins.

2 Cut the potatoes half. Heat the ghee, or olive oil and butter, in a heavy pan and cook the garlic, chillies and cumin seeds for 2–3 minutes, until they colour.

3 Add the potatoes to the pan and fry for about 5 minutes. Season with salt and pepper and stir in most of the coriander. (If serving the dish at room temperature, leave the potatoes to cool first.) Sprinkle the remaining coriander over the top and serve the potatoes from the pan with lemon wedges to squeeze over them.

Energy 174kcal/723kJ; Protein 2.4g; Carbohydrate 15.5g, of which sugars 1.2g; Fat 11.8g, of which saturates 1.7g; Cholesterol 0mg; Calcium 16mg; Fibre 0.9g; Sodium 12mg.

CHICORY IN OLIVE OIL

IN OTHER PARTS OF THE MIDDLE EAST, THIS DISH IS KNOWN AS HINDBEH BI-ZEIT, LITERALLY 'CHICORY WITH OLIVE OIL', BUT THE LEBANESE CALL IT ASOURA, MEANING 'SQUEEZED', AS THE COOKED CHICORY IS SQUEEZED BY HAND TO GET RID OF ALL EXCESS WATER. IT IS SERVED AS A MEZZE DISH OR AS AN ACCOMPANIMENT TO MEAT, POULTRY OR FISH.

SERVES FOUR

INGREDIENTS

- about 350g/12oz chicory
- 45ml/3 tbsp olive oil
- juice of 1 lemon
- sea salt and ground black pepper

1 Bring a pan of water to the boil. Drop in the chicory and boil for 10 minutes, until soft. Drain and refresh under cold running water.

COOK'S TIP

Chicory is usually eaten raw as part of a salad in Western Europe. Cooking it gives it a sweet and mellow flavour.

2 Take the chicory in your hands and squeeze tightly to remove all the excess water, so that it is almost dry. Divide it into four portions and squeeze them into tight balls. Cover and leave in the refrigerator until ready to serve.

3 Just before serving, place each ball on a plate and flatten it out a little with the palm of your hand, or the back of a wooden spoon. Drizzle each one with olive oil and a little lemon juice and sprinkle with salt and pepper.

Energy 109kcal/447kJ; Protein 0.5g; Carbohydrate 2.5g, of which sugars 0.7g; Fat 11.5g, of which saturates 1.7g; Cholesterol 0mg; Calcium 19mg; Fibre 0.8g; Sodium 1mg.

Green Beans with Cumin and Tomatoes

Adapted from the Ottoman vegetable dishes cooked in olive oil, loubia bi zeit is prepared all over Jordan, Syria and Lebanon. It can be served hot or at room temperature and often tastes better if it is cooked the day before, to allow the flavours to mingle.

SERVES FOUR TO SIX

INGREDIENTS

- 30–40ml/2–3 tbsp olive oil
- 2 onions, finely chopped
- 2–3 cloves garlic, finely chopped
- 10ml/2 tsp cumin seeds
- 450g/1lb green beans, trimmed and left whole
- 5ml/1 tsp ground cinnamon
- 5ml/1 tsp ground allspice
- 5ml/1 tsp sugar
- 400g/14oz can of chopped tomatoes
- sea salt and ground black pepper
- 1 lemon, cut into wedges, to serve

1 Heat the oil in a heavy-based pan and stir in the onion and garlic, until they begin to colour. Stir in the cumin seeds, then toss in the green beans and cook, stirring, for 2–3 minutes.

2 Add the cinnamon, allspice and sugar to the pan and stir through to cover all the beans in the spice mixture.

3 Stir the tomatoes into the pan. Cover with a lid and cook gently for 15–20 minutes, until the beans are tender but still retain a bite to them. Season to taste with salt and pepper. Serve hot or at room temperature with wedges of lemon to squeeze over them.

Energy 122kcal/507kJ; Protein 3g; Carbohydrate 10g, of which sugars 8g; Fat 8g, of which saturates 1g; Cholesterol 0mg; Calcium 64mg; Fibre 2.9g; Sodium 95mg.

STUFFED AUBERGINES IN OIL

THERE ARE MANY VARIATIONS OF STUFFED VEGETABLE DISHES THROUGHOUT THE REGION. IN LEBANON, THE LOCAL SPICE MIX, SABAA BAHARAT, A BLEND OF SEVEN SPICES, IS OFTEN USED. IF YOU CANNOT FIND IT, USE A COMBINATION OF GROUND CUMIN, CORIANDER AND CINNAMON.

SERVES FOUR TO SIX

INGREDIENTS

- 150ml/¼ pint/⅔ cup olive oil
- 1 onion, finely chopped
- 2 tomatoes, skinned, seeded and chopped
- 10ml/2 tsp sabaa baharat
- 10ml/2 tsp dried mint
- 5–10ml/1–2 tsp sugar
- 175g/6oz/¾ cup short grain rice
- 6 medium aubergines (eggplants)
- 1–2 small potatoes, sliced
- juice of 1 lemon
- sea salt and ground black pepper

1 To make the stuffing, heat 15ml/1 tbsp of the olive oil in a heavy pan and cook the onion for 2–3 minutes, until it begins to colour. Add the tomatoes, sabaa baharat, mint and the sugar and cook for 2–3 minutes.

2 Add the rice to the pan, coating it well in the oil, and pour in enough water to cover the rice by a finger's width. Season with salt and pepper and bring to the boil. Reduce the heat and simmer for 10 minutes, until all the water has been absorbed.

3 Turn off the heat, cover the pan with a clean dish towel and put on the lid. Leave the rice to steam for 10 minutes.

4 Meanwhile, prepare the aubergines. Cut off the stalks and use an apple corer to hollow out the middle. Fill each aubergine with the rice mixture and seal the opening with a slice of potato.

5 Mix the lemon juice and remaining olive oil with 100ml/3½fl oz/scant ½ cup water.

6 Stand the aubergines in a heavy pan and pour the lemon, oil and water mixture in to the pan around the aubergines. Place on medium heat.

7 Bring the liquid to the boil, reduce the heat, cover the pan and simmer for about 40 minutes. Serve the stuffed aubergines hot or at room temperature as a mezze dish, or serve as an accompaniment to roast meat dishes.

COOK'S TIPS

For this recipe, most of the aubergine flesh is removed and it is not added to the filling. It is generally discarded but could be used in another dish.

The stuffed aubergines need to stand up while cooking, so that they are surrounded by the cooking liquid but not submerged in it. Choose a pan into which they will fit fairly snugly, standing side by side.

Energy 486kcal/2023kJ; Protein 10.8g; Carbohydrate 76.2g, of which sugars 34.9g; Fat 16.8g, of which saturates 2.3g; Cholesterol 0mg; Calcium 160mg; Fibre 10.8g; Sodium 26mg.

Aubergine and Chickpea Mousaka

The principal idea of a mousaka is that the dish is prepared in layers. Originally an Ottoman dish, 'musakka' is cooked all over the eastern Mediterranean, sometimes employing courgettes (zucchini) and potatoes. The most famous and well-travelled version includes minced lamb. This meatless recipe is popular in Syria and Lebanon.

SERVES FOUR

INGREDIENTS

- 2 large aubergines (eggplants), sliced
- sunflower oil, for frying
- 30ml/2 tbsp olive oil
- 2 onions, finely chopped
- 2 cloves garlic, finely chopped
- 2 x 400g/14oz cans of cooked chickpeas, rinsed and drained
- 10ml/2 tsp ground cinnamon
- 5ml/1 tsp ground cumin
- 10ml/2 tsp pomegranate syrup
- 1 small bunch flat-leaf parsley, finely chopped
- 15ml/1 tsp tomato purée (paste)
- 10ml/2 tsp sugar
- 4–5 large tomatoes, thinly sliced
- 15ml/1 tsp butter
- 5–10ml/1–2 tsp zahtar
- sea salt and ground black pepper

1 Preheat the oven to 180°C/350°F/ Gas 4. Brush the aubergine slices with oil and griddle them on both sides.

2 Heat the olive oil in a heavy pan and stir in the onions and garlic, until they begin to colour. Stir the chickpeas for 1–2 minutes then add the cinnamon and cumin. Stir in the pomegranate syrup, toss in the parsley and season with salt and pepper.

3 Line an oven-proof dish with half of the aubergines, spoon the chickpea mixture on top, and cover with another layer of aubergines. Mix together the tomato purée and sugar and thin it with about 120ml/4fl oz/½ cup water. Pour the mixture over the layered aubergines.

4 Add the tomato slices, dot with butter and sprinkle with zahtar. Bake for 25–30 minutes and serve with bread.

Energy 467kcal/1953kJ; Protein 15g; Carbohydrate 43g, of which sugars 18g; Fat 28g, of which saturates 5g; Cholesterol 8mg; Calcium 112mg; Fibre 6.8g; Sodium 167mg.

ROASTED COURGETTES WITH VINEGAR

THE COURGETTE IS A VERY POPULAR VEGETABLE IN THE EASTERN MEDITERRANEAN REGION, AND IN THE MARKETS YOU CAN FIND MARBLED GREEN COURGETTES, YELLOW ONES AND WHITE ONES, AS WELL AS THE MORE USUAL GREEN TYPE. ANY KIND WILL DO FOR THIS RECIPE, WHICH MAKES A LOVELY SIDE DISH FOR GRILLED (BROILED) OR ROASTED MEATS AND FISH.

SERVES FOUR TO SIX

INGREDIENTS

- 4–6 courgettes (zucchini), trimmed and sliced lengthways
- 4 cloves garlic, halved and lightly crushed
- 45–60ml/3–4 tbsp olive oil
- 30ml/2 tbsp cider or white wine vinegar
- 10ml/2 tsp dried mint
- sea salt

1 Preheat the oven to 180°C/350°F/Gas 4. Place the courgette slices in an ovenproof dish with the crushed garlic clove halves.

2 Pour the olive oil over the courgettes, and roast in the oven for 25–30 minutes, until softened and lightly browned. Mix 30–45ml/2–3 tbsp of the cooking liquid with the vinegar and dried mint to make a dressing.

3 Lift the courgette slices out of the dish and arrange on a warmed serving plate. Drizzle the vinegar and mint dressing over the courgettes. Sprinkle generously with salt and serve warm or at room temperature.

Energy 78kcal/322kJ; Protein 2.7g; Carbohydrate 3.3g, of which sugars 2.1g; Fat 6g, of which saturates 0.9g; Cholesterol 0mg; Calcium 36mg; Fibre 1.3g; Sodium 2mg.

Baked Courgettes with Cheese

This is a popular supper dish throughout Lebanon, Syria and Jordan. It makes a good light meal eaten with yogurt and bread, but is also often eaten as an accompaniment to roast meat. A crumbly, tangy cheese made of ewe's milk, such as feta, is usually used for this recipe, but you can replace it with Parmesan if you wish.

SERVES FOUR TO SIX

INGREDIENTS

- 30ml/2 tbsp olive oil plus a knob (pat) of butter
- 2 onions, cut in half lengthways and sliced finely with the grain
- 5–10ml/1–2 tsp caraway seeds
- 4–6 firm courgettes (zucchini), trimmed and cut into thick slices lengthways
- 4 eggs
- 250g/9oz feta or Parmesan cheese, crumbled or grated
- 2.5ml/½ tsp paprika
- sea salt and ground black pepper

1 Preheat the oven to 180°C/350°F/Gas 4. Heat the oil and butter in a large pan. Add the onions and cook until soft. Stir in the caraway seeds and then remove from the heat.

2 Place the courgette slices in a steamer and steam for about 10 minutes until tender but not mushy. Drain well and spread half the slices in the base of an ovenproof dish. Spread the onion mixture, including the oil and butter, over the top and arrange another layer of courgettes over the onions.

3 Beat the eggs, then mix in the cheese and paprika. Season generously and pour the over the courgettes. Bake the dish for 20–25 minutes, until the top is golden brown. Serve immediately.

Energy 314kcal/1302kJ; Protein 23.3g; Carbohydrate 7.2g, of which sugars 5.4g; Fat 21.6g, of which saturates 10.2g; Cholesterol 169mg; Calcium 562mg; Fibre 1.8g; Sodium 504mg.

STUFFED COURGETTES WITH APRICOTS

STUFFING VEGETABLES OR COOKING THEM WITH FRUIT IS A FAVOURITE METHOD OF PREPARING VEGETABLES THROUGHOUT THE EASTERN MEDITERRANEAN. INSPIRED BY THE DISHES OF MEDIEVAL PERSIA THIS DISH, KABLAMA, OFFERS THE TRADITIONAL SAVOURY-SWEET TASTE THAT IS SO COVETED IN THIS PART OF THE WORLD. IT IS OFTEN SERVED AS AN ACCOMPANIMENT TO GRILLED MEAT.

SERVES FOUR

INGREDIENTS

For the filling
- 15–30ml/1–2 tbsp olive oil
- 1 onion, halved and finely sliced
- 2 cloves garlic, finely chopped
- 2–3 tomatoes, skinned, seeds removed and chopped
- 5–10ml/1–2 tsp palm sugar (jaggery) or sugar
- 1 small bunch flat leaf parsley, chopped
- 4–6 medium courgettes (zucchini), washed
- 225g/8oz dried apricots, soaked in just enough water overnight
- juice of 1 lemon
- 30ml/2 tbsp olive oil
- 30ml/2 tbsp grape molasses
- sea salt and ground black pepper
- Greek (US strained plain) yoghurt, to serve

1 Preheat the oven to 180°C/350°F/Gas 4.To make the filling, heat the olive oil in a heavy pan and stir in the onion and garlic for 1–2 minutes to soften. Add the tomatoes, sugar and parsley. Season with salt and pepper and leave to cool.

2 Slice off the stem end of the courgette and, using an apple corer, scoop out the pulp without breaking the skin.

3 Spoon the onion and tomato filling into each courgette hollow. Drain the apricots and reserve 300ml/½ pint/1¼ cups of the soaking water.

4 Look for the slit in each apricot and pull it open. Arrange half the apricots in the base of an oven-proof dish. Place the courgettes on top, and arrange the rest of the apricots over them.

5 Mix together the reserved apricot water with the lemon juice, olive oil, grape molasses and a little salt, and pour over the apricots and courgettes.

6 Cover with foil and bake for about 40 minutes. Dot the top with a little butter and return to the oven for 10 minutes. Serve warm with a dollop of thick Greek yogurt.

VARIATION

For a non-fruity version, these stuffed courgettes are also delicious topped with a layer of yogurt, topped with a mixture of breadcrumbs and grated Parmesan.

Energy 332kcal/1386kJ; Protein 7g; Carbohydrate 42g, of which sugars 40g; Fat 16g, of which saturates 2g; Cholesterol 0mg; Calcium 133mg; Fibre 7.1g; Sodium 241mg.

OKRA WITH TOMATOES AND CORIANDER

A favourite dish in Jordan, Syria and Lebanon, this is adapted from the Ottoman tradition of cooking vegetables in oil. It is a seasonal dish, prepared when okra are harvested. Some cooks simmer it until the okra releases a glutinous substance – a consistency revered by some – but here the okra are sautéed so they remain crunchy.

SERVES FOUR

INGREDIENTS

- 450g/1lb fresh okra, washed, patted dry and left whole
- juice of 1 lemon
- 30ml/1 tbsp olive oil
- 1 onion, finely chopped
- 2 cloves garlic, finely chopped
- 5–10ml/2 tbsp palm sugar (jaggery) or sugar
- 4 tomatoes, skinned and chopped
- 1 bunch fresh coriander (cilantro) leaves, finely chopped
- sea salt and ground black pepper

1 Place the okra in a bowl and toss in the lemon juice. Leave them to marinate for about 15 minutes then lift them out of the juice.

2 Heat the olive oil in a shallow, heavy pan and stir in the onion to soften. Add the garlic and toss in the okra. Fry lightly for 3–4 minutes then sprinkle with the sugar and toss in the chopped tomatoes. Add most of the coriander and cook for 1–2 minutes, until the okra are tender but still retain a bite. Season with salt and pepper.

3 Serve the okra immediately as an accompaniment to grilled or roasted meat and poultry, or leave the okra to cool and serve at room temperature as a mezze dish.

Energy 143kcal/598kJ; Protein 4g; Carbohydrate 12g, of which sugars 10g; Fat 9g, of which saturates 1g; Cholesterol 0mg; Calcium 201mg; Fibre 6.0g; Sodium 117mg.

BRAISED ONIONS WITH TAMARIND

THE TART FLAVOUR OF TAMARIND IS MUCH ENJOYED IN SYRIA AND JORDAN, PARTICULARLY WITH VEGETABLES. MEDIEVAL MANUSCRIPTS SUGGEST THAT COURGETTES (ZUCCHINI), LEEKS AND ONIONS HAVE BEEN COOKED IN TAMARIND JUICE FOR HUNDREDS OF YEARS. THE CONCENTRATED TAMARIND PASTE EMPLOYED IN THIS RECIPE IS AVAILABLE IN MIDDLE EASTERN AND INDIAN STORES.

SERVES FOUR TO SIX

INGREDIENTS

- 30–45ml/2–3 tbsp olive oil
- 450g/1lb shallots, peeled
- 15ml/1 tbsp tamarind paste
- 15ml/1 tbsp palm sugar (jaggery) or sugar
- sea salt and ground black pepper
- 1 bunch coriander (cilantro), chopped

1 Heat the oil in a shallow heavy pan and add the shallots. Sauté the shallots until they are golden brown.

2 Stir the tamarind paste into the shallots. Add the sugar and enough water to just cover the base of the pan.

3 Reduce the heat, cover the pan and simmer gently for about 15 minutes, until the shallots are tender and coated in the thick sauce.

4 Season with salt and pepper and sprinkle the chopped coriander over the top. Serve hot or at room temperature with roasted or grilled meat and poultry.

COOKS TIP

If shallots are not in season you can also use this method to cook onions, cut into chunks or slices.

Energy 117kcal/487kJ; Protein1g; Carbohydrate 12g, of which sugars 10g; Fat 8g, of which saturates 1g; Cholesterol 0mg; Calcium 25mg; Fibre 1.1g; Sodium 69mg.

SPINACH WITH YOGURT

POPULAR THROUGHOUT LEBANON, JORDAN AND SYRIA, THIS DISH IS DELICIOUS SERVED ON ITS OWN OR AS AN ACCOMPANIMENT TO MEATBALLS. AS WITH ALL TRADITIONAL FATTA DISHES, WHICH WERE PROBABLY DEVISED AS A WAY OF USING UP STALE BREAD, THE SPINACH IS SERVED ON TOASTED FLAT BREAD AND TOPPED WITH MELTED BUTTER AND PINE NUTS.

SERVES FOUR

INGREDIENTS

- 500g/1¼lb fresh spinach, washed and drained
- 15–30ml/1–2 tbsp olive oil
- 1 onion, chopped
- 5ml/1 tsp ground cinnamon
- 5ml/1 tsp paprika
- 5ml/1 tsp ground cumin
- 1 small bunch fresh coriander (cilantro), finely chopped
- 15–30ml/1–2 tbsp flaked (sliced) almonds
- 2 pitta breads, toasted
- 15ml/1 tbsp butter
- 15–30ml/1–2 tbsp pine nuts
- sea salt and ground black pepper

For the yogurt sauce

- 600ml/1 pint/2½ cups Greek (US strained plain) yogurt
- 2 cloves garlic, crushed
- 30ml/2 tbsp tahini
- juice of ½ lemon

1 To prepare the yogurt sauce, beat the yogurt with the garlic, tahini and lemon juice and season it to taste with salt and pepper. Set aside.

2 Put the washed spinach in a steamer or a large pan and cook very briefly until just wilted. Refresh under cold running water.

3 Drain the spinach and squeeze out the excess water. Transfer to a board and chop coarsely.

4 Heat the oil in a heavy pan, stir in the onion and cook for 2–3 minutes. Stir in the spices and then add the spinach, making sure all the leaves are thoroughly coated with the spiced oil.

5 Cook for a further 2–3 minutes, until the spinach is wilted. Season well with salt and pepper. Mix in the coriander and flaked almonds.

6 Break the toasted pitta bread into bitesize pieces and arrange them in a serving dish. Spread the spinach over the top of the bread and spoon the yogurt sauce over the spinach.

7 Melt the butter in a frying pan and add the pine nuts. Stir-fry until the pine nuts are golden. Tip the pine nuts, with the butter, over the yogurt and serve immediately while still warm.

Energy 435kcal/1818kJ; Protein 19.3g; Carbohydrate 45.1g, of which sugars 20g; Fat 21.3g, of which saturates 4.8g; Cholesterol 11mg; Calcium 625mg; Fibre 5.9g; Sodium 529mg.

BAKED VEGETABLE STEW

In various parts of the Middle East vegetables, are often baked or stewed with cuts of lamb to provide a hearty meal in one dish. However, when they are prepared as mezze, or as an accompaniment, the meat is usually omitted. Any seasonal vegetable can be prepared in this way, but the most popular combination includes courgettes, tomatoes and peppers.

SERVES SIX

INGREDIENTS

- 150ml/¼ pint/⅔ cup olive oil
- 6 large tomatoes
- 4–6 potatoes, peeled
- 3 courgettes (zucchini)
- 2 onions
- 2 (bell) peppers
- 1 small bunch parsley, chopped
- 1 bunch fresh mint, finely chopped
- juice of 1 lemon
- 2 cloves garlic, crushed
- 10ml/2 tsp sugar
- sea salt and ground black pepper

1 Preheat the oven to 200°C/400°F/Gas 6 and lightly grease a baking dish with a little of the olive oil.

2 Thinly slice the tomatoes and line the base of the prepared baking dish with half the slices. Finely slice the potatoes and arrange in a layer on top of the tomatoes, followed by a layer of thinly sliced courgettes.

3 Cut the onions in half lengthways, and slice with the grain, then thinly slice the peppers. Toss the onion and pepper slices together with the chopped parsley and mint, then sprinkle the mixture over the courgettes.

4 Complete the layering with the rest of the tomato slices. Combine the rest of the olive oil with the lemon juice, garlic and sugar. Season, and pour the mixture over the vegetables.

5 Cover the dish with foil and bake in the oven for about 40 minutes, then remove the foil, dot the butter over the tomatoes and return the dish to the oven to cook, uncovered, for a further 15–20 minutes.

6 Serve the baked vegetables straight away, as an accompaniment to a meat or poultry dish, or with yogurt and flat bread as a mezze.

Energy 306kcal/1280kJ; Protein 7.4g; Carbohydrate 42.7g, of which sugars 16.2g; Fat 12.8g, of which saturates 2g; Cholesterol 0mg; Calcium 101mg; Fibre 6.3g; Sodium 37mg.

Jerusalem Artichoke and Tomato Stew

Almost any vegetable is cooked with tomatoes in the Middle East. The garlicky tomato sauce can be mopped up with bread, and this method of cooking results in tender, tasty vegetables. Jerusalem artichokes are excellent cooked this way and can be served on their own or as an accompaniment to roasted meat and poultry dishes.

SERVES FOUR

INGREDIENTS

- 30–45ml/2–3 tbsp olive oil
- 2 onions, finely chopped
- 2 cloves garlic, finely chopped
- 500g/1¼lb Jerusalem artichokes, peeled and cut into bitesize pieces
- 2 x 400g/14oz cans chopped tomatoes
- 10–15ml/2–3 tsp sugar
- sea salt and ground black pepper
- 1 small bunch fresh coriander (cilantro), finely chopped, to garnish
- 1 lemon, cut into wedges, to serve

1 Heat the oil in a heavy pan, stir in the onions and cook until they begin to colour. Add the garlic and the pieces of artichoke, and toss well to make sure they are coated in the oil.

2 Add the tomatoes to the pan, together with the sugar. Cover the pan and cook gently for 25–30 minutes, until the artichokes are tender.

3 Remove the lid and bubble up the sauce over high heat to reduce it a little. Season with salt and pepper and transfer to a serving dish. Garnish with some coriander and serve with wedges of lemon to squeeze over the dish.

Energy 147kcal/619kJ; Protein 3.6g; Carbohydrate 19.8g, of which sugars 17g; Fat 6.6g, of which saturates 1g; Cholesterol 0mg; Calcium 98mg; Fibre 5.1g; Sodium 97mg.

Red Cabbage with Quince and Walnuts

Originally of Armenian origin, this dish spread throughout the eastern Mediterranean as the Armenians migrated from the Caucasus, taking with them their love of vegetables combined with fruit. Simple to prepare, this delicious dish is best served to accompany roasted lamb, duck or chicken.

SERVES FOUR TO SIX

INGREDIENTS

- 1 red cabbage, quartered, cored and chopped into bitesize pieces
- 115g/4oz/½ cup butter, melted
- 5–10ml/1–2 tsp ground cinnamon
- juice of 1 lemon
- 10ml/2 tsp pomegranate molasses
- 2 quinces
- 15–30ml/1–2 tbsp sugar
- 15–30ml/1–2 tbsp walnuts, roughly chopped
- sea salt and ground black pepper

1 Preheat the oven to 180°C/350°F/Gas 4. Grease a baking dish and arrange the cabbage in it. Pour in half the melted butter and toss with half the cinnamon, salt and pepper, lemon juice and pomegranate molasses. Cover with foil and bake for about 30 minutes.

2 Meanwhile, quarter and core the quinces. Cut them into thin slices and submerge them in a bowl of cold water mixed with a squeeze of lemon juice to prevent them from discolouring.

3 Take the cabbage out of the oven and arrange the quince slices over the top. Sprinkle them with sugar and the remaining cinnamon, and sprinkle the walnuts over the top. Pour the rest of the butter over the quinces.

4 Cover and bake for 20 minutes more, then remove the foil and return the dish to the oven for about 10 minutes to brown the top. Serve immediately.

Energy 224kcal/927kJ; Protein 2.6g; Carbohydrate 13.5g, of which sugars 12.5g; Fat 18g, of which saturates 10.5g; Cholesterol 44mg; Calcium 73mg; Fibre 3.6g; Sodium 155mg.

APRICOTS STUFFED WITH RICE

THIS IS ONE OF A NUMBER OF SAVOURY SPECIALITIES FROM THE RICH MEDIEVAL LEGACY OF SUMPTUOUS DISHES COOKED WITH FRUIT. THE APRICOTS CAN BE PREPARED WITH A FILLING OF RICE MIXED WITH MINCED LAMB, TO SERVE ON THEIR OWN OR, AS HERE, WITHOUT MEAT FOR SERVING AS AN ACCOMPANIMENT TO ROASTED MEAT AND POULTRY DISHES.

SERVES FOUR

INGREDIENTS

- 30ml/2 tbsp olive oil
- 1 onion, finely chopped
- 15ml/1 tbsp pine nuts
- 175g/6oz/¾ cup short grain or pudding rice, well rinsed and drained
- 5ml/1 tsp ground cinnamon
- 5ml/1 tsp ground allspice
- 5ml/1 tsp sugar
- 5ml/1 tsp dried mint
- 1 large tomato, skinned, seeded and finely chopped
- 16 fresh, or whole dried, apricots
- 15ml/1 tbsp butter
- sea salt and ground black pepper

For the cooking liquid

- 120ml/4fl oz/½ cup olive oil
- 50ml/2fl oz/¼ cup water
- juice of 1 lemon
- 10–15ml/2–3 tsp sugar
- 5ml/1 tsp pomegranate molasses

1 Preheat the oven to 180°C/350°F/Gas 4. Heat the oil in a heavy pan, stir in the onion and cook until it begins to colour. Add the pine nuts and cook until golden, then stir in the rice, making sure the grains are coated in the oil.

2 Add the spices, sugar, mint and tomato to the pan, season with salt and pepper, and pour in about 350ml/12fl oz/1½ cups water to cover the rice.

3 Bring to the boil, stir once, then reduce the heat and leave to simmer for 10–15 minutes, until all the water has been absorbed. Remove from the heat.

4 Meanwhile, prepare the apricots. Using a sharp knife, slit them lengthways, making sure they remain attached at one side. Remove the stone (pit) and scrape away a little of the flesh to make a bigger space for the filling.

5 Spoon a portion of the rice mixture into the hollow of each apricot, so that it looks plump and appetizing. Place the apricots upright in a lightly greased, shallow baking dish, packing them tightly together so that they support each other during cooking.

6 Mix together the ingredients for the cooking liquid and pour it over and around the apricots. Cover the dish with foil and bake for about 20 minutes.

7 Remove the foil and baste the apricots with the cooking juices. Dot each one with a little butter and return the dish to the oven to cook, uncovered, for a further 5–10 minutes. Serve straight away.

COOK'S TIP

If you are using dried apricots, soak them overnight, then poach them in the soaking water for 10–15 minutes. Drain well, and stuff the larger ones. Use the smaller ones for another dish, or chop finely and mix in with the rice before stuffing the larger apricots.

Energy 449kcal/1872kJ; Protein 6.8g; Carbohydrate 54.1g, of which sugars 16.3g; Fat 23.3g, of which saturates 4.6g; Cholesterol 9mg; Calcium 57mg; Fibre 3.8g; Sodium 37mg.

STUFFED PRUNES IN A POMEGRANATE SAUCE

With the influence of the Armenians and Ottomans, dried and fresh fruits are employed regularly in sweet and savoury dishes. Prunes, apricots and figs are often stuffed with nuts or with an aromatic rice mixture, or they are added to meat and vegetable stews. This delicious dish of prunes stuffed with walnuts makes an unusual mezze dish.

SERVES FOUR

INGREDIENTS

- 12–16 ready-to-eat, pitted prunes
- 12–16 walnut halves
- 15–30ml/1-2 tbsp ghee or olive oil with a knob (pat) of butter
- 30–45ml/2–3 tbsp pomegranate molasses
- 30ml/2 tbsp sugar
- 1 cinnamon stick
- 3–4 cardamom pods
- 2–3 cloves
- juice of 1 lemon
- 250ml/9fl oz red wine or water
- sea salt and ground black pepper
- 1 small bunch flat leaf parsley, chopped

1 Find the opening in each pitted prune and stuff it with a walnut half.

2 Melt the ghee, or olive oil and butter, in a heavy pan and toss in the prunes for 2-3 minutes, turning them over from time to time. Stir in the pomegranate molasses with the sugar and spices, and add the lemon juice and wine.

3 Season with salt and pepper and bring the liquid to the boil. Reduce the heat and simmer, uncovered, for about 15 minutes, stirring occasionally, until the prunes are tender.

4 Arrange the prunes on a serving dish and spoon the spicy pomegranate sauce over and around them. Garnish with the parsley and serve hot or at room temperature.

Energy 244kcal/1021kJ; Protein 1g; Carbohydrate 34g, of which sugars 32g; Fat 8g, of which saturates 5g; Cholesterol 21mg; Calcium 72mg; Fibre 2.7g; Sodium 116mg.

Pickled White Cabbage with Walnuts

Most cabbages grown in Lebanon are white or light green with firm, tender leaves that impart a natural sweetness to dishes. When there is a glut of these cabbages the vegetables are often preserved, and this is one of the favourite recipes for doing it.

4 Pull the top edge over the mixture, tuck in the sides and roll the leaf into a tight, pointed log shape.

5 Pack the stuffed leaves tightly into a sterilized jar and pour over the vinegar. Seal the jar, and leave the cabbage parcels to marinate for at least a week.

6 After opening, store in the refrigerator for 4–5 days. Serve as a mezze, drizzled in olive oil, or as accompaniment to cheese or grilled meats.

SERVES FOUR

INGREDIENTS

- 8 large white cabbage leaves, or 16 smaller ones
- 4 cloves garlic
- 225g/8oz/2 cups shelled walnuts, coarsely chopped
- 1 fresh chilli, seeded and finely chopped
- 15ml/1 tbsp olive oil
- 300ml/½ pint/1¼ cups cider or white wine vinegar
- sea salt

1 Steam the cabbage leaves for 5–6 minutes until softened. Refresh under cold water and drain well.

2 Using a mortar and pestle, pound the garlic with a little salt until creamy. Add the walnuts and pound to a gritty paste. Add the chilli and bind the mixture with the oil.

3 Lay the leaves on a flat surface and trim the central ribs, so that they lie flat. Place a spoonful of the walnut mixture near the top of each leaf.

Energy 440kcal/1816kJ; Protein 9.8g; Carbohydrate 7g, of which sugars 6.5g; Fat 41.5g, of which saturates 3.5g; Cholesterol 0mg; Calcium 110mg; Fibre 4.3g; Sodium 12mg.

PICKLED STUFFED AUBERGINES

AUBERGINES COME IN VARIOUS SIZES AND SHAPES AND ARE USED IN NUMEROUS SAVOURY DISHES AND SEVERAL SWEET ONES TOO. PICKLED STUFFED AUBERGINES ARE A GREAT FAVOURITE, SERVED AS A MEZZE DISH OR EATEN AS A SNACK FOLLOWED BY THE PICKLING LIQUID TO QUENCH THE THIRST.

SERVES FOUR TO SIX

INGREDIENTS

- 12 baby aubergines (eggplants), stalks removed
- 1 leek, cut in half if very long
- 225g/8oz/2 cups walnuts, finely chopped
- 1 red (bell) pepper, finely chopped
- 4 cloves garlic, finely chopped
- 1 red or green chilli, seeded and finely chopped
- 5–10ml/1–2 tsp sea salt
- 15ml/1 tbsp olive oil
- 1 small bunch flat leaf parsley
- 600ml/1 pint/2½ cups white wine vinegar

1 Bring a pan of water to the boil and add the aubergines and the leek. Cook for 10 minutes to soften, then drain and refresh under cold running water. Set aside the aubergines. Cut the leek into long thin strips and set aside also.

2 Mix together the walnuts, pepper, garlic, chilli and salt and bind with the olive oil.

3 Make a slit in the side of each aubergine and stuff the hollow with the filling. Finish with a few parsley leaves. Carefully wind a strip of leek around the aubergine to bind it and keep it intact. Pack tightly into a sterilized jar and pour over the vinegar.

4 Seal the jars and store in a cool place for 2–3 weeks. Refrigerate once opened. As long as they are kept sealed and topped up with vinegar, these aubergines will keep for several months.

Energy 324kcal/1342kJ; Protein 8.4g; Carbohydrate 8.7g, of which sugars 7.7g; Fat 28.7g, of which saturates 2.6g; Cholesterol 0mg; Calcium 82mg; Fibre 6.9g; Sodium 11mg.

Pickled Green Peppers

There are a variety of long, thin green peppers in the eastern Mediterranean, some of which are sweet and others that are slightly hot to the tongue, although not classified as a chilli. For this pickle, which is popular in Syria, Jordan and Turkey, you need the long, green peppers, often quite knobbly, available in Middle Eastern stores.

MAKES 1 X 1 LITRE JAR

INGREDIENTS

- 450g/1lb long, green peppers, washed thoroughly and patted dry
- 300ml/1 pint/1¼ cups water
- 300ml/1 pint/1¼ cups white wine vinegar
- 15ml/1 tbsp salt

COOK'S TIP

You may need to make extra pickling juice if you are pickling the peppers in several jars, as they must be completely submerged in liquid.

1 Mix the water and vinegar and salt together in a jug (pitcher). Pack the peppers tightly into a jar and pour the vinegar mixture over.

2 Seal the jar tightly and store for at least 2 weeks before opening. Serve with kebabs or with mezze dishes.

Energy 134kcal/560kJ; Protein 5g; Carbohydrate 14g, of which sugars 13g; Fat 1g, of which saturates 0g; Cholesterol 0mg; Calcium 46mg; Fibre 7.2g; Sodium 5535mg.

PICKLED CAULIFLOWER WITH CHLLIES

UP THERE WITH PICKLED PEPPERS, PICKLED CAULIFLOWER IS A GREAT FAVOURITE AT THE KEBAB AND SOUP HOUSES OF LEBANON, SYRIA AND JORDAN. IT ALSO APPEARS AS AN ADDITION TO THE MEZZE TABLE TO WHET THE APPETITE. SOME JARS OF PICKLED CAULIFLOWER ARE TINGED PINK WITH A LITTLE BEETROOT, BUT THE ONES WITH GARLIC AND CHILLI ARE STRONG IN FLAVOUR AND HAVE A GOOD NIP.

TO MAKE 2 X 1 LITRE JARS

INGREDIENTS

- 1 head of fresh cauliflower, trimmed and cut into small florets (keep any of the small light green leaves)
- 8–10 cloves garlic, peeled and left whole
- 4–6 small green or red hot chillies, left whole
- 250ml/8fl oz/1 cup white wine or apple vinegar
- 30ml/2 tbsp sea salt
- 1 litre/ 3¾ pints/4 cups water

1 Place the cauliflower in sterilized jars, alternating with the garlic cloves and chillies. If using the cauliflower leaves, add them too.

2 Mix the vinegar and salt with the water. Pour over the cauliflower and seal the jar tightly. Store in a cool place for at least 1 month before using.

Energy 225kcal/935kJ; Protein 893g; Carbohydrate 18g, of which sugars 17g; Fat 11g, of which saturates 4g; Cholesterol 0mg; Calcium 111mg; Fibre 7.5g; Sodium 23629mg.

SWEET DISHES, PUDDINGS AND CAKES

The choice of sweetmeats in the eastern Mediterranean is astounding: a tantalizing array of syrupy pastries, cakes, milk puddings, ice creams, poached or candied fruit, almond and pistachio marzipans. Cakes and sweet treats are eaten at any time of day, although some may be served at the end of a meal, such as the milk puddings, flavoured with rose or orange blossom waters, mastic or spices. These puddings look magnificent as an impressive dessert, while the cakes and sweetmeats are lovely with coffee at any time.

Dried Fruit Compote with Almonds

Served as a winter dessert, or at ceremonial feasts, khushaaf is a classic sweet dish found throughout the Middle East. When the Ottomans dined in the Topkapi Palace, khushaaf was often spooned over plain rice as a final touch to a rather splendid meal. The syrup can be flavoured with rose or orange flower water, or both, but the ancient taste of sweet scented roses is the most traditional.

SERVES SIX TO EIGHT

INGREDIENTS

- 225g/8oz dried apricots
- 175/6oz dried prunes
- 120g/4¼oz sultanas (golden raisins)
- 120g/4¼oz blanched almonds
- 30ml/1 tbsp pine nuts
- 45–60ml/3–4 tbsp sugar (measure to taste)
- 30–45ml/2–3 tbsp rose water
- 15ml/1 tbsp orange flower water

1 Put the dried fruit and nuts into a bowl and cover completely with water.

2 Add the sugar, rose water and orange flower water to the dried fruit and nuts, and gently stir until the sugar dissolves.

3 Cover the bowl and place it in the refrigerator. Leave the fruit and nuts to soak for 48 hours, during which time the liquid will turn syrupy and golden.

4 Serve this compote, chilled, on its own, or with cream or ice cream, or with rice pudding. It also makes a delicious breakfast with yogurt.

Energy 260kcal/1092kJ; Protein 5g; Carbohydrate 36g, of which sugars 36g; Fat 11g, of which saturates 1g; Cholesterol 0mg; Calcium 73mg; Fibre 3.8g; Sodium 31mg.

Pumpkin Poached in Syrup

This is a winter classic. Thought to be Kurdish, it features in every restaurant and household during the pumpkin season, when the markets and streets are alive with bustling pumpkin stalls where someone is busily peeling and preparing the flesh. Similarly, during the quince season, kitchens are filled with the sweet floral scent of fruit poaching in a clove-scented syrup. Poached pumpkin is delicious with crème fraîche.

SERVES FOUR TO SIX

INGREDIENTS

- 450g/1lb sugar
- 225ml/8fl oz/1 cup water
- juice of 1 lemon
- 6 cloves
- 1kg/2¼lb peeled and deseeded pumpkin flesh, cut into cubes or rectangular blocks

1 Put the sugar and water into a deep, wide heavy-based pan. Bring the liquid to the boil, stirring all the time, until the sugar has dissolved.

2 Boil gently for 2–3 minutes, then reduce the heat and stir in the lemon juice and the cloves.

3 Add the pumpkin pieces to the pan and bring the liquid back to the boil. Reduce the heat, put the lid on the pan, and poach the pumpkin gently, turning the pieces over from time to time, until they are tender and gleaming. Depending on the size of your pieces, this may take 45 minutes to 1 hour.

4 Leave the pumpkin to cool in the pan, then lift the pieces out of the syrup and place them on a serving dish.

5 Spoon most, or all, of the syrup over them and serve at room temperature, or chilled with cream, or crème fraîche if you like.

Energy 318kcal/1355kJ; Protein 1g; Carbohydrate 83g, of which sugars 82g; Fat 0g; Cholesterol 0mg; Calcium 57mg; Fibre 1.7g; Sodium 4mg.

BAKED STUFFED APPLES

APPLES GROWN IN SYRIA AND LEBANON HAVE BEEN HELD IN HIGH ESTEEM SINCE MEDIEVAL TIMES, WHEN THEY WERE WRITTEN ABOUT AND CALLED UPON FOR SPECIFIC RECIPES. CRISP AND FLAVOURSOME, THE FRUITS OF THIS REGION ARE DELICIOUS WHETHER THEY ARE TART OR SWEET.

SERVES FOUR

INGREDIENTS

- 4 crisp apples, tart or sweet
- juice of 1 lemon
- 300ml/½ pint/1¼ cups water
- 225g/8oz palm sugar (jaggery) or sugar
- 1–2 tbsp pomegranate or grape syrup
- clotted cream, to serve

For the filling:

- 40ml/4 tbsp blanched almonds, flaked
- 30ml/2 tbsp sultanas (golden raisins)
- 100g/3¾oz dried apricots, chopped
- 30ml/2 tbsp palm sugar (jaggery) or sugar
- 15–30ml/1–2 tsp ground cinnamon

1 Cut out the core of each apple to create a cavity, and peel around the top edge of the apples. Rub lemon juice over the peeled area. Preheat the oven to 180°C/350°F/Gas 4.

2 In a small bowl, mix together the ingredients for the filling.

3 Place the apples side by side in a lightly buttered baking dish. Spoon the prepared filling into the apples.

4 Put the water, sugar and fruit syrup into a pan and bring it to the boil, stirring all the time. Reduce the heat and simmer for 10 minutes.

5 Pour the syrup over and around the apples and bake for 30 minutes. Baste the apples and return for 10 minutes more, until tender. Transfer to a dish.

6 Bubble up the syrup in a pan to reduce and thicken, then pour over the apples. Serve with clotted cream.

Energy 507kcal/2150kJ; Protein 5g; Carbohydrate 113g, of which sugars 112g; Fat 4g, of which saturates 1g; Cholesterol 0mg; Calcium 91mg; Fibre 4.8g; Sodium 52mg.

SESAME AND PISTACHIO BISCUITS

These little biscuits, called barazek, tend to be eaten in a flash by hungry children at the end of a school day in Syria, Jordan and Lebanon. Sold in cake shops and by street vendors, the recipes vary from region to region but are always in demand.

SERVES SIX TO EIGHT

INGREDIENTS
- 115g/4oz butter
- 115g/4oz sugar
- 300g/11oz plain (all-purpose) flour

For the topping:
- 115g/4oz sesame seeds
- 30ml/1 tbsp ground pistachios
- 30ml/1 tbsp sugar
- 10ml/2 tsp ground cinnamon
- 1 egg white, lightly beaten

1 In a bowl, cream the butter until soft and then beat in the sugar until the mixture is light and fluffy.

2 Add the flour to the butter and sugar mixture, and combine with your hand to form a soft dough.

3 Lightly grease a baking tray and line with baking parchment. Take a cherry-sized portion of the dough in your hands and mould it into a ball. Flatten the ball in the palm of your hand and place it on the baking tray. Repeat with the rest of the dough until it is all used up.

4 In a small bowl, mix together the sesame seeds, pistachios, cinnamon and sugar and bind with the egg white. Brush a little of the mixture over each round of dough and place them in the oven for about 10 minutes, or until they begin to turn golden.

5 Remove the biscuits from the oven and leave to cool on the baking trays for 5 minutes. Transfer them to a wire rack and cool completely before storing in an airtight container.

Energy 406kcal/1701kJ; Protein 7g; Carbohydrate 49g, of which sugars 20g; Fat 22g, of which saturates 9g; Cholesterol 31mg; Calcium 165mg; Fibre 2.4g; Sodium 111mg.

SWEET PANCAKES WITH SCENTED SYRUP

THIS MEDIEVAL DISH OF PANCAKES DIPPED IN SYRUP, SPRINKLED WITH PISTACHIOS AND SERVED WITH THICK CLOTTED CREAM IS OFTEN PREPARED FOR RELIGIOUS FESTIVALS AND WEDDINGS.

SERVES FOUR TO SIX

INGREDIENTS
- 15g/½oz fresh yeast
- 5ml/1 tsp sugar
- 250ml/8fl oz/1 cup lukewarm water
- 225g/8oz plain (all-purpose) flour
- sunflower oil, for frying

For the syrup
- 450g/1lb sugar
- 300ml/½ pint/1¼ cups water
- juice of 1 lemon or lime
- 15–30ml/1–2 tbsp orange blossom water
- 45ml/3 tbsp pistachios, chopped, and clotted cream, to serve

1 In a small bowl, dissolve the yeast and the sugar in a little of the lukewarm water until it begins to froth.

2 When the yeast and water is frothing, sift the flour into a bowl and make a well in the centre. Pour in the yeast with the rest of the water and, drawing the flour in from the sides, beat the mixture together to form a smooth batter.

3 Cover the bowl with a cloth and leave it in a warm place for about 1 hour, until the batter rises and becomes bubbly and elastic.

4 Meanwhile, prepare the syrup. Heat the sugar and water together, stirring, until the sugar has dissolved. Bring to the boil, reduce the heat and simmer for 10–15 minutes.

5 Stir in the lemon juice and orange blossom water. Simmer for 5 minutes more until the syrup coats the back of the wooden spoon. Set aside to cool.

6 When the batter is frothy, heat a heavy frying pan with a little oil. Pour a little batter into the hot pan and roll the pan to spread to the sides. Fry for a minute, then flip over and cook the other side. Remove from the pan, fold in half and place on a serving plate.

7 Repeat until the batter is finished. Pour syrup over the pancakes. Sprinkle with pistachios and serve with cream.

Energy 474kcal/2011kJ; Protein 4g; Carbohydrate 109g, of which sugars 80g; Fat 5g, of which saturates 1g; Cholesterol 0mg; Calcium 61mg; Fibre 1.2g; Sodium 5mg.

Cream Cheese Pudding with Syrup and Nuts

This cream cheese dessert, ashtalieh, is similar to the classic milk pudding, but thicker and creamier so it can be cut into squares, which are then bathed in sugar syrup.

SERVES FOUR TO SIX

INGREDIENTS
- 1 litre/1¾ pints/4 cups whole milk
- 60ml/4 tbsp sugar
- 250g/9oz/generous 1 cup cream cheese
- 90ml/6 tbsp cornflour (cornstarch), slaked with a little extra milk
- 10–15ml/2–3 tsp orange blossom water
- 15ml/1 tbsp pine nuts and 30ml/2 tbsp blanched, chopped almonds, soaked in cold water overnight
- 30ml/2 tbsp pistachio nuts, chopped

For the syrup
- 225g/8oz/1 generous cup sugar
- juice of 1 lemon
- rind of ½ lemon, cut into fine strips

1 Heat the milk in a heavy pan with the sugar, stirring, and bring it to the boil.

2 Reduce the heat and add the cream cheese, beating it into the milk and sugar until the mixture is smooth.

3 Add a couple of spoonfuls of the hot mixture to the slaked cornflour, then pour it into the pan, whisking vigorously until the mixture thickens.

4 Add the orange blossom water and simmer gently for 10–15 minutes, until it is thick. Pour the mixture into a shallow dish and leave it to cool and set. Chill in the refrigerator.

5 To make the syrup, put the sugar in a heavy pan with 120ml/4fl oz/½ cup water and bring it to the boil, stirring constantly until the sugar has dissolved. Add the lemon juice and rind.

6 Reduce the heat and simmer for 10 minutes, until the syrup is thick enough to coat the back of a spoon. Remove from the heat and set aside.

7 When ready to serve, cut into squares and place on individual plates. Spoon some of the syrup over them and decorate with the nuts. Serve chilled or at room temperature.

Energy 431kcal/1799kJ; Protein 7.5g; Carbohydrate 43.5g, of which sugars 27.8g; Fat 28.4g, of which saturates 14g; Cholesterol 62mg; Calcium 158mg; Fibre 1.2g; Sodium 124mg.

Spiced Ground Rice Pudding

This ground rice pudding, moughli, is grainier than the traditional smooth milk puddings such as ashtalieh and mouhalabieh. Flavoured with cinnamon, which is regarded as beneficial, moughli is traditionally served in Lebanon to women who have just given birth. When you taste this sweet, sustaining and comforting pudding you will see why.

SERVES SIX

INGREDIENTS

- 300g/11oz/scant 2 cups ground rice
- 450g/1lb/2¼ cups sugar
- 30ml/2 tbsp ground cinnamon
- 10ml/2 tsp ground aniseed
- 30ml/2 tbsp desiccated (dry unsweetened shredded) coconut
- 15ml/1 tbsp pistachio nuts, chopped

VARIATION

For extra flavour and crunch you could lightly dry-roast the pistachio nuts and desiccated coconut. Let them cool before sprinkling on top of the pudding.

1 Pour 1.2 litres/2 pints/5 cups water into a heavy pan and bring it to the boil. Reduce the heat and beat in the ground rice, sugar and spices, stirring constantly to keep smooth.

2 Simmer gently for about 15 minutes, until the mixture is very thick.

3 Transfer the mixture into individual serving bowls and leave to cool and set, then chill in the refrigerator.

4 When ready to serve, top each pudding with a sprinkling of coconut and pistachio nuts and eat chilled or at room temperature.

Energy 525kcal/2219kJ; Protein 5.1g; Carbohydrate 119.4g, of which sugars 78.8g; Fat 5g, of which saturates 2.9g; Cholesterol 0mg; Calcium 56mg; Fibre 0.8g; Sodium 20mg.

MILK PUDDING WITH MASTIC

MIDDLE EASTERN MILK PUDDINGS ARE ABSOLUTELY DELECTABLE AND LOVED THROUGHOUT THE REGION. SOME ARE FLAVOURED WITH ORANGE BLOSSOM WATER, OTHERS WITH ROSE WATER, CINNAMON OR ANISEED. MASTIC, THE CRYSTALLIZED GUM FROM A SMALL EVERGREEN TREE, GIVES THIS PUDDING, 'MOUHALLABIEH', A UNIQUE RESINOUS TASTE AS WELL AS A MILDLY CHEWY TEXTURE.

SERVES FOUR TO SIX

INGREDIENTS

- 50g/2oz/½ cup rice flour
- 1 litre/1¾ pints/4 cups whole milk
- 125g/4¼oz/⅔ cup sugar
- 1–2 mastic crystals, pulverized with a little sugar
- 15–30ml/1–2 tbsp icing (confectioners') sugar, for dusting

1 Mix the rice flour with a little of the milk to form a loose paste. Pour the rest of the milk into a heavy pan and stir in the sugar. Bring the milk to boiling point, stirring all the time, until the sugar has dissolved. Reduce the heat and stir a spoonful or two of the hot milk into the rice flour paste, then transfer the mixture to the pan, stirring constantly to avoid lumps.

2 Bring the milk back to boiling point and stir in the ground mastic. Reduce the heat and simmer gently for 20–25 minutes, stirring from time to time, until the mixture becomes quite thick and coats the back of the spoon.

3 Pour the pudding mixture into serving bowls and let it cool, allowing a skin to form on top. Chill in the refrigerator and, just before serving, dust the tops with icing sugar.

COOK'S TIP

Mastic can be found in Middle Eastern food stores; it is sold in the form of crystals, which need to be broken down with a mortar and pestle before use.

Energy 613kcal/2561kJ; Protein 10.1g; Carbohydrate 70.5g, of which sugars 58.2g; Fat 33.7g, of which saturates 17.1g; Cholesterol 63mg; Calcium 279mg; Fibre 1g; Sodium 248mg.

Creamed Semolina with Cinnamon

This medieval pudding, ma'mounia, is popular throughout with the young and old alike. Warm and nourishing, it is a household winter favourite for a snack or even breakfast. To transform it into a dessert, serve with clotted cream and chopped nuts.

SERVES FOUR TO SIX

INGREDIENTS

- 250g/9oz sugar
- 500ml/17fl oz/generous 2 cups water
- juice of 1 lemon
- 100g/3¾oz butter
- 225g/8oz fine ground semolina
- 5–10ml/1–2 tsp ground cinnamon
- clotted cream, to serve

1 To make the syrup, put the sugar and water in a pan and bring to the boil, stirring. Add the lemon juice, reduce the heat and simmer for 10 minutes, until the syrup coats the back of a spoon. Turn off the heat and set aside.

2 Melt the butter in a heavy pan and slowly stir in the semolina. Continue to stir for 3–4 minutes, then gradually, add the syrup, stirring vigorously to prevent any lumps from forming and to keep the syrup from burning.

3 When the pudding has thickened, take the pan off the heat and cover with a clean dish towel, followed by the lid. Leave to steam for about 15 minutes, then serve warm with a dusting of cinnamon and whipped cream.

Energy 420kcal/1771kJ; Protein4g; Carbohydrate 73g, of which sugars 44g; Fat 14g, of which saturates 9g; Cholesterol 36mg; Calcium 27mg; Fibre 0.8g; Sodium 108mg.

Sweet Turmeric Bakes

Light and spongy with a distinctive colour and flavouring from the turmeric, these rustic cakes, called 'souf', are a feature of the mountain villages of Lebanon, where they are served for breakfast, or to accompany a mid-morning coffee or tea.

SERVES FOUR TO SIX

INGREDIENTS
- 15–30ml/1–2 tbsp tahini
- 25g/1oz/2 tbsp butter
- 75ml/5 tbsp olive oil
- 350ml/12fl oz/1½ cups milk
- 250g/9oz/1¼ cups sugar
- 250g/9oz/1½ cups semolina
- 200g/7oz/1¾ cups plain (all-purpose) flour
- 10ml/2 tsp baking powder
- 30ml/2 tbsp ground turmeric
- 30ml/2 tbsp pine nuts

1 Preheat the oven to 180°C/350°F/Gas 4. Smear the tahini over the base and sides of a 25 x 20cm/10 x 8in baking tin (pan). Melt the butter with the olive oil in a small pan.

2 Heat the milk with the sugar in a heavy pan, stirring constantly, until almost boiling. Then stir the melted butter and oil into the milk.

3 Into a bowl, sift together the semolina, flour, baking powder and turmeric. Add the mixture to the milk and beat vigorously to make a smooth batter.

4 Pour the batter into the tahini-lined tin, sprinkle the surface with the pine nuts and bake the cake in the oven for about 30 minutes.

5 Remove the cake from the oven and leave to cool, then cut it into 5cm/2in squares and serve while still warm, or at room temperature.

Energy 624kcal/2632kJ; Protein 11.4g; Carbohydrate 106.2g, of which sugars 46.8g; Fat 20.2g, of which saturates 4.6g; Cholesterol 13mg; Calcium 164mg; Fibre 2.2g; Sodium 70mg.

SEMOLINA CAKE WITH POPPY SEEDS

POPPY SEED CAKES ARE PARTICULARLY ENJOYED BY THE JEWISH COMMUNITY OF LEBANON, WHO PREPARE THEM FOR THE FESTIVAL OF PURIM. BLUE POPPY SEEDS GIVE THE CAKES A PRETTY SPECKLED APPEARANCE, OR YOU CAN USE WHITE POPPY SEEDS, AS HERE.

SERVES SIX TO EIGHT

INGREDIENTS

- 115g/4oz/½ cup butter
- 175g/6oz/scant 1 cup sugar
- 30–45ml/2–3 tbsp white poppy seeds
- 5–10ml/1–2 tsp vanilla extract
- 2 eggs
- 450g/1lb/2⅔ cups fine semolina
- 5ml/1 tsp baking powder
- 2.5ml/½ tsp bicarbonate of soda (baking soda)
- 175g/6fl oz/¾ cup Greek (US strained plain) yogurt
- 16 blanched almonds, halved

For the syrup

- 250ml/8fl oz/1 cup water
- 450g/1lb/2¼ cups sugar
- juice of 1 lemon

1 First make the syrup. Boil the water with the sugar, stirring constantly, until dissolved. Stir in the lemon juice, reduce the heat and simmer for 10–15 minutes, until the syrup coats the back of a wooden spoon. Leave to cool.

2 Preheat the oven to 180°C/350°F/Gas 4 and grease a 20 x 30cm/8 x 12in baking tin (pan).

3 Cream the butter with the sugar, beat in the poppy seeds and vanilla and add the eggs one at a time.

4 Sift the semolina with the baking powder and bicarbonate of soda and fold it into the creamed mixture, then stir in the yogurt.

5 Transfer the mixture to the tin, spreading it to the edges. Arrange the almonds on top, and bake for about 30 minutes, or until firm.

6 Pour the syrup over the hot cake. Cut into diamonds and leave to cool in the tin before lifting out.

Energy 664kcal/2809kJ; Protein 9.9g; Carbohydrate 127g, of which sugars 83.4g; Fat 16.5g, of which saturates 8.5g; Cholesterol 81mg; Calcium 120mg; Fibre 1.5g; Sodium 156mg.

Puréed Apricot Dessert

Dried fruit desserts are a feature of every household as many families have fruit trees in their yard. The most popular dried fruits include prunes, mulberries, grapes and apricots. This ancient dessert, mishmishiyya, is prepared with dried apricots.

SERVES FOUR TO SIX

INGREDIENTS

- 450g/1lb dried apricots, soaked overnight in water to just cover
- 125g/4¼oz sugar
- 200ml/7fl oz/scant 1 cup double (heavy) cream
- 15–30ml/1–2 tbsp icing (confectioners') sugar
- 15–30ml/1–2 tbsp orange blossom water
- 15–30ml/1–2 tbsp flaked (sliced) toasted almonds

1 Pour the apricots, soaking water and the sugar into a pan and bring to the boil. Simmer for 10–15 minutes.

2 When the apricots have cooled, blend them with the thin syrup in a food processor to form a smooth, slightly tart, purée. Transfer the purée to a wide, shallow serving bowl, or individual bowls, cover with plastic film and chill until completely cold.

3 Just before serving, whip the cream until it begins to thicken, then add the icing sugar and orange blossom water. Continue to whip until the cream forms thick peaks, and spoon it on to the apricot purée. Sprinkle the top with the nuts and serve.

Energy 412kcal/1731kJ; Protein 4g; Carbohydrate 59g, of which sugars 59g; Fat 19g, of which saturates 11g; Cholesterol 46mg; Calcium 91mg; Fibre 5.9g; Sodium 51mg.

Little Walnut Cakes

These little stuffed cakes, called ma'amoul, are often prepared for religious festivals, such as Ramadan for the Muslims and Easter for the Christians. Traditionally they are filled with chopped walnuts, pistachios or a date paste.

SERVES FOUR TO SIX

INGREDIENTS

- 225g/8oz plain (all-purpose) flour
- 115g/4oz butter, diced
- 15ml/1 tbsp rose water
- 15–30ml/1–2 tbsp milk
- 15–30ml/1–2 tbsp icing (confectioners') sugar

For the filling

- 115g/4oz walnuts, finely chopped
- 30ml/2 tbsp sugar
- 15ml/1 tbsp rose water

1 In a bowl, mix together the chopped walnuts, sugar and rose water for the filling, and set aside.

2 Preheat the oven to 180°C/350°F/ Gas 4. Sift the flour into a large bowl, add the diced butter, and rub it into the flour until the mixture resembles fine breadcrumbs.

3 Stir in the sugar and rose water and bind the mixture together with a little milk to form a soft, malleable dough.

4 Take a small apricot-sized lump of dough in your fingers and mould it into a ball. Carefully, hollow out the ball to form a deep cavity into which you spoon a little of the nut filling. Fold the edges over the filling, pinch the top to seal and mould into a round ball in the palm of your hand.

5 Place the ball on a lightly oiled baking sheet and press it down with the palm of your hand. Repeat with the rest of the dough and the filling until you have roughly 16–20 little cakes.

6 Prick the tops with a fork and place them in the oven for 20–25 minutes, until pale brown but still slightly soft. Leave to cool on the baking sheet before dusting with icing sugar.

VARIATION

Replace the walnut filling with the same amount of soft dried dates, finely chopped, and omit the sugar.

Energy 435kcal/1813kJ; Protein 7g; Carbohydrate 38g, of which sugars 9g; Fat 30g, of which saturates 11g; Cholesterol42; Calcium 80mg; Fibre 1.8g; Sodium 121mg.

SESAME AND HONEY BRITTLE

THROUGHOUT HISTORY, ARABS AND JEWS ARE KNOWN TO HAVE ALWAYS HAD A PASSION FOR SWEETS OF ALL KINDS. WHETHER THEY ARE JEWISH OR ARAB IN ORIGIN, THESE LITTLE SESAME SQUARES, CALLED 'SIMSIMIYY', ARE SOLD BY STREET VENDORS THROUGHOUT THE EASTERN MEDITERRANEAN.

SERVES SIX TO EIGHT

INGREDIENTS

- 450g/1lb sesame seeds
- 225g/8oz blanched almonds, finely chopped
- 225g/8oz clear honey
- 225g/8oz sugar
- 5ml/1 tsp ground cinnamon

1 Preheat the oven to 180°C/350°F/Gas 4. Spread the sesame seeds and almonds in a thin layer on a baking sheet and place in the oven for about 10 minutes, until lightly browned and emitting a nutty aroma.

2 In a heavy pan, melt the honey with the sugar, stirring all the time until it has dissolved. Stir in the cinnamon and simmer gently for about 5 minutes. Remove the pot from the heat and stir in the roasted sesame seeds and nuts.

3 Lightly grease a baking tin (pan) or tray and transfer the sesame and honey mixture to it. Press the mixture down in the tin with your knuckles to compact it and spread it evenly.

4 Leave the mixture to cool a little and to begin to set but, while it is still pliable, loosen the edge of the brittle with a sharp knife or spatula and lift the whole piece out of the dish and on to a wooden board.

5 Using a sharp knife, cut the brittle into diamond- or square-shaped pieces.

6 Leave to cool completely until the pieces are hard and brittle. Serve with tea, or store them in an airtight container for several weeks.

Energy 700kcal/2920kJ; Protein 16g; Carbohydrate 53g, of which sugars 52g; Fat 48g, of which saturates 6g; Cholesterol 0mg; Calcium 450mg; Fibre 6.5g; Sodium 20mg.

PISTACHIO BAKLAVA WITH ORANGE BLOSSOM

The Ottoman-inspired baklava is popular throughout the eastern Mediterranean and is deliciously sweet and moist if properly made. Most people buy the various sweet pastries from the pastry shops, as they take time to prepare at home, and they are sometimes bought on the spur of the moment as gifts to present to hosts. Baklava, however, really isn't so difficult to make, and is well worth the time and effort.

SERVES EIGHT

INGREDIENTS

- 175g/6oz clarified or plain butter
- 100ml/3½ fl oz/scant ½ cup sunflower oil
- 450g/1lb filo sheets
- 450g/1lb pistachios, finely chopped
- zest of 1 orange

For the syrup:

- 450g/1lb sugar
- 250ml/8fl oz/1 cup water
- 30–45ml/2–3 tbsp orange blossom water

1 In a small pan, melt the butter with the oil. Brush a little on the base and sides of a 12inch/30cm cake tin (pan). Place a sheet of filo in the bottom and brush with the melted butter and oil. Preheat the oven to 325°F/160°C/Gas 3.

2 Continue making layers of pastry, with half the quantity of filo sheets, making sure each sheet is brushed with the butter and oil. Ease the sheets into the corners of the tin and trim the edges if they flop over the rim.

3 Once you have brushed the last of that batch of filo sheets, mix the pistachios with the orange zest and spread them over the top. Then continue as before, layering the remaining filo sheets while brushing them with the butter and oil.

4 Brush the final layer as well, then, using a sharp knife, cut diagonal parallel lines through all the layers to the bottom to form small diamond-shaped portions.

5 Bake the baklava in the oven for about 1 hour, until the top is golden – if the top is still pale, turn the oven up for a few minutes at the end.

6 Meanwhile, make the syrup. Put the sugar and water into a heavy pan. Bring the liquid to the boil, stirring all the time, until the sugar dissolves. Reduce the heat, stir in the orange blossom water and simmer for about 15 minutes, until it thickens a little. Leave the syrup to cool in the pan.

7 When the baklava is ready, remove it from the oven and slowly pour the cold syrup over the piping hot pastry.

8 Put the baklava back into the oven for just 2–3 minutes – this will help it soak up the syrup – then take it out and leave it to cool in the tin.

9 When it is completely cool, lift the baklava out of the tin, and arrange on a serving dish.

VARIATIONS

Persian-inspired variations of baklava recipes often include a mixture of almonds and pistachios, while Albanian-influenced recipes use walnuts.

Energy 776kcal/3247kJ; Protein 10g; Carbohydrate 91g, of which sugars 62g; Fat 44g, of which saturates 12g; Cholesterol 31mg; Calcium 99mg; Fibre 3.2g; Sodium 272mg.

Lebanese Pudding

This pudding is called layali loubnan, which literally translates as 'nights of Lebanon'. Traditionally, it is made of layers of semolina, kashta (a scented creamy mixture), bananas and nuts, but it can also include apricot, cherry or rose petal conserves, or even tahini.

SERVES SIX TO EIGHT

INGREDIENTS

For the semolina

- 600ml/1 pint/2½ cups whole milk
- 60ml/4 tbsp sugar
- 90g/31/2oz/½ cup fine semolina
- 1–2 mastic crystals, pulverized with a little sugar

For the cream

- 15ml/1 tbsp rice flour
- 150ml/¼ pint/⅔ cup whole milk
- 300ml/½ pint/1¼ cups double (heavy) cream
- 30–45ml/2–3 tbsp sugar
- 2 slices white bread, ground to crumbs
- 15ml/1 tbsp rose water

For the topping

- 2 bananas, finely sliced
- juice of ½ lemon
- 30ml/2 tbsp chopped pistachio nuts
- 30ml/2 tbsp flaked (sliced) almonds
- 45–60ml/3–4 tbsp runny honey
- 30ml/2 tbsp orange blossom water

1 First prepare the semolina. Heat the milk and sugar in a heavy pan, stirring until the sugar has dissolved. Bring the milk to the boil, then add in the semolina and mastic, beating vigorously.

2 Reduce the heat and simmer, stirring from time to time, until the mixture begins to thicken. Pour it into a serving dish, level it with the back of a spoon and leave to cool.

3 To prepare the cream layer, mix the rice flour with a little milk, heat the rest of the milk and cream, together with the sugar, stirring constantly, until almost boiling. Stir a spoonful of the hot mixture into the rice flour mixture and then pour the rice flour mixture back into the pan.

4 Add the breadcrumbs and rose water to the pan and stir vigorously until the mixture is thick and creamy. Leave to cool a little, then spoon it over the semolina, which should have set. Leave to cool and set, then chill the pudding.

5 A short time before serving, arrange the sliced bananas in a layer over the pudding. Squeeze lemon juice over the top to prevent them from turning brown. Sprinkle the nuts on top.

6 Heat the honey with the orange blossom water and pour it over the nuts. Once the honey has cooled, chill the pudding until ready to eat.

Energy 431kcal/1799kJ; Protein 7.5g; Carbohydrate 43.5g, of which sugars 27.8g; Fat 28.4g, of which saturates 14g; Cholesterol 62mg; Calcium 158mg; Fibre 1.2g; Sodium 124mg.

PUFFED FRITTERS IN SYRUP

LEBANESE CHRISTIANS PREPARE THESE FRITTERS, OR AWAMAT, ON 6 JANUARY TO CELEBRATE THE BAPTISM OF CHRIST. THE TRADITION OF EATING FRITTERS IN SYRUP AT RELIGIOUS OCCASIONS DATES BACK TO THE MEDIEVAL FEASTS OF BAGHDAD AND, LATER, TO THE LAVISH BANQUETS OF THE OTTOMAN EMPIRE.

SERVES SIX

INGREDIENTS

- 2.5ml/½ tsp dried yeast
- 2.5ml/½ tsp sugar
- 150ml/¼ pint/⅔ cup lukewarm water
- 175g/6oz/1½ cups plain (all-purpose) flour
- 50g/2oz/½ cup rice flour
- 1–2 mastic crystals, pulverized with 5ml/1 tsp sugar
- sunflower oil, for frying
- pinch of salt

For the syrup

- 225g/8oz/1 cup sugar
- 150ml/¼ pint/⅔ cup water
- 30ml/2 tbsp orange blossom water

1 In a small bowl, cream the yeast with the sugar in the lukewarm water until frothy. Sift the flours with the salt and mastic into a bowl and make a well in the centre.

2 Pour the creamed yeast into the well and draw in a little of the flour to form a batter. Dust the surface of the batter with a little of the remaining flour, cover the bowl with a clean, damp cloth, and leave for about 20 minutes.

3 Remove the cloth and draw in the rest of the flour to make a soft, sticky dough, adding a little extra water if necessary. Cover the bowl with the damp cloth again and leave the dough to prove for about 2 hours, until doubled in size.

4 Meanwhile, prepare the syrup. Place the sugar and water in a heavy pan and bring it to the boil, stirring constantly.

5 Stir the orange blossom water into the pan, reduce the heat and simmer for about 10 minutes, until the syrup coats the back of a wooden spoon. Turn off the heat and leave the syrup to cool.

6 Heat enough sunflower oil in a pan for frying. Take a portion of the dough in your hand and squeeze it through thumb and forefinger to drop little balls of dough into the oil. Alternatively, use two teaspoons – the shapes do not need to be perfect.

7 Fry the fritters in batches until golden brown and drain on kitchen paper.

8 While still warm, soak the fritters in the cold syrup for 10–15 minutes. Scoop them out and serve at room temperature with a little of the syrup drizzled over them.

Energy 193kcal/806kJ; Protein 4.1g; Carbohydrate 30.9g, of which sugars 11.5g; Fat 6.6g, of which saturates 0.5g; Cholesterol 0mg; Calcium 23mg; Fibre 0.6g; Sodium 3mg.

WHEAT IN FRAGRANT HONEY

IN LEBANON, THIS NOURISHING DESSERT KNOWN AS KAMHIYEH IS TRADITIONALLY PREPARED WITH YOUNG GREEN WHEAT OR BARLEY TO MARK SIGNIFICANT EVENTS. FOR MUSLIMS, IT IS A DISH PREPARED FOR NURSING MOTHERS; JEWS SERVE IT TO CELEBRATE A BABY'S FIRST TOOTH; AND FOR CHRISTIANS, IT IS EATEN ON 4 DECEMBER IN HONOUR OF ST BARBARA.

SERVES SIX

INGREDIENTS

- 225g/8oz/1¼ cups whole wheat grains, soaked overnight and drained
- 1 litre/1¾ pints/4 cups water
- 60–90ml/4–6 tbsp fragrant runny honey
- 30ml/2 tbsp orange blossom water
- 30ml/2 tbsp rose water
- 30–45ml/2–3 tbsp raisins or sultanas (golden raisins), soaked in warm water for 30 minutes and drained
- 30ml/2 tbsp pine nuts, soaked in water for 2 hours
- 30ml/2 tbsp blanched almonds, soaked in water for 2 hours
- seeds of ½ pomegranate

1 Place the soaked whole wheat grains in a heavy pan with the water and bring to the boil.

2 Reduce the heat, cover, and simmer for 1 hour, until the wheat is tender, and most of the water is absorbed.

3 Meanwhile, heat the honey and stir in the orange blossom and rose waters – don't let the mixture boil. Stir in the raisins and turn off the heat.

4 Transfer the wheat grains to a serving bowl, or individual bowls, and pour the honey and raisins over the top.

5 Garnish with the nuts and pomegranate seeds and serve while still warm, or leave to cool and chill in the refrigerator before serving.

COOK'S TIP

You could try serving this for breakfast or as part of a brunch.

Energy 193kcal/806kJ; Protein 4.1g; Carbohydrate 30.9g, of which sugars 11.5g; Fat 6.6g, of which saturates 0.5g; Cholesterol 0mg; Calcium 23mg; Fibre 0.6g; Sodium 3mg.

POMEGRANATE SALAD WITH PINE NUTS

VARIATIONS OF THIS PRETTY, DECORATIVE FRUIT SALAD ARE PREPARED THROUGHOUT THE MIDDLE EAST. IT IS OFTEN OFFERED TO GUESTS ON THEIR ARRIVAL AS A MARK OF HOSPITALITY, OR IT CAN BE SERVED AS A REFRESHING DISH BETWEEN COURSES AND AS AN ACCOMPANIMENT TO OTHER SWEET DISHES, AS WELL AS A TRADITIONAL DESSERT AT THE END OF A MEAL.

SERVES FOUR TO SIX

INGREDIENTS

- 45–60ml/3–4 tbsp pine nuts
- 3 ripe pomegranates
- 30ml/2 tbsp orange blossom water
- 15–30ml/1–2 tbsp fragrant runny honey
- handful of small mint leaves, to decorate

COOK'S TIP

Pomegranates signify good luck and prosperity, which is why they are served to welcome visitors to the home.

1 Place the pine nuts in a bowl, cover with the water and leave for 2 hours.

2 Cut the pomegranates into quarters, transferring any excess juice to a bowl.

3 Extract the seeds, taking care to discard the pith and membrane, and place in a bowl with the juice. Drain the pine nuts and add them to the bowl.

4 Stir in the orange blossom water and honey, cover the bowl, and chill in the refrigerator.

5 Serve the salad chilled, or at room temperature, decorated with a few mint leaves.

Energy 82kcal/344kJ; Protein 1.3g; Carbohydrate 8.2g, of which sugars 8.1g; Fat 5.2g, of which saturates 0.4g; Cholesterol 0mg; Calcium 4mg; Fibre 1.2g; Sodium 2mg.

SNOWY WHITE ICE CREAM

Influenced by the Ottomans and their snowy white ice cream, this traditional recipe is popular throughout the Arab world. The silky, ground orchid root, sahlab, gives the ice cream its pearly white colour as well as acting as a thickening agent. Sahlab is available in Middle Eastern stores.

SERVES FOUR

INGREDIENTS

- 1.2 litres/2 pints/5 cups whole milk
- 225g/8oz sugar
- 45ml/3 tbsp sahlab
- 30–45ml/2–3 tbsp orange blossom water

1 Put the milk and sugar into a pan. Bring to the boil, stirring constantly, until the sugar dissolves. Reduce the heat and simmer for 10 minutes.

2 Put the sahlab into a small bowl. Mix it with a little cold milk, then stir in a spoonful of the hot, sweetened milk, then pour the sahlab mixture into the pan of milk, stirring all the time.

3 Stir the orange blossom water into the pan. Beat gently and continue to simmer for 10–15 minutes more.

COOK'S TIP

When serving, allow the ice cream to sit out of the freezer for 5-10 minutes so that it is easier to scoop.

4 Pour the mixture into a freezer container, cover with a dry dish towel and leave to cool. Remove the towel, cover with aluminium foil and place in the freezer. Leave it to set, beating it at intervals to disperse the ice crystals, or pour into an ice-cream maker and churn according to the instructions.

Energy 451kcal/1901kJ; Protein 11g; Carbohydrate 80g, of which sugars 73g; Fat 12g, of which saturates 8g; Cholesterol 42mg; Calcium 361mg; Fibre 0.2g; Sodium 133mg.

STUFFED DATE FUDGE

THIS IS A POPULAR ARAB SWEETMEAT PREPARED FOR ALL FESTIVE OCCASIONS. AS DATES PLAY AN IMPORTANT ROLE IN THE EASTERN MEDITERRANEAN, THERE IS RARELY A FESTIVE MEAL WHERE THEY DO NOT APPEAR. THIS ONE, KNOWN AS 'RANGINAK', IS PREPARED AS A WELCOMING TREAT FOR GUESTS AS DATES ARE REGARDED AS A GIFT OF HOSPITALITY.

SERVES FOUR TO SIX

INGREDIENTS
- 500g/1¼lb moist, pitted dates
- roughly 115g/4oz walnuts, enough halves to fill each date
- 225g/8oz butter
- 45–60ml/3–4 tbsp sugar
- 225g/8oz plain (all-purpose) flour
- 15ml/1 tbsp ground almonds
- 15ml/1 tbsp ground pistachios

1 Find the opening in each date where the stone has been extracted and stuff it with a walnut half.

2 As you work, place the stuffed dates in a lightly greased, shallow baking dish, packing them tightly together.

3 In a small pan, melt the butter with the sugar and stir in the flour.

4 Continue to stir it over a low flame until the mixture begins to turn golden brown, then pour it over the dates. Leave to set, then sprinkle the nuts over the top. Cut into little squares, each containing a stuffed date, and serve them with tea or coffee.

Energy 804kcal/3367kJ; Protein 10g; Carbohydrate 97g, of which sugars 45g; Fat 0g, of which saturates 21g; Cholesterol 80mg; Calcium 119mg; Fibre 5.3g; Sodium 246mg.

STUFFED RED DATE PRESERVE

This is a beautiful and unusual preserve, revered in Lebanon and Jordan. Dates are one of the region's most ancient staple foods, coveted for their nutritional value and their sweetness. It is said that the Bedouin are unable to sleep under fruit-laden date palms, such is their urge to pick and eat the fruit.

MAKES ENOUGH FOR 2 X 450G/1LB JARS

INGREDIENTS
- 40 fresh, ripe red dates
- 40 blanched whole almonds
- 500g/1¼lb/2½ cups sugar
- juice and rind (cut into fine strips) of 2 clementines
- 6–8 cloves

1 Place the dates in a heavy pan and just cover with water. Bring to the boil, reduce the heat and simmer for 5 minutes to soften the dates.

2 Drain the dates, reserving the water, and carefully push the stone (pit) out of each date with a sharp knife.

3 Stuff each date with an almond.

4 Pour the reserved cooking water back into the pan and add the sugar, clementine juice and rind, and cloves. Bring the water to the boil, stirring constantly until the sugar has dissolved.

5 Reduce the heat and drop in the stuffed dates. Simmer for 1 hour, until the syrup is fairly thick. Leave the dates to cool in the syrup, then spoon into jars to enjoy with bread, yogurt, milk puddings, or just on their own.

Energy 1619kcal/6871kJ; Protein 15.8g; Carbohydrate 347.4g, of which sugars 346g; Fat 28.2g, of which saturates 2.4g; Cholesterol 0mg; Calcium 318mg; Fibre 8.3g; Sodium 45mg.

Quince Preserve

Many delectable jams and syrups are made in the eastern Mediterranean, but in Lebanon quince jam is particularly sought after as the fragrant fruit is associated with love and marriage. More of a conserve than a spreadable jam, this quince preserve is best spooned generously on to freshly baked bread, or drizzled over yogurt.

MAKES ENOUGH FOR 3–4 X 450G/1LB JARS

INGREDIENTS
- 1kg/2¼lb fresh quinces, peeled (optional), quartered, cored and diced
- juice of 2 lemons
- 500g/1¼lb/2½ cups sugar

1 Place the prepared fruit in a heavy pan and sprinkle with the lemon juice to prevent it from turning brown. Pour in about 600ml/1 pint/2½ cups water – just enough to surround the fruit – and add the sugar.

2 Bring to the boil, stirring constantly until the sugar dissolves. Reduce the heat and simmer for 1–1½ hours, until the fruit has turned a deep reddish-pink. Turn up the heat and boil vigorously for 2 minutes.

3 Spoon the mixture into sterilized jars. Seal and store in a cool place for at least 6 months, if not eating immediately.

COOK'S TIP
Quince is inedible raw, and needs slow cooking to release its sweetness and aroma, but its taste is unique.

Energy 593kcal/2524kJ; Protein 1.4g; Carbohydrate 155.6g, of which sugars 155.6g; Fat 0.3g, of which saturates 0g; Cholesterol 0mg; Calcium 94mg; Fibre 5.5g; Sodium 15mg.

INDEX